ELEMENTARY
BASIC

THE ANALYTICAL ENGINE

ELEMENTARY BASIC

AS CHRONICLED BY

John H. Watson

EDITED WITH COMMENTARIES BY

Henry Ledgard

AND

Andrew Singer

Random House New York

Library of Congess Cataloging in Publication Data
Ledgard, Henry F., 1943-
Elementary Basic, as chronicled by Dr. John H. Watson.
Includes Index.
1.Basic(Computer program language)
2.Electronic digital computers—Programming.
I.Singer, Andrew, 1943-
II.Title
QA76.73.B314 1982b   001.64'24   81-69672
ISBN 0-394-70789-3   AACR2

Manufactured in the United States of America

24689753

Contents

THE LAST BOW

Preface

Henry Ledgard and I were drinking tea and discussing a paper when the trunk arrived; or rather I should say when Edwina, Henry's wife, called to tell him that a trunk had come. Edwina is English and properly speaking the trunk is hers, but I'm getting ahead of the story. At the time, neither of us thought anything of it and we immediately returned to our tea and paper.

The following day I got in late. Thinking we might have lunch, I stopped at Henry's office. As I stepped in, I noticed a distinct change in the atmosphere from the day before. My friend was clearly preoccupied. He also looked a bit disheveled and rather tired. Now this is most unusual. Henry is a person of extremely regular habits. It is rare for him to retire later than nine, and he is usually up and about well before six. He nearly always appears well rested and neat. As we walked to the university cafeteria, he said little.

Finally, overcome with curiosity, I said, "Henry, is something wrong? You don't seem yourself this morning."

"It's the trunk," he replied, with an edge to his voice.

"Trunk?"

"The trunk that came for Edwina from England yesterday."

"Oh, *that* trunk. What about it?"

"It's a very strange trunk; that is, I mean its contents are strange. The trunk is full of manuscripts."

"What's so strange about that?"

"They all seem to have been written by a certain Dr. John Watson about a certain Mr. Sherlock Holmes."

"Now really, Henry, be serious."

"I am completely serious, but I haven't told you the best part of it yet. What do you suppose the manuscripts are about?"

"I refuse to have my leg pulled in this fashion, Henry!"

"Andrew, Holmes was an ace programmer. According to Watson, he used a successor to Babbage's Analytical Engine in his work. The manuscripts are Watson's chronicles of their experiences. Holmes's insights are brilliant. His deductive powers and methodical nature made him a natural programmer."

"Henry, how did Edwina come by this trunk?"

"It was a bequest from a great-aunt. She hardly knows the woman and can't imagine why it was willed to her at all."

"Henry, how many of Edwina's family know that you're a computer scientist?"

"Most of them, I suppose."

"Do you suppose this great-aunt might have known?"

"What are you getting at?"

"Just that it's a marvellous practical joke and you've been completely taken in."

The expression on Henry's face as I spoke struck me almost as funny as the situation itself, and I burst out laughing as we headed for the cafeteria door.

The laughter seemed a bit hollow a few days later when I saw the manuscripts themselves. Faded, brittle, and written in a somewhat cluttered hand, they certainly looked authentic. An actual sample of Watson's handwriting that Henry had obtained seemed to clinch it. No one would possibly go to this much trouble for a practical joke. Here was no hoax but a fascinating discovery.

Henry handed me a small bundle of copies.

"I thought you might find them interesting reading," he said with a smile. "Unless of course you still have some doubts?"

With a pained expression, I took the copies and retreated to the library. The manuscripts had been sorted into chronological order. A separate page on top was not part of a manuscript but a note addressed to the reader from Watson himself. I have reproduced it here.

To a Reader in the Future:

Although you may or may not be familiar with my numerous short sketches describing the exploits of Mr. Sherlock Holmes, you must know that my hope in publishing these has been to make the public aware of the Science of Deduction and my friend's remarkable skill as a practitioner of it.

Naturally, some of the cases in which Holmes had the kindness to invite my participation could not be openly discussed, and thus I have deliberately suppressed my notes wherever a matter of delicacy was involved. The records which follow, however, describe an extraordinary set of cases which fall into a wholly distinct class, and I have elected not to publish them for the most unusual reason that there does not exist as yet a suitable readership for them.

Therefore, I consign them to posterity and ask only that they not be published as a curiosity but rather at such time as they may find readers to whom they will seem contemporary.

John D. Watson, M.D., L.R.C.P., M.R.C.S.

Reading the manuscripts themselves, I realized that Watson had been most perceptive. Even today, computer literacy is rare, and it would be unlikely to suppose that a popular audience for these adventures exists. Except for their dependence on the peculiar programming language used by Babbage's Engine, they constituted a most lucid and enjoyable tutorial on problem solving with a computer.

I was still absorbed in my reading several hours later when I looked up to see Henry sitting across the table.

"Incredible, aren't they?" he said quietly.

"Amazing."

"Would you publish them?"

"Not the way they are."

"What then?"

"I would edit them and translate the programs into a contemporary programming language, perhaps produce several translations for different languages, Pascal, Basic, Ada, and so on. Then I'd add some commentary to address the more detailed issues of the individual languages. Do you think it would work?"

"Yes."

"I guess Edwina's aunt knew what she was doing."

And that is how we came to publish this book. With all due respect to Watson, we have endeavored to preserve his style altogether. Many of the manuscripts deal with problems of considerable complexity. We have selected only those that would be appropriate for a tutorial. Perhaps one day we will publish an edition of the more advanced cases.

The sole objective of this book is to teach you to program in Basic, the language of this translation. We assume in this book, as Holmes assumed of Watson, that you, the reader, have probably never programmed before. Learning to program is not easy. Its essence lies in the ability to solve problems—by computer, of course.

Generally, each chapter of the book begins with one of the case studies of Sherlock Holmes. Here we see Holmes and Watson solving some problem. Following each case study, the commentary discusses in detail the issues arising from the problem presented by Holmes.

The first three chapters present Holmes's introduction to problem solving and programming. Like Watson, you are not expected to be able to duplicate the ideas presented, or even understand them fully. That will follow in due course. Hopefully, though, you will see the general effect of all that follows.

In Chapter IV, Holmes presents the first steps needed to write programs. By the end of Chapter VII, you should have completed the central issues in writing any computer program. At this point you will be well on your way.

The next five chapters should enlarge your skills considerably. In these cases, Holmes is dealing with somewhat larger problems and the programming tools needed to solve them effectively.

In the last chapter, Holmes and Watson confront a most difficult case from a computing standpoint. Holmes's solution brings into play almost all the ideas presented in this book.

In writing this text we have tried to keep to a small number of features common to almost every implementation of Basic. The portion of Basic covered in the text is summarized in the Appendix, *Basic at a Glance*. In any case, our version of Basic follows that presented in the standard for 'minimal' Basic [ANSI X3.60-1978 American National Standards Institute, New York, New York]. Several popular enhancements to this standard are also covered. Be careful—your local dialect may be ever-so-slightly different.

So come, dear reader, the game is afoot.

HENRY LEDGARD
ANDREW SINGER

Circumstantial Evidence

I

The Analytical Engine

N an incoherent and, as I deeply feel, an entirely inadequate fashion, I have endeavoured to give some account of the remarkable career of Mr. Sherlock Holmes as a criminal investigator and consulting detective. As the reader is undoubtedly well aware, my companion's interests were as broad as Nature herself and he often spoke on an amazing variety of subjects as though he had made a special study of each. In my modest chronicles of the cases that I have had the privilege to share with Sherlock Holmes, I have often alluded to his numerous publications, but I have said nothing before of his unparallelled contributions to the development of the Analytical Engine.

My first introduction to the Analytical Engine was in the late spring, shortly after the conclusion of one of the most ghastly adventures we had ever shared, which I have chronicled under the heading of "The Adventure of the Speckled Band." The entire day Holmes was in a mood that some would call taciturn. He was most unsettled, smoked incessantly, played snatches on his violin, sank into reveries, and hardly answered the casual questions that I put to him. We sat through a silent dinner together, after which, pushing his plate aside, he revealed to me the problem with which he was preoccupied.

"You can never foretell what one mind will come up with, Watson, but you can say with precision what an average person will do. Individuals vary, but percentages remain constant; and while we have not yet grasped the results that the human mind alone can attain, it has its distinct limitations. There are only particular individuals on whom we can rely to produce the same chain of logical argument from one occasion to the next."

"I certainly wouldn't argue with you, Holmes," I replied. "But as yet we haven't found a suitable replacement for human reasoning."

"Oh, on the contrary, Watson," he answered nonchalantly. "Have you ever heard of the Analytical Engine?"

"I know of no substitute for the mind of man."

Holmes chuckled. "Then you must learn of it. It is an ingenious mechanism, a machine that has displayed a considerable talent for deductive reasoning, far superior to the average logician. You recall my intervention in the matter of that notebook floating in the River Cam last month?"

"I am not likely soon to forget the sight of that bloated face staring up at me, Holmes," I replied grimly, considering the sorry state of mankind that such events should come to pass. "What connection has the late professor with this Engine?"

"HAVE YOU EVER HEARD OF THE ANALYTICAL ENGINE?"

"Well, as you may remember, my investigation led me to the Caven-dish laboratories; and it was there that I had occasion to study the Engine, if only briefly. Since then I have been in correspondence with mathematicians at Cambridge who have been conducting experiments with it. Watson, I do not exaggerate when I say that the Analytical Engine is capable of solving, within minutes, complex numerical problems that would keep five of London's finest mathematicians working for hours. Furthermore, it is adept at logic and has a perfect memory for detail.

"The Engine also has its limits," he continued. "It can only undertake problems whose solutions are spelled out in minute detail and that are presented in its own peculiar language."

"Really, Holmes, sometimes you go too far with my patience!" I exclaimed. "You expect me to believe that this device is capable of solving problems, has a perfect memory, and actually speaks a language of its own?"

"No, no, my dear Watson, you take me too literally. The Analytical Engine does indeed have a language of its own, but communications must be written out."

"Now you tell me it can read?"

"In a sense, yes."

I threw up my arms in a desperate gesture and began to rise from the table.

"I fear I am going too fast for you, Watson. Bear with me for a moment and I shall do my utmost to explain all this to you. Everything I say is true, but let me assure you that the Analytical Engine hardly resembles a human being.

"Its 'language' is actually a highly logical code, designed by mathematicians in order to operate the Engine. This code is not difficult to master, but it does require considerable discipline. It has a very small vocabulary, which is nothing to compare with the English tongue. This vocabulary is arranged into statements according to a limited set of rules.

"The major problem in communicating with the Engine is that one must use the utmost care and precision in giving it instructions, for it has no imagination whatsoever and cannot correct even trivial errors in spelling or punctuation. It is, after all, like other machines in that it has no awareness of the tasks that it performs; therefore it will obey the most unreasonable of instructions. For example, if it is told to print the number zero *ad infinitum*, it will continue to do so for hours on end, until a human being finally causes it to stop."

"But Holmes, how does one give instructions to this Engine?" I asked, scarcely crediting my companion's remarks thus far and wondering whether perhaps his penchant for cocaine had finally betrayed his reason.

"By writing a set of instructions in code and supplying them mechanically to the Engine. Such a set of instructions is called a *programme*, because it is an orderly and precise procedure for solving a problem. The art of writing programmes is called, reasonably enough, *programming*."

"Of what relevance is this strange machine to you, Holmes?"

"I intend to employ the Engine whenever possible in my future criminal cases," he replied. "As you know, I have been rather overburdened with work in recent months, so the Engine's speed and potential accuracy are most attractive to me. It has a great capacity for dealing with large amounts of information as well."

"But, Holmes," I interrupted, "do you truly expect this device, if it is as unimaginative as you say, actually to solve crimes?"

"Not at all, my dear Watson," said Holmes with a laugh. "I daresay it is not clever enough to replace my brain; but it will be useful for storing information, as well as for performing certain repetitive tasks that absorb too much of my time. Of most interest to me is that it will provide a means of expressing my logical methods in a rigorous form, and perhaps be useful in communicating to others my modest attempts at formulating a Science of Deduction."

1.1 Commentary

Actually, Charles Babbage and his collaborator, Lady Augusta Ada Lovelace (Lord Byron's daughter), had between them worked out most of the fundamental principles upon which modern computing is based. The Analytical Engine was indeed the forerunner of today's computers.

Holmes's insight into the promises and pitfalls of the computer is striking. The ability to handle great amounts of data, to remember even the tiniest detail, to make extremely accurate calculations, and to obey instructions over and over again are all well recognized.

What are not so well recognized are the pitfalls: the often endless details, the intolerance to error, the annoying idiosyncrasies, and the need for unremitting rigor.

Your first attempt at programming is likely to be a frustrating experience. The demanding precision to which Holmes alludes is quite unfamiliar to most people. You must struggle to piece together a variety of computer instructions, making changes almost randomly and hoping somehow the program will work. You might desperately put a line into your program that says:

```
PRINT THE ANSWER
```

CHARLES BABBAGE

and expect the computer to print the correct result. This would be futile. To get a computer to do your bidding, you must tell it precisely what you want it to do in exactly the proper way.

When you do this, you have at your command a kind of modern genie.

LADY LOVELACE

For example, this entire book has been typed using a specialized computer called a *word processor*. This computer has made it possible for us to modify the text in small and large ways and then print out revised versions quickly for study and further improvement. When we were finished revising the manuscript, this computer reproduced our text in a form that made it possible for another computer to typeset the book automatically. Babbage would be especially satisfied if he were alive today, for it was his desire to eliminate error from tide tables that led him to develop the Difference Engine from which the Analytical Engine evolved. In fact, this early computer was designed to set type to enable the printing of the tables.

In the chapters that follow, Holmes will introduce all that you need to know in order to write first-rate computer programs yourself. In the first adventure, "Murder at the Metropolitan Club," you will observe as Holmes writes an algorithm. The concept of an algorithm is the most fundamental idea you need to grasp in order to write programs. Having introduced the subject, Holmes then presents his algorithm coded in Basic. It is there that we begin to discuss the subject of programming languages and how they are used to solve problems.

II

Murder at
the Metropolitan Club

O Sherlock Holmes it was always *the* Engine. His precise and admirably balanced mind was eclipsed only by this mechanism of wood and metal—a series of gears, wheels, and levers, finely adjusted and exclusive of all human temperament. It came as no surprise, then, that he was deeply attracted to the potential of the Engine in his criminal investigations, and its development occupied his immense faculties and extraordinary powers for many of the years that I had the privilege of knowing him and following his cases.

It was only a short time after our first discussion of the Engine that he found a practical use for it. All of London was interested, and the fashionable world dismayed, by the murder of a renowned art dealer at the Metropolitan Club under most unusual and inexplicable circumstances. The crime was of interest in itself, but for Holmes it was also an opportunity to experiment with the Analytical Engine; and it was for this purpose only that he agreed to assist the official police in the matter.

The public were allowed to know certain particulars of the crime, but a good many of the facts, as they dealt with prominent members of society, were suppressed. It is not my task at this time to fill in the missing links, as I am under a specific prohibition from the lips of Sherlock Holmes, but rather to give some explanation of how the great detective was able to employ the extraordinary Engine. Let me say from the first that the case was solved without use of the device, as were so many of his cases. Following its conclusion, Holmes retraced his steps, outlining the circumstances attendant on the investigation to see whether the Engine would arrive at the same results as he himself had.

"You recall our visit last week to the Metropolitan Club in the Strand," he began, "and the renowned subject under investigation.

"An initial enquiry by Scotland Yard yielded four suspects," he said, recounting the case. "The four were registered in adjoining rooms above the club. One of them was Sir Raymond Jasper, a noted member of the bar, and another an accountant by the name of Robert Holman. The other two, a Colonel Reginald Woodley and a Mr. James Pope, were visitors from Northumberland, unconnected with each other, I should add. The police assembled a list of facts concerning the crime and these four gentlemen, but in their usual manner failed to recognise the singularities of these trifles and thus entirely overlooked their importance. I can never bring them to

"YOU RECALL OUR VISIT TO THE METROPOLITAN CLUB."

realize the importance of a man's sleeves or the great issues that may hang from a bootlace.

"Here, then, is a partial floor plan of the club's boarding rooms and the list of clues we assembled."

I have duplicated the floor plan here.

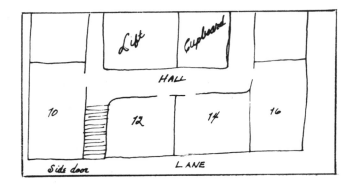

The clues were as follows :

1. Sir Raymond Jasper occupied Room 10.
2. The man occupying Room 14 had black hair.
3. Either Colonel Woodley or Sir Raymond wore a pince-nez.
4. Mr. Pope always carried a gold pocket watch.
5. One of the suspects was seen driving a four-wheel carriage.
6. The man with the pince-nez had brown hair.
7. Mr. Holman wore a ruby signet ring.
8. The man in Room 16 had tattered cuffs.
9. Mr. Holman occupied Room 12.
10. The man with tattered cuffs had red hair.
11. The man in Room 12 had grey hair.
12. The man with a gold pocket watch occupied Room 14.
13. Colonel Woodley occupied a corner room.
14. The murderer had brown hair.

"Well, my friend," I said, after examining the list, "these may be very good clues, but a glance at them does not tell me who the murderer was."

"Precisely why the police neglected them, and that is where the Analytical Engine comes into use. These clues are worthless unless we can determine the particular relationship of one to another and see how they fit into a larger scheme. To do so we need to devise an *algorithm* that both we and the Engine can follow."

"This all sounds very mathematical, Holmes," I suggested.

"It is, Watson," he replied. "But the mathematics themselves are childishly simple. Our algorithm may be compared to a recipe—a set of instructions to be carried out in a specific order. Our ingredients and how they are to be used, however, must be stated explicitly and rigorously if the Engine is to follow them correctly. There are a few items of importance concerning algorithms that I must relate to you. First and foremost, only one instruction is performed at a time; and secondly, after each instruction, the next step must be made absolutely clear. Finally, there must be a clearly defined stopping place, indicating that the problem has been solved and that the execution of the algorithm ends."

"But, Holmes," I asked, "since the clues themselves are steps by which one logically arrives at the solution, why do they not constitute an algorithm?"

"This is the key, Watson. The clues are *data*, not *instructions*. They have no orderly arrangement that shows their inter-relationship. It is just such an orderly arrangement that the algorithm confers. Now, Watson, if you wish to follow my future investigations, you would do well to learn the technique of creating algorithms yourself, for there is really no other way to understand the Analytical Engine's operation."

"Very well, Holmes," I replied. "But what must I do to start?"

"The first step," said Holmes, "is to try to imagine how you would tell someone else to solve the problem."

"Naturally I would keep track of all the relevant facts of the case," I ventured, "and then carefully examine all the clues that might relate to each of them."

"But think, Watson, to 'keep track of the facts' would mean to keep a table of the established facts; to 'examine the clues' would then mean to enter the facts in appropriate places in the table. Let us use this method in the first stage of developing an algorithm to solve the particular case with which we are concerned."

Holmes took a sheet of paper and began writing out what I had proposed. "Perhaps this is what you have in mind, Watson," he said, handing me the paper. It read :

1. Look at the next clue.
2. If the clue establishes a fact then
    record the fact
  else
    dismiss the clue.
3. Repeat this process until the murderer is found.

"Yes," I replied. "This seems to be a plausible method. Could we place these facts in some form of table to better illustrate this method?"

Beneath the algorithm I sketched the table that I have reproduced here.

SUSPECT.	COLONEL WOODLEY.	MR. HOLMAN.	MR. POPE.	SIR RAYMOND.
Hair Colour.				
Transport.				
Attire.				
Room.				

Holmes gave it a quick glance.

"Indeed, Watson, this approach is excellent; but there is a minor problem. We need a clearer, more rigorous attack. What does it mean, for instance, to say 'if the clue establishes a fact'? Some of the clues establish facts directly, whereas others do not; and exactly what does it mean to 'look at the next clue'? The Analytical Engine would certainly not be able to make any clear interpretation of these instructions, let alone follow them."

"Really, Holmes!" I cried. "One moment you are praising my efforts, the next I appear to be the fool."

"My apologies, Watson, I do not mean to try your patience, but it is essential that our approach to this problem be made without error. Bear with me and I will make it clear how we can put your efforts to good use. Let us consider two obvious clues. The first, 'Sir Raymond Jasper occupied Room 10,' means that we should set the room number of Sir Raymond to 10 in the table. This is an example of a known fact provided directly by a clue.

"Now, consider 'the man occupying Room 14 had black hair.' This means if the room of some suspect is 14, then set the hair colour of this same suspect to black in the table. This clue does not disclose a fact immediately, but only after some other fact has been established.

"Moreover," he continued, "we must assume initially that nothing in the table is known; to illustrate this we initially leave each space empty.

Gradually, as we examine our list of clues, we assign the proper item to each place in the table. Finally, we must state that the algorithm's result is to be the name of the murderer.

"I know all this seems rather fussy to you, but in designing an algorithm one must state the overall strategy carefully and in considerable detail. Here is a general sketch of how we require the algorithm to operate," he said, as he began writing again. When finished, he presented me with this summary :

1. Assume that nothing is known.
2. Establish the known clues.
3. Do the following:
   try the remaining clues
   until the murderer is known.
4. Give the name of the murderer.

"An essential item in our algorithm, concerning which I have said nothing, is this third instruction. It is the command we give the Engine to try every clue repeatedly until one of them produces the solution. This is known among the mathematicians at Cambridge as a *loop*, and I shall provide you with a fuller account of its role at a later date. For now, let us return to our problem."

"But this version doesn't appear to be any more specific than the last, Holmes," I ventured.

"Absolutely correct, Watson. Even this version is too general for our purposes. As I have already told you, the Engine must be instructed as to exactly what to do at each step. We must, for example, specify which of the table entries can be set directly from our list of clues and how the remaining clues can be used to establish facts.

"Consider the clue 'Sir Raymond Jasper occupied Room 10.' This is a known clue and can be more precisely stated as:

Let ROOM of SIR_RAYMOND = 10

Likewise, 'The man occupying Room 14 had black hair,' one of the remaining clues, can be stated as:

If ROOM of some SUSPECT = 14 then
   let HAIR of SUSPECT = BLACK

Do you see the gist of it now, Watson?"

"Yes, Holmes," I said. "I am beginning to understand the phrasing of algorithms; but it still seems to be a laborious procedure."

"Laborious, yes—but after all, we want to state each clue *explicitly*, giving names to the persons and to the properties associated with each of them."

My companion's enthusiasm for the task fired me and thus for the remainder of the evening I busied myself tediously pairing off the available facts. At last my results ran this way :—

Assume all table entries are unknown

Let ROOM of SIR_RAYMOND = 10 . . . . clue 1

Let ATTIRE of MR_POPE = GOLD_WATCH . . . . clue 4

Let ATTIRE of MR_HOLMAN = RUBY_RING . . . . clue 7

Let ROOM of MR_HOLMAN = 12 . . . . clue 9

Do the following:

    if ROOM of some SUSPECT = 14 then . . . . clue 2
        let HAIR of SUSPECT = BLACK

    if SUSPECT = COL_WOODLEY or SIR_RAYMOND then . . . . clue 3
        let ATTIRE of SUSPECT = PINCENEZ
    let TRANSPORT of some SUSPECT

        = FOURWHEEL_CARRIAGE . . . . clue 5
. . .   .

    if HAIR of some SUSPECT is BROWN then . . . . clue 14
        let MURDERER = SUSPECT
until the murderer is known

Give the name of the MURDERER

Expectantly, I reviewed my deductions, but, alas, found that this algorithm did not, however I chose to look upon it, reveal the murderer's name. I retired with a heavy feeling of dissatisfaction.

    The following morning, rising earlier than usual, I found Holmes already engaged in breakfast. He sat quietly munching his toast as I approached the table with a long foolscap document in my hand.

    "Well, Watson," he said, pushing aside his plate, "what have you to report?"

    "I fear my efforts have been wasted, Holmes. I can see nothing from this," I confessed.

    "On the contrary, Watson, you can see everything. You, however, like Scotland Yard, fail to reason from what you see. You are too timid in drawing your inferences. Let's examine it further," he suggested, "for in this field errors often lead to improved understanding."

I presented the document to him and a revised table that I have duplicated below.

SUSPECT.	COLONEL WOODLEY.	MR. HOLMAN.	MR. POPE.	SIR RAYMOND.
Hair Colour.				
Attire.		RUBY RING	GOLD WATCH	
Room.		12		10

Heartened by his reaction, I ventured an observation that had troubled me when I had tried to fit the list of clues into an algorithm.

"This fifth clue, Holmes, I believe is irrelevant to the case," I suggested. "That one of the suspects is known to have driven a four-wheel carriage does not, in my estimation, have any bearing on the circumstances we are investigating."

"Splendid, Watson!" cried Holmes. "You have just discovered another important property of algorithms: they must contain *no superfluous instructions* and no loose ends."

He stood for a moment examining the document.

"Really, you have done very well indeed. You have correctly assumed that each suspect has a different attire characteristic. It is true, however, that you have made an error that could lead us entirely off the track."

I was deeply dismayed.

"Now think carefully, Watson," he continued. "Your statement

If SUSPECT = COL_WOODLEY or SIR_RAYMOND then
   let ATTIRE of SUSPECT = PINCENEZ

does *not* embody the meaning of the third clue, which states that one of these two suspects wore just such an eyepiece. Your algorithm will give us the wrong answer. What we need here is a clearer translation of this clue. I would suggest,

If ATTIRE of SIR_RAYMOND ≠ PINCENEZ then
   let ATTIRE of COL_WOODLEY = PINCENEZ
If ATTIRE of COL_WOODLEY ≠ PINCENEZ then
   let ATTIRE of SIR_RAYMOND = PINCENEZ

You see, Watson, only when we know that one of these suspects does not wear a pince-nez can we establish that the other suspect has the eyepiece.

"The important point is that the algorithm must be absolutely *correct*, which means it must solve the problem you intend it to solve. The Analytical Engine will never know if your algorithm is correct or not. It will only obey your instructions.

"Now let us re-organize the clues, bearing in mind these last observations," said Holmes, sketching on a fresh sheet of paper the chart I have replicated here :

Clues establishing known facts:

1. Sir Raymond Jasper occupied Room 10.
2. Mr Pope always carried a gold pocket watch.
3. Mr. Holman wore a ruby signet ring.
4. Mr. Holman occupied Room 12.

The remaining clues:

5. The man occupying Room 14 had black hair.
6. Either Colonel Woodley or Sir Raymond wore a pince-nez.
7. The man with the pince-nez had brown hair.
8. The man with tattered cuffs had red hair.
9. The man in Room 16 had tattered cuffs.
10. The man in Room 12 had grey hair.
11. The man with the gold pocket watch occupied Room 14.
12. Colonel Woodley occupied a corner room.
13. The murderer had brown hair.

We spent the remainder of the morning reconstructing the algorithm based on the arrangement of facts Holmes had outlined at our breakfast table. The result is reproduced here as Exhibit 2.1.

As he scanned the now complete algorithm, Holmes puffed at his pipe with satisfaction. "Excellent, Watson, I daresay that with a few days' study of the Engine's special language you'll be ready to test your algorithm on the Engine itself."

"Is it a difficult language?" I enquired.

"I should say that it will prove far less formidable to you than did Latin or Greek at Wellington. The important thing is that you now understand the key principle on which the Engine's operation rests."

"And I now know the murderer's true identity!" I exclaimed.

"Indeed," replied Holmes dryly.

Definitions:

HAIR   : row of hair colours for the suspects
ATTIRE · row of attire characteristics for the suspects
ROOM   : row of room numbers for the suspects
SUSPECT, MURDERER: one of the suspects

Algorithm:

Set all table entries and **MURDERER** to unknown

Let ROOM of SIR_RAYMOND = 10
Let ATTIRE of MR_POPE = GOLD_WATCH
Let ATTIRE of MR_HOLMAN = RUBY_RING
Let ROOM of MR_HOLMAN = 12

Do the following:
  if ROOM of some SUSPECT = 14 then
    let HAIR of SUSPECT = BLACK
  if ATTIRE of SIR_RAYMOND ≠ PINCENEZ then
    let ATTIRE of COL_WOODLEY = PINCENEZ
  if ATTIRE of COL_WOODLEY ≠ PINCENEZ then
    let ATTIRE of SIR_RAYMOND = PINCENEZ
  if ATTIRE of some SUSPECT = PINCENEZ then
    let HAIR of SUSPECT = BROWN
  if ATTIRE of some SUSPECT = TATTERED_CUFFS then
    let HAIR of SUSPECT = RED
  if ROOM of some SUSPECT = 16 then
    let ATTIRE of SUSPECT = TATTERED_CUFFS
  if ROOM of some SUSPECT = 12 then
    let HAIR of SUSPECT = GREY
  if ATTIRE of some SUSPECT = GOLD_WATCH then
    let ROOM of SUSPECT = 14

  if ROOM of some SUSPECT = 10
  and SUSPECT ≠ COL_WOODLEY then
    let ROOM of COL_WOODLEY = 16
  if ROOM of some SUSPECT = 16
  and SUSPECT ≠ COL_WOODLEY then
    let ROOM of COL_WOODLEY = 10

  if HAIR of some SUSPECT = BROWN then
    let MURDERER = SUSPECT
until the MURDERER is known

Print the name of the MURDERER

Exhibit 2.1 *Final Algorithm for the Metropolitan Club Murder*

2.1   Algorithms Reviewed

Of all the topics we will discuss in this book, the most fundamental is the concept of an *algorithm*. Over a century ago Holmes realized that people are accustomed to taking many things for granted when they deliver instructions to others, and he warned against making the same error when designing an algorithm for the Engine.

The rigor demanded by a computer algorithm is the essence of programming, no matter which special language you are working in. Let's quickly review the properties of an algorithm discussed by Holmes, for his treatment of the subject in this chapter gives us the key to all that we will take up in later pages.

Generally, an algorithm is a sequence of instructions given to solve some problem. Any algorithm must have the following characteristics:

1.   *It must be organized properly.*   An algorithm reflects some sequence of instructions carried out in the real world. Accordingly, the instructions must be arranged in some meaningful way in order to solve the problem at hand.

2.   *It must go step by step.* Each instruction in the algorithm must be some form of imperative statement to carry out a given step in the problem solution. After each step, the next step in the solution must be unambiguous.

3.   *It must be precise.* The instructions given in an algorithm can leave no room for ambiguity. Thus it must be possible to interpret the instructions in only one way.

4.   *It must make the data explicit.* Each item we choose to include in our algorithm must be clearly identified. For example, if an algorithm has something to do with suspects and room numbers, and these are calculated during the course of the algorithm, then these items need to be described explicitly.

5.   *It must contain no irrelevant information.* There can be no loose ends, no extraneous instructions, no frills. The algorithm must state only the relevant instructions needed to be carried out.

6.   *It must be correct.* An algorithm is always directed toward its single goal—to establish results that will be known upon its completion. The results must be exactly what you want.

All of these features are things that we often take for granted. In an algorithm, we must be rigorous to the last detail.

Before going on to the next chapter and discussing how we express algorithms in Basic, let's review a few last steps in the algorithm to solve the murder at the Metropolitan Club.

As you recall, Watson prepared a table containing facts established by the known clues. In Table 2.1 we show the effects of executing the algorithm further.

In particular, Table 2.1 shows the entries established after two successive executions of the repeated instructions given in Holmes and Watson's algorithm. After executing the instructions once, the facts given in Table 2.1a are established; after another execution, the facts given in Table 2.1b are established. Thus the algorithm slowly fills the table with newly established facts. We leave it to you to execute the instructions again in order to establish the identity of the murderer.

TABLE 2.1   *Facts Established after Two Executions of the Loop*

(* denotes a fact obtained during the given execution of the loop.)

a.   Facts established after first execution:

Suspect	Colonel Woodley	Mr. Holman	Mr. Pope	Sir Raymond
Hair Color		GREY*		
Attire		RUBY RING	GOLD WATCH	
Room	16*	12	14*	10

b.   Facts established after second execution:

Suspect	Colonel Woodley	Mr. Holman	Mr. Pope	Sir Raymond
Hair Color		GREY	BLACK*	
Attire	TATTERED CUFFS*	RUBY RING	GOLD WATCH	
Room	16	12	14	10

III

Holmes Gives a Demonstration

HERLOCK Holmes had spent several days in bed, as was his habit from time to time, and emerged one morning with several documents in his hands. He had a horror of destroying papers, especially those connected with his past cases, and I thought at first sight that he had been sifting through some old notes; but he announced as he entered the room that what he held was a new version of the algorithm we had worked out concerning the dreadful business at the Metropolitan Club. This rendering, he informed me, was composed entirely in the Engine's special language, Basic.

Holmes seemed quite pleased with his work and offered the documents for my study. I have duplicated them here as Exhibit 3.1.

"You expect me to make sense of this ineffable twaddle, Holmes?" I exclaimed, for this new version appeared to be written with the oddest assortment of English terms, numbers, and punctuation marks tossed about at random.

Holmes walked to the mantelpiece and began filling his pipe with that abhorrent shag he kept in the toe of a Persian slipper.

"These six lines, for instance," I said, tapping the papers, "the ones at the beginning of the programme; these hardly appear to be written in code at all and do not have the cryptic appearance of the rest of this document."

"Those are *remarks*, Watson," replied Holmes as he lit his pipe. "In Basic, all remarks begin with the symbol REM, and occupy a complete line. Here they are used to make observations on the programme's content, entirely for the human reader's enlightenment. They contain no instructions to the machine, and have no effect on the programme's meaning. You might consider them as asides to communicate in ordinary English any information the programmer wishes to include concerning the programme."

"I can hardly imagine how the deuce you arrived at these results," said I, still amazed at the complexity of this latest document.

"I reached this one," said Holmes, pointing to the papers with the stem of his briar, "by sitting upon five pillows and consuming an ounce of shag. You have not, I hope, learned to despise my pipe and my lamentable tobacco? It must take the place of food these days if I am to master this Engine.

"Now, the succession of lines beginning with 0080 and running through 0180 are also remarks. You will see that each of our suspects is represented by a number—suspect number 1 is Colonel Woodley; suspect 2, Mr. Holman; 3 is Mr. Pope; and 4, Sir Raymond."

"But, Holmes," I asked, "how does this make a pennyworth of difference to us?"

"For reasons you will understand better as we proceed, Watson. In writing a programme one must choose names for all the entities of the algorithm. Here, for example, S is the programme name used for a suspect, M the programme name for the murderer. These names are called *variables*, because the values associated with them will vary as the programme progresses. For instance, the value associated with S will depend on which suspect is being examined.

"Now, Watson, for your table. Each row is represented by an *array*, defined in line 0190. The row of hair colours by the array H$, the row of attire characteristics by A$, and the row of room numbers by R$. Each row has four entries, one for each suspect. The actual entries in each row are represented by character strings. For example, the colour black is denoted by "BLACK" and a gold watch by "GOLD_WATCH". When an entry is unknown, it has the value "UNKNOWN"."

"This seems a bit much to digest at once, Holmes," I protested.

"It will all become clear to you, Watson, as we work further with the Engine. For the moment, let us study the structure of a programme, using our work on the affair at the Metropolitan Club as a guide.

"Allow me to summarize for you exactly what the main body of the programme accomplishes. It begins with the line:

```
0220 LET M = 0
```

This sets the value of M to 0, meaning an identity for the murderer has not been established. The next lines

```
0010 REM  -- THIS PROGRAMME EXAMINES THE CLUES
0020 REM  -- GIVEN FOR THE MURDER IN THE METROPOLITAN CLUB.
0030 REM  -- THE THREE ARRAYS, H$ FOR HAIR, A$ FOR ATTIRE, AND
0040 REM  -- R$ FOR ROOM, ARE USED TO ESTABLISH THE FACTS
0050 REM  -- AS THEY ARE DETERMINED.
0060 REM  -- THE PROGRAM PRINTS THE NAME OF THE MURDERER.
0070 REM
0080 REM  -- DICTONARY OF NAMES:
0090 REM
0100 REM  -- S    ONE OF THE SUSPECTS, 1 THROUGH 4
0110 REM  -- M    THE MURDERER, A SUSPECT FROM 1 TO 4; 0 IF UNKNOWN
0120 REM  -- H$   ARRAY OF HAIR COLOURS
0130 REM  -- A$   ARRAY OF ATTIRE CHARACTERISTICS
0140 REM  -- R$   ARRAY OF ROOM NUMBERS
0150 REM
0160 REM  -- 1 DENOTES COLONEL WOODLEY, 2 DENOTES MR. HOLMAN
0170 REM  -- 3 DENOTES MR. POPE,        4 DENOTES SIR RAYMOND
0180 REM
0190      DIM H$(4), A$(4), R$(4)
0200 REM
0210 REM  -- ASSUME NOTHING IS KNOWN
0220      LET M = 0
0230      FOR S = 1 TO 4
0240         LET H$(S) = "UNKNOWN"
0250         LET A$(S) = "UNKNOWN"
0260         LET R$(S) = "UNKNOWN"
0270      NEXT S
0280 REM
0290 REM  -- ESTABLISH KNOWN CLUES
0300      LET R$(4) = "ROOM_10"
0310      LET A$(3) = "GOLD_WATCH"
0320      LET A$(2) = "RUBY_RING"
0330      LET R$(2) = "ROOM_12"
0340 REM
0350      LET S = 1
0360 REM  -- REPEATEDLY TRY THE REMAINING CLUES
0370         IF R$(S) <> "ROOM_14"    THEN 0390
0380            LET H$(S) = "BLACK"
0390         IF A$(4) = "UNKNOWN"     THEN 0420
0400         IF A$(4) = "PINCENEZ"    THEN 0420
0410            LET A$(1) = "PINCENEZ"
```

Exhibit 3.1   *Holmes's Programme for the Metropolitan Club Murder*

```
0420        IF A$(1) = "UNKNOWN"     THEN 0450
0430        IF A$(1) = "PINCENEZ"    THEN 0450
0440          LET A0(4) = "PINCENEZ"
0450        IF A$(S) <> "PINCENEZ" THEN 0470
0460          LET H$(S) = "BROWN"
0470        IF A$(S) <> "TATTERED_CUFFS" THEN 0490
0480          LET H$(S) = "RED"
0490        IF R$(S) <> "ROOM_16"    THEN 0510
0500          LET A$(S) = "TATTERED_CUFFS"
0510        IF R$(S) <> "ROOM_12"    THEN 0530
0520          LET H$(S) = "GREY"
0530        IF A$(S) <> "GOLD_WATCH" THEN 0550
0540          LET R$(S) = "ROOM_14"
0550        IF R$(S) <> "ROOM_10"    THEN 0580
0560        IF S = 1                 THEN 0580
0570          LET R$(1) = "ROOM_16"
0580        IF R$(S) <> "ROOM_16"    THEN 0610
0590        IF S = 1                 THEN 0610
0600          LET R$(1) = "ROOM_10"
0610        IF H$(S) <> "BROWN" THEN 0650
0620          LET M = S
0630 REM
0640 REM     -- TRY NEXT SUSPECT
0650        IF S = 4 THEN 0680
0660          LET S = S + 1
0670          GOTO 0700
0680          LET S = 1
0690          GOTO 0700
0700     IF M = 0 THEN 0370
0710 REM
0720 REM     -- PRINT THE NAME OF THE MURDERER
0730     IF M <> 1 THEN 0750
0740       PRINT "THE MURDERER IS COLONEL WOODLEY."
0750     IF M <> 2 THEN 0770
0760       PRINT "THE MURDERER IS MR. HOLMAN."
0770     IF M <> 3 THEN 0790
0780       PRINT "THE MURDERER IS MR. POPE."
0790     IF M <> 4 THEN 0810
0800       PRINT "THE MURDERER IS SIR RAYMOND."
0810     STOP
0820 END
```

Exhibit 3.1 *Continued*

```
0230 FOR S = 1 TO 4
0240    LET H$(S) = "UNKNOWN"
0250    LET A$(S) = "UNKNOWN"
0260    LET R$(S) = "UNKNOWN"
0270 NEXT S
```

set each entry in the table to unknown; first for suspect 1, then for suspect 2, suspect 3, and finally suspect 4. In the next segment we make a note of our known clues. For instance, the line

```
0320 LET A$(2) = "RUBY_RING"
```

explicitly sets the **MR. HOLMAN** entry of our attire array A$ to "RUBY_RING".

"As for the remaining clues, the suspect S is initially set to 1, Colonel Woodley; notice that this departs slightly from our original algorithm. Then each remaining clue is tested. For instance, consider the two instructions:

```
0370 IF R$(S) <> "ROOM_14" THEN 0390
0380    LET H$(S) = "BLACK"
```

"This first line tells us that if the room number of the suspect S is not 14, we continue with the instruction at line 0390. If, however, the room number of the suspect is equal to 14, we move on to the next instruction, which sets the hair colour of the suspect S to black.

"Now suppose we have gone through and tested all of these clues against a particular suspect, arriving at last at line 0650. Here we set the suspect S to be the next person whom we wish to investigate. In line 0700 the murderer M is tested to see if it is zero. If this is still the case, we run through the clues against our next suspect, and we continue to test them, one by one, until we arrive at a value other than zero for the murderer M.

"How often have I said that when you have eliminated the impossible, whatever remains, however improbable, must be the truth? This process of elimination is exactly what our programme will do for us, Watson. You may recall in our earlier discussions that this repetition of instructions is called a *loop*, and I compared it to a simple recipe."

Although this exposition of the programme seemed to follow readily from our algorithm, I remained confused by some of the odd grammar and vocabulary of this programme. Ordinary words like LET or IF seemed to take on entirely new meanings in Basic and I questioned Holmes on this point.

"The words that baffle you, Watson," he explained, "are known as *keywords*, and are the framework for constructing logical operations within the language itself. Once you have learned more of the grammar of Basic you will be able to write simple programmes of your own with little difficulty."

"Very well, Holmes, but what of the names such as A$ or S? As you chose these names yourself, I surmise they are not part of the special Basic lexicon. Yet are there not some restrictions as to how such names may be conceived?"

"Certainly." agreed Holmes. "There are specific rules governing the formation of names. A name must be written as a letter or a letter followed by a digit, as is the case with S and S1. If a name stands for a string, it must be appropriately identified as such."

He pointed to the $ symbol and then to A$ as an example of a name representing a string.

"Unfortunately, these names are hardly illuminating, especially to someone other than the programme's author. Some of the mathematicians are developing versions that allow longer names like SUSPECT or ATTIRE$. I hope they succeed, for writing programmes with longer names will greatly enhance their understanding."

"LET US TALK OF LIGHTER MATTERS."

"The line numbers make little sense to me," I protested. "Some are referenced in the programme, and some are not. Why, it is quite impossible to see what happens after an instruction that branches off to another."

Holmes seemed a trifle disconcerted at this remark and returned the programme to the pile of earlier versions on the table.

"Oddly enough, Watson, the use of line numbers *is* somewhat confusing, and impossible to encapsulate briefly. Come now, let us talk of lighter matters, for Basic is a subject that is best absorbed in moderate doses at the outset."

3.1 General Program Structure

We now have a working model of a basic Basic program. We have seen a problem, in this case a search for the identity of a criminal, presented as an algorithm and translated into Basic. If you find this program a bit overwhelming, hang in there—our intent here is only to give you a taste of what we'll be getting into later.

As you have probably already observed, the writing of programs requires that you know a number of sometimes odd conventions. Watson's mystification at some of the things mentioned by Holmes is true of us all. For starters, let's examine some of the major components of Holmes's program.

Let's first look at the overall structure of the program for the murder at the Metropolitan Club:

```
0010  REM -- THIS PROGRAMME EXAMINES THE CLUES
...   ...
0220  LET M = 0
...   ...
0820  END
```

All programs consist of a sequence of lines. Each line has a line number and a *statement*. Thus all programs have the form:

```
line-number   statement
line-number   statement

. . .
```

line-number   statement
line-number   END

Depending on the version of Basic you are using, a line number can consist of 1 to 4 or 5 digits. Here, all line numbers will consist of 4 digits, a common practice accepted by almost every version of Basic. The line numbers must be in sequential order. Increasing line numbers are often given in increments of 10, a convention we will also follow. This convention allows you to make small changes to a program without changing all the line numbers.

The last statement in a program must be an END statement, such as:

0930 END

This statement signifies the end of the complete program text.

The first group of lines in the program, lines 0010 through 0180, are remark lines describing the overall purpose of the program and some characteristics of its behavior. Importantly, each name used in the program is itemized, and its role is documented. For instance, the remark

0100 REM -- S   ONE OF THE SUSPECTS, 1 THROUGH 4

describes a numeric variable S. This variable can take on values from 1 through 4.

Remark lines are not required in a program; their use is purely for the human reader. As we shall often demonstrate, remarks can be an indispensable addition to a program.

The first line of the program that is not a remark line is a *dimension* statement:

0190   DIM H$(4), A$(4), R$(4)

This statement specifies the three rows of Watson's table. For instance, the row of hair colors, H$, is denoted by:

H$(4)

Here the $ in H$ means that the entries will have string values, and the 4 in parentheses means there are four such values.

Next, we come to the algorithm portion of the program. An algorithm is written as a sequence of statements. There are several kinds of statements in Basic. Each of them specifies some action to be carried out by the computer. For example, the statement in line 0220,

0220 LET M = 0

sets the value of the murderer M to 0. Other statements in Basic allow complex actions to be specified. For example, the lines having the form

```
0230 FOR S = 1 TO 4
        actions taken for a given suspect S
0270 NEXT S
```

specify a series of actions to be executed repeatedly, once for each value of S successively set to the values 1 through 4.

Next consider the statement in line 0370:

```
0370 IF R$(S) <> "ROOM_14" THEN 0390
```

This statement tests if the room of a suspect S is "ROOM_14". When S is 1, the entry for Colonel Woodley will be tested; when S is 2, the entry for Mr. Holman will be tested; and so on. If the test is true, execution of the program will continue at line 0390. If the test is false, execution will continue at the following statement, the one in line 0380. This statement

```
0380 LET H$(S) = "BLACK"
```

will set the entry for the hair color of S to black. The net effect of the pair of statements is to set hair of suspect S to "BLACK" if the room of S happens to be "ROOM_14".

This is enough for digestion now. All of these points will be taken up in greater detail in later chapters by Holmes and we too shall give them greater attention. For the remainder of this chapter, however, let's take a closer look at the individual components of a program.

3.2   The Units of a Basic Program

At the most elementary level, a Basic program consists of a sequence of symbols. The possible symbols are given in Table 3.1. The arrangement of symbols is subject to numerous and sometimes complex conventions that you will have to learn as we go along. Here we pin down a few of the more primitive conventions, including the rules for writing identifiers, numbers, character strings, and comments.

Identifiers

An *identifier* is a name created by the programmer. It consists of a letter, or a letter followed by a digit. If the identifier stands for a string value, it must have a dollar sign ($) after it. Some examples are:

```
S      C$
S1     A$
M      R$
X      N1$
Y      N2$
```

In Basic, S and S$ are considered as different identifiers.

Some implementations of Basic are much more generous in the rules for writing identifiers, allowing lengthy identifiers, and sometimes even a special character (normally an underscore) for separating the parts of a compound name. For example, the above identifiers might be better written as:

```
SUSPECT          COLOUR$
OTHER_SUSPECT    ATTIRE$
MURDERER         ROOM$
X_COORDINATE     FIRST_NAME$
Y_COORDINATE     LAST_NAME$
```

If your version of Basic allows long identifiers, use them, *generously*. We cannot begin to say how much we would have preferred to write this text with these longer names. Unfortunately, the reality that many popular versions of Basic do not support long identifiers weighed against us.

Keywords

In Basic there are a number of words that have a special significance in a program. These are called *keywords*. A keyword is a special word that tells the computer what to do. For example, the keyword REM introduces a remark.

You don't have to memorize all the keywords. The important point is that each has a specific role. Furthermore, the keywords in Basic are usually "reserved," meaning that you may not use the the keywords as identifiers in your program even if your version of Basic supports long identifiers; for example, you might be able to change the name S to SUSPECT but could not change the name S to REM or NEXT, which would be quite senseless in any case.

Numbers

Suppose you wish to compute the number of feet to the scene of a crime or an amount of money embezzled in a series of bank transactions. Basic, like any other programming language, has a rather fixed set of conventions for writing numbers.

TABLE 3.1   *Basic Symbols*

Digits

0 1 2 3 4 5 6 7 8 9

Letters

A B C D E F G H I J K L M
N O P Q R S T U V W X Y Z

Special Symbols

+   –   *   /   =   <>   <   >   >=   <=

^ $ "   .   ,   :   ;   (   )

Keywords

DATA	GOSUB	ON	STEP
DEF	GOTO		STOP
DIM		PRINT	
	IF		TO
END	INPUT	RANDOMIZE	THEN
		READ	
FOR	LET	REM	
		RESTORE	
	NEXT	RETURN	

The first kind of number you can write is an *integer*, which means a whole number. An integer is represented by a sequence of digits, possibly preceded by a plus or a minus sign, like so:

0	10
1776	+10
100000	−10

Negative numbers can be used to represent things like a temperature of minus 10 degrees or a bank balance that is in the red.

The second kind of number you can write in Basic is sometimes called a *real number*. A real number has either a decimal point, a letter E followed by a scale factor (which means "times ten to the power of") or both. For example, you may write the numbers

```
12.34
1234E-2
0.1234E2
0.1234E+2
```

all of which stand for the same real number.

These are the only conventions you can use for writing numbers. Be careful, for as much as you would like, you cannot write numbers like:

```
1,000      -- you must write 1000
$123       -- you must write 123
```

Whatever number you have in mind, you must represent it as either an integer or as a real number. Normally you use integers to represent whole quantities (the number of suspects or the scheduled time of a train arrival, for example), and real numbers to represent quantities that cannot be determined exactly (the number of feet to the scene of a crime or the weight of a molecule, for example).

Character Strings

Often when you use a computer program, the computer asks you for some data and then prints some results. Since you will surely want to know what data are requested or what the results mean, your program should print messages telling you what is going on. You can do this with *character strings*, such as:

```
"ENTER YOUR PASSWORD:"
"THE MURDERER IS MR. POPE."
```

To print a character string, you simply include it in a PRINT statement, just like

```
PRINT "THE MURDERER IS MR. POPE."
```

in Holmes's program.

A character string consists of a sequence of characters enclosed by quotation marks (").

The characters that you can put in a character string can be any character that your computer recognizes, even such characters as ? and %. What if you would like to have a quotation mark itself as part of a character string? Usually you can't. If you want, you can use an apostrophe (single quote) instead. Thus we may have:

```
"THE MURDERER'S HAIR IS BROWN"
"NOTE THE APOSTROPHE ABOVE"
```

```
"STRINGS MAY CONTAIN SPECIAL CHARACTERS"
"LIKE ? AND %"
"as well as lower case letters in some implementations"
```

Each string must fit on the line in which it occurs.

Remarks

One of the most useful features of programming languages is the ability to annotate your program with *remarks*. For example, in the sequence

```
0290 REM  -- ESTABLISH KNOWN CLUES
0300      LET R$(4) = "ROOM_10"
0310      LET A$(3) = "GOLD_WATCH"
0320      LET A$(2) = "RUBY_RING"
0330      LET R$(2) = "ROOM_12"
```

the first line is a remark.

A remark consists of the word REM followed by the text of a remark. The text of your remark may include anything you like, but must fit on a line. Thus we may have:

```
0010 REM  LONG REMARKS CAN BE WRITTEN, BUT
0020 REM  EACH LINE IN A LONG REMARK MUST
0030 REM  BEGIN WITH THE WORD REM.
```

Normally we will begin the text of each remark with a pair of hyphens, as in:

```
0010 REM  -- FOR READABILITY, THE TEXT OF A REMARK
0020 REM  -- OFTEN BEGINS WITH A PAIR OF HYPHENS.
```

As far as running your program is concerned, if execution reaches a REM statement, execution proceeds to the next line with no other effect.

3.3 Spacing and Layout

It is much easier to read

```
0210 REM  -- ASSUME NOTHING IS KNOWN
0220      LET M = 0
0230      FOR S = 1 TO 4
0240          LET H$(S) = "UNKNOWN"
0250          LET A$(S) = "UNKNOWN"
0260          LET R$(S) = "UNKNOWN"
0270      NEXT S
0280 REM
```

```
0290 REM   -- ESTABLISH KNOWN CLUES
0300      LET R$ (4) = "ROOM_10"
0310      LET A$ (3) = "GOLD_WATCH"
```

than

```
0210 REM--ASSUME NOTHING IS KNOWN
0220 LET M=0
0230 FOR S=1 TO 4
0240 LET H$(S)="UNKNOWN"
0250 LET A$(S)="UNKNOWN"
0260 LET R$(S)="UNKNOWN"
0270 NEXT S
0280 REM--ESTABLISH KNOWN CLUES
0290 LET R$(4)="ROOM_10"
0300 LET A$(3)="GOLD_WATCH"
```

The only difference between the two examples is simply the use of spacing. The computer will ignore blank spaces and blank remark lines, but the human reader will not. In fact, the proper spacing of programs can go a long way in making your intent clear.

There are a few restrictions on the placing of blank spaces. These restrictions need not concern you very much, as it is reasonably obvious just what these restrictions are. For example, you may not put blank spaces between the characters of an identifier or between the < and the > of a <>. And, of course, at least one blank must be inserted between adjacent words, such as between the LET and M above.

Moreover, you have to remember that each statement must fit on one line. All of these rules follow common intuition, and generally speaking, you may insert blank spaces and blank remark lines wherever convenient.

Unfortunately, some implementations make the use of program spacing difficult. You may be working with a small video screen, or your computer may execute more slowly when you put in extra spaces or remark lines. On small computers, extra spaces and remark lines may take up memory space from other program instructions. Some versions of Basic even remove all of the extra spaces you put in. If you have any of these problems, you will have to decide what you want to do. But at least, recall how much you would like to read the programs in this book were all the extra spaces removed.

Finally, notice the line,

```
0280   REM
```

in the first sequence given above. This is a remark statement with no text, and has the effect of a "blank line". Such lines can be inserted freely in a program to improve its readability. In the text to follow, we will make generous use of such blank lines to separate groups of related statements.

The Game Afoot

IV

The Adventure
of the Bathing Machine

HE summer following the little matter of the Vatican cameos was made memorable by three cases of interest, in which I had the privilege of being associated with Mr. Sherlock Holmes and of studying his methods in the use of the Analytical Engine. In glancing over my somewhat jumbled notes of these cases, I find they brought him the fewest personal opportunities in his long and admirable career. Each, however, did provide him with a chance for testing out the Engine's varied capabilities, including a telegraphic arrangement he made at considerable expense for communicating with the Engine over great distances. To Holmes the cases were of themselves of only secondary interest; and although he saved Scotland Yard a good deal of embarrassment in the first of these, the official police took full credit for concluding the affair.

Upon attending one of my new patients one fine June morning, I returned to Baker Street to find Holmes packing his valise in those high spirits that told me he was off on some new adventure.

"You are preparing for a trip," I remarked, eager to display my own deductive faculties.

"Yes, Watson," replied Holmes. "And perhaps your native shrewdness can deduce my destination?"

I studied his packages for a moment. "Off on some scholarly pursuits, I see. Perhaps to Cambridge and the Analytical Engine."

"There is such a delightful freshness about you, my dear Watson. You've really done very well indeed."

I was immensely pleased.

"It is true, however," he continued, "that you have missed everything of importance. As it happens, I leave this afternoon for the Yorkshire coast. Now, Watson, would you care to join me?"

I hesitated for a moment, and then replied. "Indeed I would, Holmes. There is a lull in my practice just now and I could benefit from a change of scene. You have a case, then?"

"A small matter, but not without points of interest," replied Holmes. "We can consider it on the train. Can you meet me at King's Cross at noon?"

"Yes of course, Holmes."

Holmes departed, and I hurried away to pack my bags for a few days by the sea.

As our train lurched northwards, Holmes was deep in thought. Framed in his ear-flapped travelling cap, he hardly spoke until we had passed well out of London. As the grey of the city turned to the green of the countryside, he proceeded to sketch for me the events in an extraordinary matter which had become a topic of conversation the length and breadth of England.

"HE PROCEEDED TO SKETCH FOR ME THE EVENTS."

"I take it you are familiar, Watson, with this matter of the disappearance of the Baroness of Whitelsey?" asked Holmes.

"Only what I have learned from what the *Telegraph* and the *Chronicle* have had to say."

"Well then," he began, "let us review what the papers have reported thus far. It seems that the Baroness was spending a few days at the seaside resort of Scarborough and was daily taking the healthful waters of the North Sea. On each occasion she was taken down to the water's edge in a hired bathing machine, and on each occasion she was accompanied by the same attendants. At her request they would retire to the beach side of the machine while the Baroness dipped into the waters. Now, on the morning of the third

"SHE WAS TAKEN DOWN IN A HIRED BATHING MACHINE."

of July, the attendants, at the conclusion of this minor ritual, hauled the machine back over the beach only to find it empty. A quick search of the shore revealed nothing, and the matter was placed in the hands of the local police. Needless to say, the Baroness has not been seen since."

After a brief pause, I casually remarked that the accusing finger of the law would certainly point in the direction of these attendants.

"Yes, Watson," he answered. "Our dear Inspector Lestrade has been called in by the local police and he naturally suspects foul play on the part of these fellows, all of whom were detained. Of course he does not have a shred of evidence, but remains adamant about a conviction. The family of one of these unfortunate attendants has asked me to look into the matter."

"Isn't it possible," I suggested, "that the Baroness met with an accidental end and that the attendants tried to conceal her drowning?"

"Possible, yes, and highly probable," replied Holmes. "But it is a capital error to theorize before one has collected one's data. However, as Lestrade has already settled upon this theory, it is up to me to look for an alternative."

With that Holmes lapsed into silence for much of the remainder of our journey, sinking into that deep concentration that some might think morose but that I knew to be a sign that he was pondering a most difficult case.

We arrived without incident and took furnished rooms in the hotel at which the Baroness had been staying. I found the trip fatiguing, but Holmes left immediately to pursue his investigations without so much as unpacking his bag. I dined alone and retired early. Lulled by the seaside air and a single glass of port, I slept late into the next morning.

I awoke to find that Holmes had already breakfasted and gone out again, leaving behind this note :

> *Watson — I've gone to Whitby, some 20 miles up the coast. Kindly establish a connection with the Analytical Engine through the local telegraph office.*
>
> *Holmes*

The director of the local telegraph office was most helpful, but in spite of this, I was occupied with filling this request for most of the morning.

When Holmes returned, he appeared elated. "A most profitable morning, Watson. The mystery of the Baroness of Whitelsey is solved to my satisfaction, but we need to resolve one final point. This provides us with an admirable opportunity for testing our new telegraph arrangements for communicating with the Engine.

"Now, the one bit of information we need to determine is the state of the tide at the time that the Baroness vanished. Let us establish this as a problem for the Engine.

"As you know, Watson, tides vary according to a 12 hour and 25 minute cycle. Since high tide today is at 11.00 A.M., tonight it will occur at 11.25 P.M. Let us define the problem in terms of what we know, what is given, and what we wish to determine :

The knowns:	Tides recur every 12 hours and 25 minutes.
The givens:	It is now July 28, and high tide is at 11.00 A.M. The Baroness disappeared on July 3, at 9.00 A.M.
To find:	The state of the tide at the time of the mysterious disappearance.

"Well, Watson, this begins to define the problem. Let me present my algorithm for solving it. First I will explain generally how the algorithm works and then explain some key ideas illustrated by it."

Holmes then presented his simple algorithm, which I have reproduced in Exhibit 4.1.

"First, we express the time for a complete tide cycle in minutes."

"But why in minutes, Holmes?" I asked.

"That is due to a limitation of the Engine, Watson. It cannot work directly with dates and times the way we can. For example, it is inconvenient to read in a date and time such as July 28th, 11.00 A.M.; thus in my algorithm all dates and times are converted to minutes. As you will see, in dealing with dates we can readily express them in terms of the total number of minutes that have elapsed since the beginning of the month.

"We read in TODAYS_DATE as the number 28, representing the 28th of the month. The TIDE_HR is read as 11, for 11.00 A.M. Similarly, the EVENT_DATE and EVENT_HR are read in as 3 and 9, respectively, representing July 3rd and 9.00 A.M., the last time the Baroness was seen. In order to do our computations, we must first convert our dates and times to minutes that have elapsed since the beginning of the month. Thus our first calculation is:

Let MINS_TO_HIGH_TIDE = (TODAYS_DATE - 1) * MINS_PER_DAY

Today's date is 28, but only 27 full days have gone by this month. Thus we subtract 1 and multiply by the number of minutes in a day. This gives the number of minutes in the 27 complete days that have elapsed since the beginning of the month.

"We must also consider the 11 hours between midnight and high tide today. So we use a second calculation,

Let MINS_TO_HIGH_TIDE = MINS_TO_HIGH_TIDE +
                  (TIDE_HR * MINS_PER_HR)

to add the number of minutes that have gone by today to our previous total. We now have the total number of minutes from the beginning of the month until high tide today.

"Next, we follow an identical procedure to arrive at a figure in minutes for the time of the swim and subsequent disappearance."

"But Holmes, why do you calculate from the beginning of the month?"

"That is arbitrary, Watson. I need some date as a reference, and the first of the month is convenient since it allows us to express our input in terms of days of the month.

"We now have the time of today's high tide and also the time of the disappearance, expressed in minutes.   We subtract one from the other.

Definitions:

— Express the knowns:
MINS_PER_HR is 60 minutes
MINS_PER_DAY is 1440 minutes
MINS_PER_TIDE_CYCLE is 745 minutes

Algorithm:

— Obtain the givens:
Input TODAYS_DATE, TIDE_HR, EVENT_DATE, EVENT_HR

— Convert times to minutes since the beginning of the month:
Let MINS_TO_HIGH_TIDE = (TODAYS_DATE - 1) * MINS_PER_DAY
Let MINS_TO_HIGH_TIDE = MINS_TO_HIGH_TIDE +
                        (TIDE_HR * MINS_PER_HR)

Let MINS_TO_EVENT = (EVENT_DATE - 1) * MINS_PER_DAY
Let MINS_TO_EVENT = MINS_TO_EVENT +
                    (EVENT_HR * MINS_PER_HR)

— Find elapsed time:
Let ELAPSED_TIME - MINS_TO_HIGH_TIDE - MINS_TO_EVENT

— Find the number of elapsed tide cycles:
Let TIDE_CYCLES = ELAPSED_TIME / MINS_PER_TIDE_CYCLE

— Output the result:
Print TIDE_CYCLES

Exhibit 4.1 *Holmes's Algorithm for Calculating Tides*

Let ELAPSED_TIME = MINS_TO_HIGH_TIDE - MINS_TO_EVENT

to find the elapsed time in minutes.

"The rest is simple. We divide the elapsed time by the number of minutes in a complete tide cycle, thus giving the number of tide cycles that have taken place in the interim. In this way, our final answer will be expressed in terms of high tide as a reference point.

"Watson, this algorithm demonstrates several key ideas about programming that I would like to explain to you, if you will hear them."

"Of course."

"Very well," Holmes continued. "The first thing to understand is the idea of a *variable*. Each variable we use in the program will have a name that we give to it. Think of a variable as a piece of information that can vary as the program progresses, such as the depth to which the parsley had sunk into the butter that hot day when the dreadful business of the Abernetty family was first brought to my attention."

"But what will cause the variables to change in value?" I asked.

"We will set and change the values of all the variables by the way we write the program," Holmes replied. "They will be completely under our control. Look again at the algorithm for our problem. Here you see several variables, for example, the variables named TODAYS_DATE and TIDE_ CYCLES.

"Next, we have the idea of an *expression*. An expression is a formula for computing a value. You can see some examples in my algorithm. Consider the statement:

Let MINS_TO_HIGH_TIDE = (TODAYS_DATE - 1) * MINS_PER_DAY

Here MINS_TO_HIGH_TIDE is a variable whose value we are trying to establish. We use the expression

(TODAYS_DATE - 1) * MINS_PER_DAY

to express the fact that we want the Engine to subtract 1 from TODAYS_ DATE and multiply the result by the number of minutes in a day."

"Does it not strike you as curious, Holmes, that the asterisk should represent multiplication?"

"Not at all, Watson. The Engine would have difficulty in sorting out the letter 'x' from the usual multiplication symbol."

"A statement used to set a variable based on an expression is termed an *assignment*, because it assigns a value to a variable. You can think of an assignment as establishing a fact about a variable. In the algorithm, all assignments have the form:

Let *variable* = *expression*

That is, an assignment consists of an expression to be computed and a variable that is to take on the value of the expression.

"It is very important to notice, Watson, that the values of variables may change as the program progresses. We use assignments to elaborate progressive states of knowledge about the data. Consider, for example, the two statements from my algorithm:

```
Let MINS_TO_HIGH_TIDE = (TODAYS_DATE   1) * MINS_PER_DAY
Let MINS_TO_HIGH_TIDE = MINS_TO_HIGH_TIDE +
                        (TIDE_HR * MINS_PER_HR)
```

The first we have already discussed. When it is evaluated, the variable MINS_TO_HIGH_TIDE will be given a value consisting of the number of minutes from the beginning of the month until midnight last night. In the second assignment, the variable is revised to include also the number of minutes that have elapsed today. Notice especially that the expression in the second assignment contains the variable MINS_TO_HIGH_TIDE, the same variable whose value is to be changed.

"Here," he said, pushing a sheet of paper my way, "I have already written out my algorithm in the language of a Basic programme. You shouldn't find it at all difficult to decipher."

I studied it for a moment. It was quite a short programme, and I have replicated it here as Exhibit 4.2.

"I take it that the names given in your algorithm must be encoded according to the rules of the Engine's language."

"Precisely," replied my companion. "In Basic, instead of

```
Let MINS_TO_HIGH_TIDE = (TODAYS_DATE - 1) * MINS_PER_DAY
```

we must write something like:

```
LET M1 = (D1 - 1) * 1440
```

"I must admit, however, that the elements of originality and enterprise are not too common to the scientific world. The terse names are, indeed, distinctly unreadable."

"Now, Watson, let us enter the data to the programme by using this telegraph arrangement. We shall soon have our answer."

It was a brisk walk in the bracing sea air to the telegraph office. In a matter of minutes our connections were established. Holmes then carefully telegraphed the numbers

```
28,  11,  3,  9
```

representing

July 28   11.00 am   July 3   9.00 am

```
0010 REM   -- THIS PROGRAMME READS IN A DAY OF THE MONTH AND
0020 REM   -- THE HOUR OF HIGH TIDE, AS WELL AS THE DAY AND
0030 REM   -- THE HOUR OF SOME EARLIER EVENT.
0040 REM   -- THE PROGRAMME COMPUTES THE NUMBER OF TIDE CYCLES
0050 REM   -- DURING THE ELAPSED TIME.
0060 REM
0070 REM   -- NOTE:  THERE ARE 1440 MINUTES IN A DAY, AND 745
0080 REM   -- MINUTES IN AN AVERAGE TIDE CYCLE.
0090 REM
0100 REM   -- DICTIONARY OF NAMES:
0110 REM
0120 REM   -- D1    TODAY'S DATE
0130 REM   -- D2    EVENT DATE
0140 REM   -- H1    HOUR OF TODAY'S HIGH TIDE
0150 REM   -- H2    HOUR OF DISAPPEARANCE
0160 REM   -- M1    MINUTES OF TODAY'S HIGH TIDE
0170 REM   -- M2    MINUTES TO DISAPPEARANCE
0180 REM   -- T     TOTAL ELAPSED TIME
0190 REM   -- N     NUMBER OF TIDE CYCLES
0200 REM
0210 REM
0220       PRINT "ENTER TODAY'S DATE, HIGH TIDE HOUR, ";
0230       PRINT "EVENT DATE, EVENT HOUR:"
0240       INPUT D1, H1, D2, H2
0250 REM
0260       LET M1 = (D1 - 1) * 1440
0270       LET M1 = M1 + (H1 * 60)
0280 REM
0290       LET M2 = (D2 - 1) * 1440
0300       LET M2 = M2 + (H2 * 60)
0310 REM
0320       LET T = M1 - M2
0330       LET N = T / 745
0340 REM
0350       PRINT "THE NUMBER OF TIDE CYCLES IS ", N
0360 END
```

Exhibit 4.2 *Holmes's Programme for Calculating Tides*

After a few minutes the results of his programme came clacking back at us over the telegraph. He began scribbling down numbers on a small pad of paper and finally tore the sheet loose.

"Precisely what I had expected," he exclaimed. "There have been nearly forty-eight and a half tide cycles between today's high tide and that fateful episode. This means, Watson, that the tide then differed by roughly half a cycle, which places the mysterious bathing machine well out of reach of the sea. Low tide, Watson! We can turn this little bit of information over to Lestrade and save these poor attendants from any further humiliation."

"But how does this possibly remove them from suspicion?" I asked.

"Elementary, Watson. If the attendants had drowned her, the incoming tide would have washed her body onto the shore to be discovered later. But it was not discovered. No, Watson, there is more to it, as her family has suggested privately. The Baron Whitelsey is known as a cruel man who abused his wife; I venture to say that the Baroness swam out to sea and made good an escape with the help of a confederate. Let us wish her well in her new life. I doubt that she will be seen on these shores again."

4.1 Variables and Assignment

If there is one concept that is central to all programmes, it is the concept of a variable and its twin concept, assignment. A variable is a name for a piece of information that varies as the program progresses. An assignment is an action that changes this information.

The dominant feature of Holmes's program for calculating tides is the use of names to refer to values needed in the course of the computation. This is a characteristic of all computer programs. For example, we may have:

```
D1 - 1     -- the value of D1 minus 1
2 * V      -- 2 times the value of V
SIN(X/4)   -- the sine of X/4
```

In each of these forms a piece of information (for example, some number of days) is associated with a name (for example, D1). This piece of information is called a *value*. This value is not given directly (for example, the value may be 28), but instead is referred to by a name (for example, D1). This name is called a *variable* since the value associated with the name will be established or changed during the course of the program.

An *assignment* is the means by which we establish or change the value of a variable. For example, we may have:

```
LET N = 0
LET N = N + 2
LET M1 = (D1 - 1) * 1440
```

In the first case, the value of N is set to zero. In the second case, the value of N is incremented by two. In the third case, the value of M1 is set to the value computed by the given formula.

The point of all of these assignments is identical. At each step in our program we have established certain facts about the state of our knowledge. An assignment reflects the fact that we have established a new state of knowledge.

The general form for writing all assignment statements is simple:

LET *variable* = *expression*

When this statement is acted upon by the computer, it means the following:

1. Compute the value of the expression
2. Then associate this value with the variable

While the rules are simple, you must be careful to obey them precisely.

Consider the following sequence of assignment statements, where the variables A and B have initially unspecified values.

```
LET A = 0       -- value of A is 0,  B is unspecified
LET B = 1       -- value of A is 0,  B is 1
LET A = 2       -- value of A is 2,  B is 1
LET B = A       -- value of A is 2,  B is 2
LET B = 2*A     -- value of A is 2,  B is 4
```

We see here that each statement in the sequence is executed step by step. Furthermore, each assignment establishes a new value for only one variable.

The assignment

```
LET N = N + 2
```

given above perhaps deserves a little special attention. Here the variable also occurs in the expression given on the right side of the statement. This causes no problems. First, the value of the expression is obtained; then this value is assigned to the variable, just as before. This statement has exactly the same effect as the following sequence:

```
LET Z = N + 2
LET N = Z
```

In both cases, the value of N has been incremented by two.

Basic, like all programming languages, has a number of rules regarding the use of variables. One such rule is that numeric variables can only be assigned numeric values, and string variables can only be assigned string values.

For instance, suppose the variable N is supposed to stand for a number of suspects, and P$ for a person's name. While you can say

```
LET N = 4
LET P$ = "WATSON"
```

you cannot say:

```
LET N  = "WATSON"    -- error, N must be assigned an integer value
LET P$ = 4           -- error, P$ must be assigned a string value
```

If you do, the computer will complain, and it should.

Watch out, though, for the following anomaly. You can assign any kind of numeric value to a numeric variable, and any kind of string value to a string variable. Thus the computer will be perfectly happy if you say

```
LET N = 12.6
```

even though 12.6 is certainly senseless as a number of suspects. Similarly, you can say

```
LET P$ = "FOUR%"
```

even though FOUR% is hardly a person's name. All of this means that you must be careful to write programs that make sense, which is the object of the game in the first place.

4.2 Expressions

In every program we want to analyze data or compute some results. To do this we need to write expressions. An *expression* is a formula for computing a value.

Consider the very simple expression:

```
D1 - 1
```

This expression subtracts one from the existing value of the variable D1. In this expression, we have a subtraction operator and two operands, D1 and 1. Next, consider the expression:

```
T / 745
```

Here we have a division operator and two operands, T and 745. Here the value of the expression is the real number that is equal to the quotient of two values.

Both of these expressions illustrate properties that are common to all expressions. First, an expression contains some special symbols like + and / called *operators*. Second, the operators are applied to the values of the *operands*. The operands may be numbers, variables, or other parenthesized expressions. Third, when an operator is applied to operands, a result is computed. In the first expression above, an integer result is computed, and in the second a real result is computed.

The arithmetic operators available in Basic are the following:

+   addition
−   subtraction
*   multiplication
/   division
^   exponentiation

Most of these operators are familiar; the operator ^ is used to compute *powers* of numbers.

For instance, we may have:

```
14 + 7       -- result is 21
4.1 + 5      -- result is 9.1
0.01 + 4.1   -- result is 4.11

14 - 7       -- result is 7
4.1 - 5      -- result is -0.9
4.36 - 1.1   -- result is 3.26

7 * 5        -- result is 35
7.1 * 5      -- result is 35.5
1.1 * 1.1    -- result is 1.21

7/5          -- result is 1.4
36/6         -- result is 6
3.14/4       -- result is 0.785

3^2          -- result is 9
3.1^2        -- result is 9.61
3^4          -- result is 81
```

There are a few little details you may want to know about. The first is called *rounding*. When you tell the computer to perform some arithmetic operation, it will only be accurate to some fixed number of digits. For instance, suppose your computer is accurate to six digits. If you write

```
PRINT 2/3
```

the computer may round out the result and print

```
.666667
```

or truncate the result and print:

.666666

It doesn't even matter how many digits you write yourself, for even if you write

```
LET X = .66666666666
PRINT X
```

the computer will still print

.666667

or:

.666666

The second point has to do with very large or very small numbers, which might arise if you are trying to calculate the distance between two planets or the weight of a molecule. In these cases, the computer will print results using the E notation (often called *scientific* notation or *floating point* notation). All of this means that

```
123000000000000
0.0000000000000456
```

will be printed as:

```
1.23E+14
4.56E-14
```

This saves you from counting zeros to find how big or how small a number is.

The operators plus and minus may also be used with a single operand. This is allowed only at the beginning of an expression, as in:

```
-10.0
+10.0
-10.0 + 3.14
```

Compound Expressions

Of course, you will often want to write expressions with several operands and operators, just as you do in conventional arithmetic. For example, you may wish to write

```
(D1 - 1) * 1440
```

or

```
A + B - C - D
```

To do things like this you have to remember a few rules. The rules are:

■   Parenthesized operands are evaluated before unparenthesized operands.

■   The exponentiation operator ˆ is applied before * and /.

■   The operators * and / are applied before – and +.

■   Otherwise, evaluation proceeds in textual order from left to right.

These rules are intended to make the writing of expressions easier. Thus if you write

```
1 + N*2
```

and N is 3, the result is 7 (which is what you want) and not 8.

To make sure that you have these rules straight, consider the following pairs of expressions. The expression on the left will give the same value as the expression on the right:

```
1 + 2 + 3      (1 + 2) + 3      -- value is 6
1 - 2 - 3      (1 - 2) - 3      -- value is -4
1 + 2 * 3      1 + (2 * 3)      -- value is 7
1 * 2 + 3      (1 * 2) + 3      -- value is 5
- 1 - 2 - 3    ((-1) - 2) - 3   -- value is -6
```

This may look a bit tricky, but in normal practice you should have no problem. With proper spacing you can write your expressions like

```
1 + N*2
```

rather than

```
1+N * 2
```

so that you and the reader will have no doubt as to what you mean.

Furthermore, whenever there is a problem, just put parentheses in your expressions to make your intent exactly clear. For example, it is probably not a good idea to write something like:

```
- A - B - C
```

You can make things look better simply by writing

```
- (A + B + C)
```

which leaves no mystery for the reader.

Using Predefined Functions as Operands

Consider the expression:

```
SQR(5.0) + 1.0
```

This expression adds 1.0 to the square root of 5.0. Our interest here centers on the SQR in:

```
SQR(5.0)
```

In mathematical parlance, SQR is called a function, in this case a function to compute the square root of its argument.

In Basic there are a number of such functions that are predefined in the language. For example, you may compute the absolute value of a number or its mathematical sine. A list of all of these functions is given in Table 4.1. To use these functions, you simply write the name of the function and its argument enclosed in parentheses, as shown above. All of this works just as you would expect, and should cause no problems. Your version of Basic is likely to have other predefined functions, and it is worth a quick check to see what they are.

The function INT deserves a special note. This function, which gives the integer part of a result, can be quite handy. For example, suppose you are standing in a train station and the time T on the clock is 1432. In more familiar notation, you take this as 2:32 p.m. How would you get this in Basic? You would write something like:

```
LET H = INT(T/100)
LET M = T - H*100
```

This determines the number of hours H and the number of minutes M in the given train time. Furthermore, if you know that the number of hours is greater than 12 (for example 14), you may compute the corresponding p.m. hours P with:

```
LET P = H - 12
```

Quite reasonable.

The function RND, which computes so-called "random" or "pseudo-random" numbers, also deserves a special mention. Each time the function is called, it gives a new number in the range 0.0 to 1.0.

TABLE 4.1   *Predefined Arithmetic Functions in Basic*

(*x* denotes an expression whose value is a number.)

ABS(*x*)   The absolute value of *x*. For example ABS(-4.6) is 4.6, and ABS(4.6) is 4.6.

ATN(*x*)   The principal value of the arctangent of *x* (in radians).

EXP(*x*)   The exponential of *x*, that is the value of the base of natural logarithms (e = 2.71828...) raised to the power of *x*. Result is a real number.

INT(*x*)   The largest integer not greater than *x*. For example INT(2.4) is 2 and INT (-2.4) is -3.

LOG(*x*)   The natural logarithm of *x*, where the value of *x* must be greater than zero.

RND   The next pseudo-random numbers in a sequence of pseudo-random numbers uniformly distributed between 0.0 and 1.0. Sometimes RND(0) is used.

SGN(*x*)   The algebraic sign of *x*, that is -1 if *x* is negative, 0 if *x* is zero, and +1 if *x* is positive.

SIN(*x*)   The sine of *x*, where *x* is expressed in radians.

SQR(*x*)   The positive square root of *x*, where *x* must be non-negative.

TAN(*x*)   The tangent of *x*, where *x* is expressed in radians.

Before going on, we must clear up a few little details that you have to know when you write an expression. The first, and the most important, is that if you use a variable in an expression it must have already been assigned a value. If you haven't, the computer will not know what to do and, most likely, your program will come to a stop or give some strange results. For example, if you write

```
LET X = N + 1
```

and you have not already given a value to N, the result will be trouble.

Second, you may occasionally write expressions that cause the computer other problems. For instance, if you attempt to divide a number by zero or take the square root of a negative number, the results are unpredictable. In these cases, you most likely have made an error or have read in some data that you did not expect.

4.3   Reading and Writing Information

In almost every program you write, you are going to want to read in some data and print some results. Doing this is easy. Consider the statement:

```
INPUT D1, H1, D2, H2
```

When the computer executes this statement, it will ask you for four values. You may give it something like:

```
28,  11,  3,  9
```

Notice that the values are separated by commas. When you give it these values, the four variables will be assigned the values that you typed in. This is exactly the same as writing

```
LET D1 =  28
LET H1 =  11
LET D2 =  3
LET H2 =  9
```

in your program. That is, reading of data is exactly the same as assigning values to variables.

The general rule for reading data is thus quite simple. You simply use the name INPUT followed by the list of variables whose values you want to read.

For printing your results, the process is just the opposite. For example, consider the statement:

```
PRINT N
```

When the computer processes this statement, it will simply print the value of N. If you want, you can say:

```
PRINT "THE NUMBER OF TIDE CYCLES IS", N
```

In this case, your program will write the characters THE NUMBER OF TIDE CYCLES IS followed by the value of N.

More generally, you may print out any character string or the value of any expression, provided that each of these items is separated by commas. Thus all of the following statements are acceptable.

```
PRINT "SOME INTRODUCTORY MESSAGE"
PRINT "YOU CAN PRINT CHARACTERS LIKE $ AND +"
PRINT A, B, C
PRINT "N divided by 4 is ", N/4
```

There is an old computer adage: you input variables and print expressions. It really is just about that simple.

Some closing details. When you are typing in data and give something the computer doesn't understand, for instance typing your name when the computer is looking for a number, the computer will either give up or ask you again for the data.

When you are using PRINT, the computer will print the output values so as to put several values on a line. The computer has its own way of printing your data, and the results may not always be nice to look at. Each printed line is divided into zones with a fixed size; the number of zones varies from four to eight, depending on your terminal or printer. A comma after an item causes printing of the next item to begin in the next zone. For instance, if you say

```
PRINT "SUSPECT", N, "IS THE MURDERER."
```

and N is 4, your output may look like:

```
SUSPECT        4               IS THE MURDERER.
```

If you want to control the situation a bit more, you can use a semicolon to separate the items given in a PRINT statement. Then the computer will print the items immediately after each other. Thus if you say

```
PRINT "SUSPECT"; N; " IS THE MURDERER."
```

your output will be:

```
SUSPECT 4 IS THE MURDERER.
```

Each PRINT statement above will cause printing to start on a new line. If you want to prevent this, you can put a comma or semicolon after the last item. Thus

```
PRINT A, B,
PRINT C
```

has the same effect as

```
PRINT A, B, C
```

and

```
PRINT "THIS LONG STRING WILL APPEAR ON A SINGLE ";
PRINT "LINE WHEN PRINTED."
```

has the same effect as:

```
PRINT "THIS LONG STRING WILL APPEAR ON A SINGLE LINE WHEN PRINTED."
```

We will take all this up in much greater detail in Chapter 11, but this should suffice for now. The exact behavior of input and output depends upon the implementation you are using, and no doubt you will have to check your manual or try out some examples to pin it down.

Summing Up

Many of the ideas we have just talked about are illustrated in the program of Example 4.1. This program reads in six integer values, representing the number of pennies, nickels, and so forth, and prints the value of the coins in dollars and cents. This program illustrates the use of variables, the writing of expressions, and the reading and printing of data in a somewhat natural setting.

This program, like all of the others in this book, was written with a great concern for you, the reader. You will see that when programs are well written, the need for remembering the many detailed conventions of Basic is greatly diminished. You now should be able to write programs just like this.

```
0010 REM  -- THIS PROGRAM READS IN SIX INTEGER VALUES, RESPECTIVELY
0020 REM  -- REPRESENTING THE NUMBER OF PENNIES, NICKELS, DIMES,
0030 REM  -- QUARTERS, HALF DOLLARS, AND SILVER DOLLARS IN COINAGE.
0040 REM  -- THE PROGRAM OUTPUTS THE TOTAL VALUE OF THE COINS IN
0050 REM  -- DOLLARS AND CENTS.
0060 REM
0070 REM  -- DICTIONARY OF NAMES:
0080 REM
0090 REM  -- N  A NUMBER OF COINS, FOR INSTANCE THE NUMBER OF DIMES
0100 REM  -- T  TOTAL CHANGE
0110 REM  -- D  NUMBER OF DOLLARS
0120 REM  -- C  NUMBER OF CENTS
0130 REM
0140 REM
0150      LET T = 0
0160 REM
0170      PRINT "NUMBER OF PENNIES IS:"
0180      INPUT N
0190      LET T = T + 01*N
0200 REM
0210      PRINT "NUMBER OF NICKELS IS:"
0220      INPUT N
0230      LET T = T + 05*N
0240 REM
0250      PRINT "NUMBER OF DIMES IS:"
0260      INPUT N
0270      LET T = T + 10*N
0280 REM
0290      PRINT "NUMBER OF QUARTERS IS:"
0300      INPUT N
0310      LET T = T + 25*N
0320 REM
0330      PRINT "NUMBER OF HALF DOLLARS IS:"
0340      INPUT N
0350      LET T = T + 50*N
0360 REM
0370      PRINT "NUMBER OF SILVER DOLLARS IS:"
0380      INPUT N
0390      LET T = T + 100*N
0400 REM
0410      LET D = INT(T/100)
0420      LET C = T - 100*D
0430      PRINT "CHANGE IS "; D; " DOLLARS AND "; C; " CENTS."
0440 END
```

Example 4.1   *Counting Change*

V

A Study In Cigar Ash

YOU see, Watson," remarked Sherlock Holmes, as we sat together one frosty evening considering a recent report that the missing Baroness of Whitelsey had been seen in Vienna, "I attribute much of my professional success to the fact that I regard detection as a science as well as an art; and unlike most of my colleagues, I have never regarded it as drudgery. Detection takes its purest form as deductive reasoning and is comparable only to mathematics in its elegance and intellectual challenge. For this reason, the Analytical Engine, based as it is upon mathematical principles, has seemed a most attractive tool for my labours."

"What is your next plan for using the Engine?" I asked, sensing that my friend was ready to launch some new idea.

"My plan, Watson, is to use this remarkable Engine as a storehouse for some of the minutiae that clutter my mind. Take for instance my monograph, 'Upon the Distinction Between the Ashes of the Various Tobaccos,'" he said, gesturing to a dusty volume that lay before us on the table.

"In this treatise I have described and classified a hundred and forty types of cigarette, cigar, and pipe tobaccos, with coloured plates illustrating the various sorts of ashes. Although I took a special interest in retaining such details as, say, the exact appearance of MacDuffy versus Lunkah cigar ash, most investigators would lack the patience to do so; and I cannot say I blame them.

"The brain is after all like an attic of vast but limited capacity that we fill with whatever matter we deem important for the future. Since the walls of this attic cannot be stretched like India rubber, as we amass more and more information some of the old is jostled out to make room for the new. It would be helpful if we had a device to remember vast quantities of data for us and to supply us with information pertaining to these data whenever we so request. I claim, Watson, that the Analytical Engine is wonderfully suited to this task.

"As an exercise to test my idea, I have prepared a table listing the properties of the ten most commonly smoked cigars in London."

Holmes's table of ash properties is given here.

CIGAR TYPE.	TEXTURE.	COLOUR.	PARTICLES.	NICOTINE.
Espanada	Caked	Dark	No	++
Heritage	Flaky	Light Grey	No	++
Latino	Varied	Dark	Yes	+
Londoner	Caked	Brown Tint	No	++
Lunkah	Granular	Dark Grey	No	++
MacDuffy	Flaky	Dark Grey	No	++
Old Wood	Varied	Brown Tint	Varied	+++
Top Hat	Caked	Dark Grey	No	++
Trichinopoly	Flaky	Dark	No	++
West Country	Fluffy	Light Grey	No	++

While I studied his document, Holmes walked over to the fire and took down a small brass box from the mantlepiece. This he opened, and quietly he smelled the single cigar which it contained.

"I should like to design a programme that would identify the cigars bearing certain specified ash characteristics. Moreover, if the specified characteristics did not match any of these ten cigars, the Engine should indicate this so that I could then research the matter myself."

"I take it, then, that there are particular characteristics of this programme that are of interest?" I queried, for I still had little experience in constructing programmes.

"Precisely, Watson," replied my friend. "The central issue is the need to make decisions and take appropriate actions as the consequence of a given condition. Of course, this is a very common problem in the work of detection.

"There are any number of combinations we can make of the various conditions. We may, for example, specify that a certain action be taken under a certain set of circumstances, such as:

if texture is caked then
    — *perform action A*

Another situation that arises is that of two possible actions, with the choice between them depending upon a single condition. For instance:

if texture is caked then
    — *perform action A*
else
    — *perform action B*

Finally, we may be faced with a number of possible courses of action, with our choice depending upon one of several conditions:

if texture is caked then
    — *perform action A*
else if texture is flaky then
    — *perform action B*
else if texture is granular then
    — *perform action C*
else (if none of the conditions above are met)
    — *perform action D*

"I understand what you are saying, Holmes, but how do you solve this problem in terms comprehensible to the Analytical Engine?"

"Quite simply, Watson," said Holmes. "All we must do is organize the decisions in the form of a consistent algorithm and then translate the algorithm into the machine's language. Here I have listed all the choices of properties for a cigar. Notice that the normal cigar has no particles and has a nicotine content marked with two plus signs. Furthermore, there are two basic kinds of cigar ash. There is Stock 1, which is flaky or caked, and Stock 2, whose characteristics are fluffy or granular."

"HE SMELLED THE SINGLE CIGAR WHICH IT CONTAINED."

Holmes's ash classification is reproduced here as follows :

Colour . . . . Dark, Dark Grey, Light Grey, Brown Tint
Texture . . . . Flaky, Caked, Granular, Fluffy
Particles . . . . No, Yes
Nicotine . . . . +, ++, +++

```
Normal Strength    . . . . . ++, no particles
Stock 1 Cigar      . . . . . Flaky or Caked
Stock 2 Cigar      . . . . . Granular or Fluffy
```

"My strategy," Holmes continued, "is to command the Engine to read a list of properties pertaining to cigar ash. The programme will then determine whether the cigar is of normal strength and whether it is of Stock 1 or Stock 2. With these questions settled, it will then be able to determine whether the cigar is one of the ten types listed in the table. If so, it will name the cigar; if not, it will report this and merely indicate the cigar's strength or class."

Holmes then produced his algorithm, which is given in Exhibit 5.1. It seemed entirely clear, and I followed his logic almost instantly.

"But surely, Holmes, the Engine does not recognise the properties of cigar ash. How could the Engine distinguish between those with a flaky or those with granular texture?"

"Very true, Watson. It is up to the programmer to distinguish the properties of cigar ash and then interpret this information for the Engine in terms it will understand. The distinctive properties will be ciphered as character strings and read by the device in this form. Thus, for example, I shall use "FLAKY" for flaky, and "DARK_GREY" for dark grey. The Engine will read character strings corresponding to each of the properties texture, colour, particles, and nicotine respectively, as I shall show you."

Definitions:

```
COLOUR      :  a texture of ash
TEXTURE     :  a colour of ash
PARTICLES   :  an indication of particles
NICOTINE    :  a result of a nicotine test
STOCK       :  a class of cigar
NORMALITY   :  an indication of particles and nicotine
```

Algorithm:

```
Input COLOUR, TEXTURE, PARTICLES, NICOTINE

If TEXTURE = FLAKY or TEXTURE = CAKED then
    let STOCK = 1
else
    let STOCK = 2
```

Exhibit 5.1   *Holmes's Algorithm to Identify Cigar Ash*

If NICOTINE = ++ and PARTICLES − NO then
   let NORMALITY = NORMAL
else
   let NORMALITY = ABNORMAL

If NORMALITY = NORMAL and STOCK = 1 then
   if COLOUR = DARK and TEXTURE = FLAKY then
      print "CIGAR IS A TRICHINOPOLY"
   else if COLOUR = DARK and TEXTURE = CAKED then
      print "CIGAR IS AN ESPANADA"
   else if COLOUR = DARK_GREY and TEXTURE = FLAKY then
      print "CIGAR IS A MACDUFFY"
   else if COLOUR = DARK_GREY and TEXTURE = CAKED then
      print "CIGAR IS A TOP HAT"
   else if COLOUR = LIGHT_GREY and TEXTURE = FLAKY then
      print "CIGAR IS A HERITAGE"
   else if COLOUR = BROWN_TINT and TEXTURE = CAKED then
      print "CIGAR IS A LONDONER"
   else
      print "*** UNIDENTIFIED NORMAL CIGAR OF STOCK 1"

If NORMALITY = NORMAL and STOCK = 2 then
   if COLOUR = DARK_GREY and TEXTURE = GRANULAR then
      print "CIGAR IS A LUNKAH"
   else if COLOUR = LIGHT_GREY and TEXTURE = FLUFFY then
      print "CIGAR IS A WEST COUNTRY"
   else
      print "*** UNIDENTIFIED NORMAL CIGAR OF STOCK 2"

If NORMALITY = ABNOMAL then
   if COLOUR = BROWN_TINT and NICOTINE − +++ then
      print "CIGAR IS AN OLD WOOD"
  else if COLOUR = DARK and NICOTINE = + and PARTICLES = YES then
      print "CIGAR IS A LATINO"
   else
      print "*** UNIDENTIFIED ABNORMAL CIGAR"

Exhibit 5.1   *Continued*

Holmes thereupon produced a sheet of paper and sketched the following example:

Sample Input: DARK, FLAKY, NO, ++
Sample Output: CIGAR IS A TRICHINOPOLY

"They say, Watson, that genius is an infinite capacity for taking pains. It is a bad definition, but it does apply to programming. What relief the Analytical Engine will bring us!" he remarked. "I propose to devote some years to the composition of a text which shall present the whole art of detection and the special uses of the Analytical Engine into a single volume."

"A massive undertaking," I replied. "Surely, Holmes, this will be your greatest contribution to science and humanity."

A flush of colour sprang to my companion's cheeks, and he bowed slightly, like the master dramatist who receives the homage of his audience. The same singularly proud and reserved nature that turned away with disdain from popular notoriety was capable of being moved to its depths by spontaneous wonder and praise from a friend.

As for our study of cigar ash, Holmes applied the programme shown in Exhibit 5.2 to test the Engine's performance against his own powers. I have had no keener pleasure than in following Sherlock Holmes in his professional investigations and in admiring his rapid deductions—as swift as intuitions, yet always founded on the same logical basis on which the Engine operated—with which he unravelled the many problems that were submitted to him.

```
0010 REM  -- THIS PROGRAMME READS IN FOUR PROPERTIES OF CIGAR ASH.
0020 REM  -- THE PROPERTIES ARE GIVEN AS CHARACTER STRINGS.
0030 REM  -- THE PROGRAMME ATTEMPTS TO IDENTIFY THE ASH ACCORDING TO ITS
0040 REM  -- PROPERTIES, AND PRINTS A MESSAGE GIVING THE FINDINGS.
0050 REM
0060 REM  -- DICTIONARY OF NAMES:
0070 REM
0080 REM  -- C$   COLOUR: EITHER "DARK", "DARK_GREY", "LIGHT_GREY"
0090 REM  --      OR "BROWN_TINT"
0100 REM  -- T$   TEXTURE: "FLAKY", "CAKED", "GRANULAR", OR "FLUFFY"
0110 REM  -- P$   PRESENCE OF PARTICLES: "YES" OR "NO"
0120 REM  -- N$   NICOTINE CONTENT: "+", "++", OR "+++"
0130 REM  -- S    STOCK OF CIGAR: 1 OR 2
0140 REM  -- M$   NORMALITY OF CIGAR: "NORMAL" OR "ABNORMAL"
0150 REM
0160 REM
```

Exhibit 5.2   *Holmes's Programme to Identify Cigar Ash*

```
0170       PRINT "ENTER COLOUR, TEXTURE, PARTICLES, NICOTINE:"
0180       INPUT C$, T$, P$, N$
0190       IF T$ = "FLAKY" THEN 0230
0200       IF T$ = "CAKED" THEN 0230
0210          LET S = 2
0220          GOTO 0270
0230          LET S = 1
0240          GOTO 0270
0250 REM   END IF
0260 REM
0270       IF N$ <> "++" THEN 0310
0280       IF P$ <> "NO" THEN 0310
0290          LET M$ = "NORMAL"
0300          GOTO 0350
0310          LET M$ = "ABNORMAL"
0320          GOTO 0350
0330 REM   END IF
0340 REM
0350       IF M$ <> "NORMAL" THEN 0640
0360       IF S  <> 1         THEN 0640
0370          IF C$ <> "DARK"   THEN 0410
0380          IF T$ <> "FLAKY" THEN 0410
0390             PRINT "CIGAR IS A TRICHINOPOLY"
0400             STOP
0410          IF C$ <> "DARK"   THEN 0450
0420          IF T$ <> "CAKED" THEN 0450
0430             PRINT "CIGAR IS AN ESPANADA"
0440             STOP
0450          IF C$ <> "DARK_GREY" THEN 0490
0460          IF T$ <> "FLAKY"     THEN 0490
0470             PRINT "CIGAR IS A MACDUFFY"
0480             STOP
0490          IF C$ <> "DARK_GREY" THEN 0530
0500          IF T$ <> "CAKED"     THEN 0530
0510             PRINT "CIGAR IS A TOP HAT"
0520             STOP
0530          IF C$ <> "LIGHT_GREY" THEN 0570
0540          IF T$ <> "FLAKY"      THEN 0570
0550             PRINT "CIGAR IS A HERITAGE"
0560             STOP
0570          IF C$ <> "BROWN_TINT" THEN 0610
0580          IF T$ <> "CAKED"      THEN 0610
0590             PRINT "CIGAR IS A LONDONER"
0600             STOP
0610          PRINT "*** UNIDENTIFIED NORMAL CIGAR OF STOCK 1"
0620          STOP
```

Exhibit 5.2   *Continued*

```
0630 REM
0640     IF M$ <> "NORMAL" THEN 0770
0650     IF S  <> 2         THEN 0770
0660        IF C$ <> "DARK_GREY" THEN 0700
0670        IF T$ <> "GRANULAR"  THEN 0700
0680           PRINT "CIGAR IS A LUNKAH"
0690           STOP
0700        IF C$ <> "LIGHT_GREY" THEN 0740
0710        IF T$ <> "FLUFFY"     THEN 0740
0720           PRINT "CIGAR IS A WEST COUNTRY"
0730           STOP
0740        PRINT "*** UNIDENTIFIED NORMAL CIGAR OF STOCK 2"
0750        STOP
0760 REM
0770     IF M$ <> "ABNORMAL" THEN 0900
0780        IF C$ <> "BROWN_TINT" THEN 0820
0790        IF N$ <> "+++"        THEN 0820
0800           PRINT "CIGAR IS AN OLD WOOD"
0810           STOP
0820        IF C$ <> "DARK" THEN 0870
0830        IF N$ <> "+"    THEN 0870
0840        IF P$ <> "YES"  THEN 0870
0850           PRINT "CIGAR IS A LATINO"
0860           STOP
0870        PRINT "*** UNIDENTIFIED ABNORMAL CIGAR"
0880        STOP
0890 REM
0900 END
```

Exhibit 5.2 *Continued*

5.1 Sequence of Execution

Before moving into the area of decision making in Basic, we pause to make note of a simple, but important concept for writing programs—its sequence of execution. In the previous chapters we have looked at assignment statements as well as statements to read and write data. As we have seen, these statements are executed one after another, in the order in which they are written.

In the discussion of decision making to follow, we will encounter new kinds of statements in which a statement may transfer execution to another statement in the program. In this category we will find, for example, the goto statement. Consider the following:

```
0010   PRINT "START"
0020   GOTO 0040
0030   PRINT "MIDDLE"
0040   PRINT "FINISH"
```

When this sequence is executed on the computer, the program will print

```
START
FINISH
```

and not:

```
START
MIDDLE
FINISH
```

The key line here is:

```
GOTO 0040
```

When this statement is reached, execution continues at line 0040, and not at the following line (line 0030).

More generally, a goto statement has the form:

```
GOTO line-number
```

Whenever execution reaches a goto statement, execution continues at the given line number. The goto statement is one of several statements in Basic that causes a *transfer* of execution from one line to another.

Execution of a program terminates when a STOP statement is reached or in its absence, when the END statement marking the end of the program is reached. A STOP statement consists solely of the word

```
STOP
```

and may appear anywhere in a program.

This leads us to the following rules about Basic:

■ Execution of a program begins at the first statement in the program, and normally, continues in sequence.

■ Execution of a transfer statement interrupts normal execution and causes execution to continue at a specified place.

■ Execution terminates when a STOP statement or END statement is reached.

Now let's continue with the means for making decisions in Basic.

5.2 Making Decisions

The ability to make decisions is fundamental to programming. Depending upon one or more circumstances, we want to take appropriate actions. The basic mechanism for making choices in Basic is the IF statement. This statement has the following form:

> IF *condition* THEN *line-number*

This statement means:

> If the condition is true, transfer execution to the statement with the given line number; otherwise do nothing and go on to the following statement.

Most often, an IF statement will appear in a sequence of statements. As a result, if the condition is not true the next statement is processed. For example, we may have

> *statement-1*
> IF *condition* THEN *line-number*
> *statement-2*

which means:

> 1. Execute statement 1.
>
> 2. Execute the IF statement: that is, if the condition is true, transfer to the designated line.
>
> 3. Otherwise, execute statement 2.

Notice here that if the condition is false, statements 1 and 2 are executed in sequence. If the condition is true, statement 1 is executed and then execution continues elsewhere.

The ability to include IF statements within a program has far reaching possibilities. While the basic mechanism is extremely simple, we can produce rather elaborate or even confusing effects. To use it effectively, we need to look at matters a little more closely.

Consider the following:

```
0010 REM  -- CASE 1
0020      PRINT "ENTER WEATHER CONDITION:"
0030      INPUT W$
0040      IF W$ <> "RAIN" THEN 0080
0050          PRINT "MESSAGE DESCRIBING WHAT TO"
0060          PRINT "DO WHEN IT IS RAINING."
```

```
0070 REM
0080      PRINT "ENTER TEMPERATURE:"
```

Here the lines

```
0050      PRINT "MESSAGE DESCRIBING WHAT TO"
0060      PRINT "DO WHEN IT IS RAINING."
```

describe an action to be taken. If W$ is RAIN, the action is performed, and execution continues at line 0080. Otherwise (the weather condition is not rain), the action is skipped and execution continues at the same line, 0080.

Next consider:

```
0010 REM  -- CASE 2
0020      PRINT "ENTER WEATHER CONDITION: "
0030      INPUT W$
0040      IF W$ <> "RAIN"  THEN 0080
0050        PRINT "MESSAGE DESCRIBING WHAT TO DO"
0060        PRINT "WHEN IT IS RAINING."
0070        GOTO 0120
0080        PRINT "MESSAGE DESCRIBING WHAT TO"
0090        PRINT "DO OTHERWISE."
0100        GOTO 0120
0110 REM
0120      PRINT "ENTER TEMPERATURE:"
```

Here the lines

```
0050  PRINT "MESSAGE DESCRIBING WHAT TO"
0060  PRINT "DO WHEN IT IS RAINING."
```

describe one action, and the lines

```
0080  PRINT "MESSAGE DESCRIBING WHAT TO"
0090  PRINT "DO OTHERWISE."
```

describe another action. As in the previous example, if the weather is rain the first action is performed; otherwise the second action is performed. In both cases, execution continues at line 0120.

Finally, consider:

```
0010 REM  -- CASE 3
0020      PRINT "ENTER WEATHER CONDITIONS:"
0030      INPUT W$
0040      IF W$ <> "RAIN"  THEN 0080
0050        PRINT "MESSAGE DESCRIBING WHAT TO "
```

```
0060        PRINT "DO WHEN IT IS RAINING."
0070        GOTO 0160
0080     IF W$ <> "SNOW"  THEN 0120
0090        PRINT "MESSAGE DESCRIBING WHAT TO"
0100        PRINT "DO WHEN IT IS SNOWING."
0110        GOTO 0160
0120        PRINT "MESSAGE DESCRIBING WHAT TO"
0130        PRINT "DO OTHERWISE."
0140        GOTO 0160
0150 REM
0160     PRINT "ENTER TEMPERATURE:"
```

Here the lines

```
0050  PRINT "MESSAGE DESCRIBING WHAT TO"
0060  PRINT "DO WHEN IT IS RAINING."
```

describe one action, lines

```
0090  PRINT "MESSAGE DESCRIBING WHAT TO"
0100  PRINT "DO WHEN IT IS SNOWING."
```

describe a second action, and lines

```
0080  PRINT "MESSAGE DESCRIBING WHAT TO"
0130  PRINT "DO OTHERWISE."
```

describe a third. If it is raining, the first action is taken; if it is snowing, the second; otherwise the third action is performed. In all cases, after the action takes place, execution continues at line 0150.

Each example above follows the same basic pattern; depending on one or more conditions, a given action takes place. In the above examples we have:

1. condition   → action A

2. condition   → action A
    else   → action B

3. condition-1   → action A
    condition-2   → action B
    else   → action C

In all cases, execution continues immediately after the condition-action pairs. This kind of scheme will be used throughout.

5.3 Conditions

Execution of an IF statement depends on the truth or falsity of some given condition. We now turn to the rules for writing conditions in Basic.

The simplest of all conditions is the testing of values to see if they are equal. For example, we may write:

```
IF S = 1 THEN ...              -- test if stock is 1
IF T$ = "FLAKY" THEN ...       -- test if texture is flaky
IF R$(S) = "ROOM_14" THEN ...  -- test if room of suspect is 14
IF N + 1 = 10 THEN ...         -- test if a value is equal to 10
```

In each of these constructs the condition has the form:

expression-1 = *expression-2*

A condition always evaluates to true or false.

Testing for the equality of two values is not the only operation we can perform in conditions. Each of the following operators may be used:

```
=     -- equal
<>    -- not equal
<     -- less than
>     -- greater than
<=    -- less than or equal
=>    -- greater than or equal
```

For instance, to see if one value is less than or equal to another, we may write:

```
N <= 10
```

This condition tests if the value of N is less than or equal to 10.

The operator <> appears particularly strange. This is the operator for testing for inequality. Thus, while you might be tempted to say

```
IF T$ ≠ "FLAKY" THEN ...    -- Illegal
```

which looks perfectly logical, you can't. Instead you have to write:

```
IF T$ <> "FLAKY" THEN ...    -- Legal
```

The rationale here is that a < followed by a > stands for "less or greater than" or "not equal." So much for that.

One of the most annoying features of many (but not all) versions of Basic is that you cannot write compound conditions. That is, you cannot write something like

```
IF T$ = "FLAKY" OR T$ = "CAKED" THEN 0200
```

or:

```
IF N > 1 AND N < 10 THEN 0400
```

You can achieve such effects without using OR and AND, but you have to twist things around a bit.

Consider the following excerpt taken from Holmes's algorithm of Exhibit 5.1:

```
if TEXTURE = FLAKY or TEXTURE = CAKED then
    let STOCK = 1
else
    let STOCK = 2
```

This excerpt can be coded in Basic as follows:

```
0190      IF T$ = "FLAKY" THEN 0230
0200      IF T$ = "CAKED" THEN 0230
0210          LET S = 2
0220          GOTO 0270
0230          LET S = 1
0240          GOTO 0270
0250 REM END IF
0260 REM
0270 ...
```

Notice here that two IF statements are required.

Next consider the excerpt:

```
if NICOTINE = ++ and PARTICLES = NO then
    let NORMALITY = NORMAL
else
    let NORMALITY = ABNORMAL
```

Here two conditions are joined by "and." This can be coded as:

```
0270      IF N$ <> "++" THEN 0310
0280      IF P$ <> "NO" THEN 0310
0290          LET M$ = "NORMAL"
0300          GOTO 0350
0310          LET M$ = "ABNORMAL"
0320          GOTO 0350
0330 REM END IF
0340 REM
0350 ...
```

Here again two IF statements are required. Furthermore, the tests for nicotine and particles are stated in the negative. If you think it's a bit tricky, it is, but such is life with Basic.

The general point here is that IF statements can be grouped together, each branching to the same line when an individual condition is true. Collectively, the conditions can be treated as a unit.

5.4   On-Goto Statements

The decision structures above provide a logical method for taking actions based on the truth or falsity of a condition. Another statement in Basic, the ON-GOTO statement, provides a similar ability for making decisions, only here the action taken depends on the value of a numeric expression.

For example, consider the lines:

```
0010      ON D  GOTO 0020, 0040, 0060, 0080, 0100, 0120, 0140
0020          PRINT "TODAY IS MONDAY, START ON A NEW CASE"
0030          GOTO 0170
0040          PRINT "TUESDAY, KEEP WORKING"
0050          GOTO 0170
0060          PRINT "WEDNESDAY, TAKE A BREAK"
0070          GOTO 0170
0080          PRINT "THURSDAY, SEE THE NEW CLIENT"
0090          GOTO 0170
0100          PRINT "FRIDAY, SUMMARIZE THE FACTS"
0110          GOTO 0170
0120          PRINT "SATURDAY, TRY SOMETHING NEW"
0130          GOTO 0170
0140          PRINT "SUNDAY, TAKE A COMPLETE REST"
0150          GOTO 0170
0160 REM CONTINUE
0170      . . .
```

Here we assume the integer variable D represents a day of the week and thus can take on one of the seven values 1 through 7. The line numbers given in the ON-GOTO correspond to the possible values of the variable D. Thus, when D is 1, line 0020 is executed; when D is 2, line 0040 is executed; and so on.

This example illustrates the general use of ON-GOTO statements. After the keyword ON, you can write any numeric expression; if need be, the value of the expression is rounded to obtain an integer value. After the GOTO, you can write a list of line numbers; the first line number is used if the value of the expression is 1, the second if 2, and so on.

Notice above that line numbers are given for each of the seven possible values of D. You do not always need to do this, but you will get an error if the value of D does not correspond to one of the line numbers. For instance, if you give only six line numbers and the value of D is 7, the computer will complain.

VI

The Adventure
of Clergyman Peter

HAT do you make of this, Watson?", asked Holmes, as he tossed a small telegram in my direction. It read :

Oxford

Must meet with you on a temporal matter of grave concern. Will arrive by one o'clock today.

Peter Cowesworthy

"A temporal matter," I replied, studying the message. "I wonder what he could mean by that. I am inclined to think that the man wants your help."

"It's just after twelve now," replied Holmes. "I would say, Watson, that a matter grave enough to carry our mysterious cleric all the way from Oxford to seek my services is more of a corporeal concern than one of the spirit. I should certainly hope that my own little practice is not degenerating into an agency for clergymen to consult me concerning their next sermon. In any event, we shall soon know for certain, for I discern two gentlemen and our landlady ascending the stair."

As he spoke there came a knock on the door, after which Mrs. Hudson admitted two visitors. The elder was a man in priestly attire, a short, bird-like man with thinning white hair and nervous eyes peering from behind gold-rimmed spectacles, and obviously in considerable distress. His younger companion was a tall, lanky fellow with a bulging Adam's apple, protruding nose, and thin lips.

"Gentlemen, I am Sherlock Holmes and this is Dr. Watson, who has been my associate and helper in many matters. How may we be of service to you?"

"Oh my," replied the clergyman, somewhat startled. "This is my Deacon, Mr. Huxtable Penwether."

"Ah, yes, Mr. Penwether, I perceive that you have recently journeyed from the Midlands," observed Holmes.

"CLERGYMAN PETER COWESWORTHY."

"Oh, no, you are mistaken, sir," he said. "I have been in London this past week, on errands for the rector."

"Indeed, he has hardly been out of my sight, Mr. Holmes," observed the clergyman.

"Yes, of course," replied Holmes, as he busied himself by filling his pipe. "Well, as Watson can attest, my deductions occasionally miss their mark." With that Holmes bade our visitors over to the basket-chair and armchair beside the empty fireplace.

The clergyman had hardly settled in his chair when abruptly he sprang to his feet and exclaimed, "Mr. Holmes, if your deductions should fail in this matter we must abandon all hope! You are the only man in the whole of England who can help us. The Mazarin Bible has vanished!" With his exclamation concluded, Cowesworthy sank back into his chair.

"Yes, the Mazarin Bible," replied Holmes, "a vellum edition, is it not, a rare Schoeffer type with hand-coloured illuminations? It is a devastating loss, indeed."

Sherlock Holmes had an almost hypnotic power when he wished, and he was an accomplished master at the art of putting a humble client at his ease.

"It was taken from your rooms?" he asked.

"Often it is in my rooms, but I bring it into the church from time to time to inspire the parishioners. It was there last Sunday, but hidden carefully. No one could have known where."

"Rector, I will endeavour to assist you. Please rest assured that Watson and I will do everything within our power to recover your Mazarin Bible. Where are you staying in London, so that we may contact you and report developments as our investigation proceeds?" asked Holmes.

"We have taken two rooms at Anderson's Hotel in Fleet Street."

The next remark astonished me, for Sherlock Holmes was the least romantic of men.

"I commend a walk in Regent's Park to you. It should prove a tonic to your strain, especially on a day as fresh as this one."

When they were gone, Holmes turned to me and said, "Come quickly, Watson, we must get to Anderson's and search Penwether's room. He was surely lying. The discoloration on his boots clearly places him in Birmingham within the past few days."

We proceeded at once to Fleet Street where a sovereign for the hall porter led us quickly to Penwether's door. "I suppose that I am committing a felony," commented Holmes, as he forced the lock, "but it is just possible that I am saving a soul. There we are," he said, pushing open the door. "I don't mind confessing that I have always thought I would make a highly efficient criminal. It is certainly fortunate for society that I have chosen otherwise."

Inside the room no Bible could be found, but the missing volume did not appear to be my companion's chief concern as he occupied himself studying Penwether's soiled clothing.

Back in our rooms at Baker Street, Holmes took me deeper into his confidence.

"An excellent case for the Analytical Engine, Watson. We know that Penwether was in Birmingham and journeyed to London in a total time of four hours. Oxford is on the route, and the fastest transportation from the station there to Cowesworthy's rooms would take half an hour each way. Could Penwether have journeyed from Birmingham to London in four hours with an hour or more in Oxford?"

"But how do you know it took four hours?" I asked.

"His collar and shirt bore the grime of a long journey," said Holmes. "Allowing for an hour stop at Oxford, the amount of railway grime on his cuffs would suggest a four-hour journey. Assuming that this is the case, what do you think of our friend not taking a first-class carriage, a man of his standing?"

"Because he feared being recognised by some fellow traveller?" I suggested.

"Precisely, Watson," he replied. "Now, here I have the timetables for all of London's main-line stations, and I have arranged these in a form that the Analytical Engine can read directly."

Holmes handed me a sheet of paper to which the stations for the Birmingham-to-London timetable had been copied. As examples it had:

BI   Birmingham
WA   Warwick
OX   Oxford

"I see that each city is given a two-letter code," I remarked.

"Yes, Watson, each stop is coded by a two-letter abbreviation, such as BI for Birmingham.

I nodded my understanding.

"Now," continued Holmes, "we enter the tables into the Engine according to this organized scheme. Look here and you will see how the stations and times are encoded. The first entry

BI 5.10

becomes

BI 510

and thus the time is entered as an integer number."

I then studied Holmes's notes and the sample timetable, which are sketched in Exhibit 6.1.

I. Sample timetable for two Birmingham-to-London trains;
    A — means no stop for the given train:

Station.	Train 1.	Train 2.
Birmingham	5.10	8.05
Warwick	5.30	8.25
Stratford	5.45	8.55
Chipping Norton.	6.15	—
Oxford	6.25	9.20
Didcot	6.40	—
Goring	6.55	—
Reading	7.15	10.05
Maidenhead	—	—
London.	7.55	10.45

II. City codes:

BI	Birmingham	DI	Didcot
WA	Warwick	GO	Goring
ST	Stratford	RE	Reading
CN	Chipping Norton	MA	Maidenhead
OX	Oxford	LO	London

III. Sample input, encoding the times of train 1:

```
BI,  510   WA,  530   ST,  545   CN,  615   OX,  625
DI,  640   GO,  655   RE,  715   MA,  000   LO,  755
```

Exhibit 6.1 *Sample Timetable and Input Representation*

"Now as you recall, our intent is to see whether it is possible to make a four-hour journey from Birmingham to London with an hour's stop in Oxford. To determine this myself, I would carefully examine the schedule for each train, searching through the timetable until I came to Oxford. I would then search for the next train to see if it makes a connection in an hour or more. And even if I found such a train, I would still have to discover how long it took to reach London and so have the length of the total journey. This is a tedious procedure involving much examination and repetitious calculation. Far better to let the Analytical Engine handle it.

"What I want as output is a table where each train is identified by a number, the length of time for a connection at Oxford to the next train, and the total journey time."

A sample sketch of Holmes's output table is given here :

DEPARTING TRAIN	OXFORD CONNECTION	TOTAL JOURNEY
1	255	535
2	50	345
. . .	. . .	. . .

BIRMINGHAM TO LONDON TIMES, STOPPING AT OXFORD

"It has never been my habit to hide any of my methods from you, Watson," Holmes continued. "If you will permit me there are some points here that may interest you."

"Proceed, my dear Holmes."

He paused a moment. "What we need, Watson, is a way to tell the Engine to repeat the same sort of calculation over and over again. As you may remember, such repeated calculations are called *loops*. A loop must continue until the answer has been found or until some other condition has been met. Two things are needed: a means of instructing the Engine to perform a series of calculations repetitively and a means of controlling the number of repetitions."

"I say, Holmes, without the second point you would be in much the same situation as the sorcerer's apprentice who knew the magical spell to make brooms fetch pails of water, but knew not the incantation which would make them stop."

"Quite so," replied Holmes. "In fact, that is just the sort of thing that often happens to beginning programmers; and, I might add, even to experienced programmers.

"There are two sorts of loops, depending on which strategy of control one employs.

"A *conditional loop* involves a set of instructions that are to be repeated until some condition is met: for example

As long as CITY ≠ LONDON, do the following:
  input CITY, ARRIVAL_TIME

or

Do the following:
  get another clue
  examine the clue
until MURDERER ≠ UNKNOWN

As you can see, Watson, when the first loop is completed, the last city read must be London. Similarly, when the second loop is completed, the identity of our murderer is no longer a mystery.

"There is also a second sort of loop called a *for loop*, involving a set of instructions that are to be repeated some fixed number of times. As an example we might say :

For each of the next nine trains, do the following:
  read the times of the train
  compute the connection and journey duration

When this loop is completed, nine trains will have been processed."

I thought about this for a moment and then asked how he would keep track of how many times the loop had been repeated.

"Elementary, Watson. We have a variable that is identified with the loop and is automatically incremented each time the loop is repeated. You will see an example of this in a moment.

"Here is a sketch of my algorithm for solving our problem," he said. The sketch ran :

Print the result table headers
Input the times of the first train

For each of the next 9 trains, do the following:
  input the times of the train
  compute the connection and journey duration
  print the results

Print the caption for the result table

Holmes's algorithm is shown in Exhibit 6.2. I did not follow it immediately. "But, Holmes," I queried, "what is the significance of the number 40?"

Definitions:

CITY   : a code for a city
TRAIN_NUM: the number of a train
CONNECTION, JOURNEY: intervals of time

START_TIME, STOP_TIME, ARRIVAL_TIME,
NEXT_START_TIME, NEXT_STOP_TIME, NEXT_ARRIVAL_TIME: train times

Algorithm:

-- Set up for first train
Print the result table headers
Input CITY, START_TIME
As long as CITY ≠ OXFORD do the following:
   input CITY, STOP_TIME
As long as CITY ≠ LONDON do the following:
   input CITY, ARRIVAL_TIME

-- Handle each connecting train
Successively setting TRAIN_NUM to 2 through 10, do the following:
   input CITY, NEXT_START_TIME
   as long as CITY ≠ OXFORD do the following:
      input CITY, NEXT_STOP_TIME
   as long as CITY ≠ LONDON do the following:
      input CITY, NEXT_ARRIVAL_TIME

   let CONNECTION = NEXT_STOP_TIME - STOP_TIME
   if minutes of STOP_TIME > minutes of NEXT_STOP_TIME then
      let CONNECTION = CONNECTION - 40

   let JOURNEY = NEXT_ARRIVAL_TIME - START_TIME
   if minutes of START_TIME > minutes of NEXT_ARIVAL_TIME then
      let JOURNEY = JOURNEY - 40

   print TRAIN_NUM - 1, CONNECTION, JOURNEY

   -- Prepare for handling the next train
   let START_TIME = NEXT_START_TIME
   let STOP_TIME = NEXT_STOP_TIME

Print the caption for the result table

Exhibit 6.2 *Algorithm for Calculating Train Connections*

"There are indeed some subtle points here. Our train times are expressed as decimal numbers. Thus the difference of the two train times

935 - 625

is 310, which is correct; but

920 - 625

is 295, which is not correct for our purposes. In the second case, the answer should be 255, because there is a 2 hour and 55 minute time difference between 9.20 A.M. and 6.25 A.M. If you look at the algorithm, Watson, you will see that in these cases I have subtracted 40 minutes to correct this difficulty. It is simply a question of doing arithmetic with hours and minutes.

"A second subtlety in the algorithm involves preparing for the next train each time the loop repeats. Thus for the second train, we must subtract the time of the first. For the third train, we subtract the time of the second, and so on. Before dealing with the next train, we must save the times of the train we are presently using. Now, Watson, the algorithm should be quite clear."

It was the next day when he produced the final programme, which I offer as Exhibit 6.3.

"Holmes," I remarked, after considerable study, "in line 0430 you divide an interval of time by 100 and then take its integer part. I deduce from your algorithm and programme that this must be Basic's way of calculating the number of hours."

"My dear Watson, you are such an ideal student and helpmate, a confederate to whom each new development comes as a perpetual surprise; and your grand gift for scientific enquiry makes you an invaluable companion in these endeavours. Let us run the programme and check the output, shall we?"

I was not completely certain how I was to interpret this remark, but I interrupted him no further as he ran the data through the Engine. He sat back while the Engine worked its calculations, but suddenly sprang up in his chair, taking his pipe in his lips, and bounding like an old hound who hears the view-holloa.

"Yes, indeed," he said. "Our friend Penwether most certainly had the opportunity to betray his superior. Let us see how this evidence sits with him, shall we? For now, it remains a matter between the deacon and his creator. We shall give him a short time to decide whether he cares to discuss this with the police."

But our meeting with the deacon was not to be. Within the hour a visit from the Reverend Cowesworthy brought with it the missing Bible and news of Penwether's confession.

"When one tries to rise above Nature," Holmes commented, "one is liable to fall below it. The highest type of man may revert to criminal means if he leaves the straight road of destiny."

```
0010 REM  --  THIS PROGRAMME INPUTS THE TRAIN TIMES ON THE ROUTE
0020 REM  --  FROM BIRMINGHAM TO LONDON.
0030 REM  --  THE PROGRAM CALCULATES THE TOTAL TIME OF A JOURNEY FROM
0040 REM  --  BIRMINGHAM TO LONDON, ASSUMING A STOP AT OXFORD.
0050 REM
0060 REM  -- DICTIONARY OF NAMES:
0070 REM
0080 REM  -- C$      CITY CODE
0090 REM  -- N       NUMBER OF A TRAIN
0100 REM  -- D1      DURATION FOR OXFORD CONNECTION
0110 REM  -- D2      DURATION OF TOTAL JOURNEY
0120 REM  -- H1, H2  NUMBER OF HOURS IN A TIME DURATION
0130 REM  -- S1, S2  STARTING TIMES FOR TWO SUCCESSIVE TRAINS
0140 REM  -- X1, X2  OXFORD TIMES FOR TWO SUCCESSIVE TRAINS
0150 REM  -- A1, A2  ARRIVAL TIMES FOR TWO SUCCESSIVE TRAINS
0160 REM
0170 REM
0180 REM  -- SET UP FOR FIRST TRAIN
0190      PRINT "DEPARTING     OXFORD       TOTAL"
0200      PRINT "  TRAIN      CONNECTION   JOURNEY"
0210      PRINT "--------     ----------   -------"
0220      PRINT
0230 REM
```

Exhibit 6.3 *Programme for Calculating Train Times*

```
0240      INPUT C$, S1
0250      IF C$ = "OX" THEN 0280
0260          INPUT C$, X1
0270          GOTO 0250
0280      IF C$ = "LO" THEN 0330
0290          INPUT C$, A1
0300          GOTO 0280
0310 REM
0320 REM  -- HANDLE EACH CONNECTING TRAIN
0330      FOR N = 2 TO 10
0340          INPUT C$, S2
0350          IF C$ = "OX" THEN 0380
0360              INPUT C$, X2
0370              GOTO 0350
0380          IF C$ = "LO" THEN 0420
0390              INPUT C$, A2
0400              GOTO 0380
0410 REM
0420          LET D1 = X2 - X1
0430          LET H1 = INT(D1/100)
0440          LET M1 = D1 - H1*100
0450          IF   M1 < 60 THEN 0470
0460              LET D1 = D1 - 40
0470          LET D2 = A2 - S1
0480          LET H2 = INT(D2/100)
0490          LET M2 = D2 - H2*100
0500          IF   M2 < 60 THEN 0530
0510              LET D2 = D2 - 40
0520 REM
0530          PRINT "    "; N - 1, D1, D2
0540 REM
0550 REM  -- PREPARE FOR HANDLING NEXT TRAIN
0560          LET S1 = S2
0570          LET X1 = X2
0580      NEXT N
0590 REM
0600      PRINT "BIRMINGHAM TO LONDON TIMES, STOPPING AT OXFORD"
0610 END
```

Exhibit 6.3 *Continued*

6.1   Looping

The concept of looping is so central to problem solving on a computer that it is hard to imagine any self-respecting computer program that does not contain at least one loop. Looping, in fact, is similar to many everyday situations, as the following informal statements illustrate:

- Duplicate the following pattern eight times.

- While the cat is asleep, let the mouse play.

- Repeat with each ingredient until the mixture thickens.

- Search through the trunk until all items are found.

- As long as a king has not been crowned, continue advancing forward.

Each of these statements implies a set of instructions to be obeyed repeatedly until a particular condition is met.

We thus see the two basic characteristics of every loop:

1.   It has a *body*: the instructions to be executed repeatedly.

2.   It has a *termination condition*: an event that must happen to signal the end of the repetition.

In Basic there are several ways for expressing loops; the choice depends upon the problem at hand.

6.2   Conditional Loops

Perhaps the simplest form of loop in Basic is embodied by the following example:

```
0250   IF C$ = "OX" THEN 0280
0260      INPUT C$, X1
0270      GOTO  0250
0280   ...
```

The body of this loop consists of the single statement

```
INPUT C$, X1
```

which is executed repeatedly as long as the condition

```
C$ = "OX"
```

remains unsatisfied.

It is important to be precise here, for understanding the meaning of even this simple loop is elementary to all that follows. When the above statements are executed, the following takes place.

1. A test is made to see if the value of the variable C$ is equal to "OX".

2. If the result of the test fails, the body of the loop (in this case the INPUT statement) is executed and the whole process begins again from step 1.

3. Otherwise (the condition is true), execution continues at line 0280, i.e. the loop is terminated.

The net effect of our simple loop is that cities and arrival times at each city are successively read in until the city happens to be Oxford, at which point execution of the loop is complete.

Obviously, there are many cases where we want to specify several actions in the body of a loop. This is easy; for example, we may have:

```
0010 IF C$ = "OX" THEN 0050
0020    INPUT C$, X3
0030    PRINT "ANOTHER CITY HAS BEEN ENTERED"
0040    GOTO 0010
0050 ...
```

The above loops illustrate the following general form:

```
line-A   IF condition THEN line-B
             statements
             GOTO line-A
line-B   ...
```

In particular, each loop begins with a condition. The condition describes some fact about our data. Each loop also contains one or more statements. The statements tell which actions are to be carried out repeatedly. As long as the condition remains false, the statements are executed. Upon termination of the loop, the condition is known to be true. Notice that if the condition is initially true, the statements in the body of the loop are not executed.

The condition given at the head of the loop has the same form as those given for all IF statements. For example, we may have:

```
line-A   IF N = 100 THEN line-B
              what to do as long as N does not equal 100
              GOTO line-A
line-B   ...
line-A   IF M <> "UNKNOWN" THEN line-B
              what to do as long as the murderer M is unknown
              GOTO line-A
line-B   ...
line-A   IF B <= 0 THEN line-B
              what to do as long as the bank balance B is not in the red
              GOTO line-A
line-B   ...
```

Just as before, we may express more complex conditions by using several IF statements at the head of a loop, as in:

```
line-A   IF T < 10.00 THEN line-B
         IF T > 12.00 THEN line-B
              what to do when the time T is between 10 a.m. and noon
              GOTO line-A
line-B   ...
```

In all cases, the body of the loop is executed repeatedly as long as the condition is not satisfied.

There is a very simple variant of this kind of loop where the condition is tested at the end of the loop. Such loops have the form:

```
line-A   statement
              possibly other statements
              IF condition THEN line-A
line-B   ...
```

This loop is executed as follows:

1. Execute the statements in the body of the loop.
2. If the condition is then true, repeat the process again.
3. Otherwise, continue at line-B, i.e. terminate the loop.

Notice here that the condition is tested *after* executing the body of the loop. Notice also that the condition is given the other way around; that is, the body of the loop is executed as long as the condition remains true.

For instance, consider:

```
0010 REM -- TRY THIS
0020        INPUT C$,X1
0030    IF C$ <> "OX" THEN 0020
0040 REM ...
```

This loop tells us to keep reading in cities and arrival times until we find a city whose value is "OX". These statements have exactly the same effect as:

```
0010 REM -- AND THIS
0020    INPUT C$, X1
0030    IF C$ = "OX" THEN 0060
0040       INPUT C$, X1
0050       GOTO 0030
0060 REM ...
```

Here we can readily see that the condition used to control the repetitions of the loop is stated in just the opposite way from the previous example.

Notice, however, one difference between testing the condition after versus before the loop. When the test is made after, the loop is always executed at least once. When the condition is tested first, the body of the loop may not be executed even once if the condition is initially true. Obviously, the problem at hand will govern your choice.

6.3   For Loops

There is yet another form of loop that you can write in Basic and this is called a FOR loop. Consider the statements

```
0330 FOR N = 2 TO 10
0370    INPUT C$, S2
...
0570    LET X1 = X2
0580 NEXT N
```

which we have borrowed from Holmes's program. Here we have a series of actions that are to be executed exactly nine times. The actions are specified between the FOR and NEXT statements. Each time the actions are executed, the variable N takes on a new value. Its first value is 2, its second value is 3, and so forth, up to 10.

Such loops are handy in cases like this where a sequence of actions is to be executed a fixed number of times. For example, we may have:

```
FOR S = 1 TO 4
   -- what to do for each of the four suspects
NEXT S

FOR M = 1 TO 12
   -- what to do for each month M
NEXT M
```

```
FOR C = (C1 + 1) TO (C2 - 1)
   -- what to do for all medial columns C between C1 and C2
NEXT C
```

In general, a FOR loop has the form:

```
FOR variable = initial-value TO final-value
   statements
NEXT variable
```

The initial and final values given in the header of the loop determine the number of times the statements are executed.

A word of caution. Each FOR loop contains a variable given in its header. This variable is called the *control variable*, and conceptually captures the state of the loop's execution. The initial and final values of the control variable are specified by expressions. Of course, the final value must be greater than the initial value; otherwise the loop has no effect.

The body of the loop is executed once for each value, starting with the initial value and continuing up to and including the final value. Upon each iteration, the value of the control variable assumes the corresponding value between the initial and final values.

Two other small points worth remembering: first, within the body of the FOR loop you should never assign a new value to the control variable. This would only add confusion. Second, when the entire loop is complete the value of the control variable retains the same value it had when the loop was terminated. Simply put, you can recycle the variable if you choose— but watch out for surprises.

Summary

There is no question that, as you progress with your programming skills, loops become an important problem-solving tool. Repeated calculations are intrinsic to almost any useful computer problem.

Here's a simple strategy for deciding which kind of loop to use. Whenever you want some actions to be repeated until you arrive at some specified result, use a conditional loop with the condition signifying the happening of the event; whenever you want certain actions to be repeated only a fixed number of times, use a FOR loop.

One point of caution: since the statements within a loop can include any statement, it is possible to have loops within loops. Since statements can also be conditional statements as well, you can have nested decision structures within loops and vice versa. When situations such as this arise, you have to be extremely careful to make the intent of your program clear.

We now revisit our program for counting change. This program is given in Example 6.1. Here a loop is used to subtract 100 from the value of

```
0010 REM  -- THIS PROGRAM READS IN SIX INTEGER VALUES, RESPECTIVELY
0020 REM  -- REPRESENTING THE NUMBER OF PENNIES, NICKELS, DIMES,
0030 REM  -- QUARTERS, HALF-DOLLARS, AND SILVER DOLLARS IN COINAGE.
0040 REM  -- THE PROGRAM OUTPUTS THE TOTAL VALUE OF THE COINS IN
0050 REM  -- DOLLARS AND CENTS.
0060 REM
0070 REM  -- DICTIONARY OF NAMES:
0080 REM
0090 REM  -- N  A NUMBER OF COINS, FOR INSTANCE THE NUMBER OF DIMES
0100 REM  -- T  TOTAL CHANGE
0110 REM  -- D  NUMBER OF DOLLARS
0120 REM  -- C  NUMBER OF CENTS
0130 REM
0140      LET T = 0
0150 REM
0160      PRINT "NUMBER OF PENNIES IS:"
0170      INPUT N
0180      LET T = T + 01*N
0190 REM
0200      PRINT "NUMBER OF NICKELS IS:"
0210      INPUT N
0220      LET T = T + 05*N
0230 REM
0240      PRINT "NUMBER OF DIMES IS:"
0250      INPUT N
0260      LET T = T + 10*N
0270 REM
0280      PRINT "NUMBER OF QUARTERS IS:"
0290      INPUT N
0300      LET T = T + 25*N
0310 REM
0320      PRINT "NUMBER OF HALF DOLLARS IS:"
0330      INPUT N
0340      LET T = T + 50*N
0350 REM
0360      PRINT "NUMBER OF SILVER DOLLARS IS:"
0370      INPUT N
0380      LET T = T + 100*N
0390 REM
0400      LET D = 0
0410      LET C = T
0420      IF C < 100 THEN 0460
0430         LET C = C - 100
0440         LET D = D + 1
0450         GOTO 0420
0460      PRINT "CHANGE IS "; D; " DOLLARS AND "; C; " CENTS."
0470 END
```

Example 6.1 *Counting Change Using Loops Instead of* INT

the change C and add 1 to the number of dollars D until the value of C is less than 100. This is exactly the computation provided by the arithmetic function INT given in the previous program.

In closing, consider the great detective's observation that "the simplest things are invariably the more important, the more powerful, and more often, the more difficult to bring home."

Like Dr. Watson, you now have at your disposal the tools for solving some very complex problems. Though simple in nature, these ideas are the most powerful you may come across. With this behind you now, from a programmer's point of view, the game is truly afoot.

VII

Holmes's Method Revealed

With the conclusion of the Adventure of Clergyman Peter, you, like Dr. Watson, should have a firm grasp of the elementary principles of programming. You should be able to write programs for solving a wide variety of problems.

We have been fortunate to observe Holmes in a number of programming situations; and in reviewing these, we will see that the great detective's methods are not at all mysterious. In the following pages we'll take a closer look at some of these ideas, drawing again on the reminiscences of Watson when they suit our purposes.

A word of caution is in order before continuing, however—do *not* be misled by the apparent simplicity of these ideas. True, they are, in and of themselves, very simple. But keep in mind Holmes's remark to Watson in their first case together, *A Study in Scarlet:* "To a great mind, nothing is little."

7.1 An Exception Disproves the Rule

"I had already perceived that Holmes had trained himself to see what others overlooked. He took great pains in preparing each problem, examining every detail of its performance, checking against all possible errors, and even drawing up an elaborate facsimile of the input and its corresponding output before approaching the Engine.

" 'I never make exceptions, Watson,' he once said when I remarked how tedious his precautions appeared. 'An exception disproves the rule.' "

It is a mistake to think that as soon as you have a good general idea of the problem you may as well start developing the program; you can handle those points you initially overlooked later on. Shortcuts sometimes pay off, but for the most part they don't. Starting with an absolutely solid problem definition is the best way to get future rewards.

When starting a new problem, there are many forces at work that encourage a programmer to abandon thoughtful and effective techniques for unproven shortcuts. If you try to get speedy results, you will only have to pay the price in time and energy later on.

The place to focus your attention at the beginning, as difficult and tedious as it may seem, *must* be on the problem definition itself. If you allow some little detail to escape you, ignore some odd case, or dwell on irrelevant information, you will find yourself playing host to some larger problems down the road.

As Holmes has demonstrated, one of the best techniques is to construct a sample of the input and output for each program before attempting to solve the problem. Among the benefits of this technique are:

■ It forces you to consider the details of the problem.

■ It can help to uncover any special or annoying cases that will surely turn up later.

■ It often forces you to restructure the problem, sometimes ever so slightly, making the program easier to write.

■ Above all, it gives you a clear idea of the intent of the entire program.

This may sound too obvious; but you will find that excellent problem definitions are as rare as excellent detectives, excellent food, or excellent anything. You will recall Holmes's remark that "Excellence is an infinite capacity for taking pains. It is a bad definition, but it does apply to programming." Writing good problem definitions requires plain hard work; there's no way around it. You must take the time to specify the inputs, the outputs, and the exact task the program is to perform. What is needed is persistence and discipline; or as Edison once remarked, "one percent inspiration, ninety-nine percent perspiration."

7.2   If Matters Become Difficult

"After clearly detailing the problem comes the next step, solving the problem in the most general terms. He uses a great many psychological techniques. I have heard him think aloud, talk about similar problems, or consider the problem as if there were no Engine at all. He is certainly not reticent about discussing the problem with me. And if matters become difficult, he ignores the problem for days."

Certainly the hardest task in problem solving is developing an overall strategy. There is little sense in pretending that the methods in problem solving are very scientific; nevertheless, there are known psychological techniques to help you over these first crucial steps.

Once you have a problem firmly fixed in your mind, it is a grave mistake to believe that this is the time to start programming. What it is the time to do is to start *thinking*.

Thinking means just that—thinking. You need to think about alternative ways to solve the problem. You need to examine various approaches in enough detail to discover the possible trouble spots that may be difficult to program. You should always look for possible errors and provide against them. It is the first rule of programming just as it is the first rule of criminal investigation. You need to polish any proposed solution before attempting to carry on. Remember, it is certainly easier to discard poor thoughts than poor programs.

You may have heard it said before, and that's because it's true: it always takes longer to write a program than it first appears. On the other hand, you can safely assume that the sooner you start writing code, rather than thinking about the problem, the longer it will take to complete the task.

One of the best thinking aids is *analogy*. Presumably the problem you are about to solve is not so unfamiliar that you have not seen anything like it before, and you should recall solutions to similiar problems. You may recognize portions of the problem that have been solved in some similiar fashion, or perhaps you have solved a similar problem that had nothing to do with computers. In each of these situations, the point is the same: look to previous solutions, for in them you may find the seeds to the solution of the new problem.

In attempting to solve a problem on a computer, there is a tendency to become heavily involved with the oddities of the programming language itself. Although the final solution must be programmed in some language, the best solutions are those for which there is a direct analogy to the world in which the problem is presented. To do this you should attempt to solve the problem without regard to the final computer implementation. Freed from the idiosyncrasies of a programming language, you can concentrate on the essence of the problem.

Holmes is a master of this technique. We see in his cases a tendency to think of the problem in the highest possible terms, often without any special regard to the final program. His mind remains free and uncluttered to employ techniques that he has found useful in the solution of many criminal investigations.

Recall the murder at the Metropolitan Club and the algorithm Holmes developed to solve the case. Although Holmes is well aware of the intense rigor required for programming, he concentrates on the organization of the clues, the sequence in which the clues are examined, and the construction of the tables of information. This is a powerful technique, not only for designing an original solution to a problem, but also for ensuring that the final program will reflect the real-world solution it was intended to solve in the first place.

Some problems are not at all easy to solve. It has long been an axiom among programmers that in difficult situations two heads are better than one. Working with someone else, customarily known as *brainstorming*, and simply talking about your problem has become a classic programming technique.

Holmes's conversations with Watson are more than idle chatter. In the process of discussing the problem, Holmes himself often finds inspiration. He is not afraid to expose the problem at hand and to listen to himself when he proposes a solution. It is remarkable how often the simple exposure of an idea to someone else can lead to a clearer, better formulated solution.

Of course, if your mind is already made up and your solution is well in hand, you can go right ahead. But take care—supposedly good ideas have been known to show serious flaws when put into action.

Sooner or later you will find yourself in a situation where there appears to be no reasonable solution to a particular problem. You may have tried repeatedly with a given idea, each time finding some new flaw. What should you do when all hope seems lost?

Take a break.

The technique of putting aside a problem for some period of time is generally known as *incubation*. This is a subtle but potentially powerful psychological technique. A complete distraction, a weekend away from a problem, a good night's rest, or some frivolous entertainment can often have far-reaching effects in solving difficult problems.

Our brain is supposedly at work on problems even though we are not consciously aware of it. Rest from a problem is often the predecessor of an inspiration. We have all experienced this in other areas of our lives.

In sum, there are a great many psychological techniques for solving problems. You should use these techniques to improve your problem solving skills in programming.

7.3   A Curious Language of His Own Invention

"Once Holmes had a particular solution in mind he would put to use a curious language of his own invention. His objective, apparently, was to write an algorithm at a very high level."

All solutions start from the problem and not from some programming language. Assuming that you have a solid idea of a solution, you must now take your first step towards a concrete program.

Holmes uses a simple device to sketch his ideas, writing out his solution in a very high level language of his own. His language is a programming "interlingua," a language somewhere between English and Basic. On the one hand, Holmes borrows extensively from English, coining phrases at will, unconstrained by a programming language.

For example, he might write

Do the following 10 times:
   -- *actions to be performed 10 times*

or

Print the values in the table

On the other hand, the language he chooses is guided by the knowledge that the final program must be written in Basic. He may, for example, conceptualize a variable, say the number of suspects, and write

Let NUM_SUSPECTS = 0

or

If NUM_SUSPECTS > 4 then
   -- *what to do if more than 4 suspects*

In Basic, the first statement can be expressed by a LET statement, the second by an IF statement.

The point of this example is to capture some written form of a solution. This form retains the high level of discourse of the problem domain, yet is specific enough to capture the essence of the algorithm that is being expressed.

7.4   Programs as Human Communication

"We had a pleasant dinner together, during which Holmes would talk about nothing but the use of different names he might assign to the variables in a programme. As always, he emphasized that programmes must be considered as elements of human communication, and that the choosing of names in a programme should serve its author's ends."

Assume for the moment that you were presented with two computer programs. Each performs the same, presumably very important, task for you. You will have to use one of the programs for the next several years, probably making modifications as time goes on. You are told that the programs, from a performance point of view, are absolutely identical; that is, they perform the same input and output, they run at approximately the same speed, and each has been tested thoroughly and shown to be correct.

You are not allowed to look inside and see the actual programs. The only additional information you have about the programs is that the first one required over a hundred changes in order to make it correct, while the second worked correctly the very first time it was run.

Now the obvious question. Which program would you choose?

This question leads to another: What are the characteristics of a program that would work correctly on its first test? We might conclude that the persons who wrote the program were highly skilled programmers or very lucky. But surely there is more, for there must be some element present in the second program that is lacking in the first. Our only logical conclusion is that the second program was written with such crystal clarity that it allowed its authors to comprehend it as easily as you can read these lines of text. In short, the program must be so transparent that "even a Scotland Yard official can see through it."

In all of Holmes's programs, we see an almost obsessive concern for clarity. A program is not just a set of instructions that must be understood by some computer, but a description of an algorithm that must be understood by human beings, especially the person writing and using the program.

The factors that go into making a program well suited for human comprehension are numerous. They include the design of clear algorithms, choice of control structures, the sequence in which operations are performed, and many other issues. Here we take up a few points that are mainly a matter of style.

It is almost impossible to be rigorous when it comes to deciding on good programming style. Yet, some programs are much easier to read and understand than others. One noteworthy problem arises in trying to overcome the extreme terseness of Basic. Short identifiers, reliance on line numbers, and the primitiveness of Basic constructs can easily lead to cryptic programs.

One line of attack is the use of remarks. Remarks are a form of internal documentation that allow you to describe the workings of a program. We admit the Basic convention for remarks is often inconvenient. You must use an entire new line for a remark that might be more informative if placed at the end of a statement line. It would be nice for instance, to write something like:

```
LET D1 = D1 - 40    -- ADJUST MINUTES
```

Nevertheless, remarks are invaluable for illuminating the logic of a program.

One strategic place to annotate a program is at the very beginning. Here you can describe its general intent, make note of any special cases, or even give your name and telephone number in case someone who uses it has problems. All of the programs here make use of such remarks—their purpose is so that you, the reader, have some clue to the events.

Another important use of remarks is for the description of the names used in a program. Consider

```
REM  -- DICTIONARY OF NAMES:
REM
REM  -- N  A NUMBER OF COINS, FOR INSTANCE THE NUMBER OF DIMES
REM  -- T  TOTAL CHANGE
REM  -- D  NUMBER OF DOLLARS
REM  -- C  NUMBER OF CENTS
```

taken from our program to count change. Here each name is listed, and a brief indication of its role is given. A reader who sees a statement like

```
LET T = T + 25*N
```

can readily decipher this statement with a glance at the dictionary of names. In a large program with many names, this is indispensible. Even for small programs, like most of those here, imagine trying to read the programs if each dictionary of names were removed.

Although the value of using remarks can be illustrated over and over again, programmers are often tempted not to use them. After all, when a program is being written, who needs them? But what if you have to go back to try to figure out what has happened and what is left to do? And what about the next day? Or the next week? Or the occasion when you have to change someone else's program? Enough said.

One last point—temperance is moderation in all things. Remarks can be overused as well as misused. It is far better to write clear programs in the first place than rely on copious remarks. Remarks should contain useful information. Frequent comments like

```
REM  -- A GETS B PLUS C
     LET A = B + C
```

not only clutter up your program but discourage anyone from trying to wade through it.

In short, remarks can really make a difference. Use them, temperately.

7.5   The Seemingly Insignificant Blank Space.

"It has long been an axiom of mine," said Holmes, "that the little things are infinitely the most important. I can never bring you to realize the importance of every single character in a programme, and, most notably, the seemingly insignificant blank space."

You have probably observed in all of Holmes's programs a rather generous use of both blank lines (remark lines with no text) and blank spaces. This is no accident. Like the use of remarks to annotate your program, the use of judicious spacing is primarily to assist human comprehension of a program.

Basic, like many languages, is a "free format" language, in that there are no column restrictions on statements. Such languages allow the programmer to write a program in any way that emphasizes its logical structure. The use of spacing conventions to illuminate structure is often called "prettyprinting."

Prettyprinting is a vital ingredient in reading programs. With good spacing rules, typing errors are much easier to detect and the meaning of portions of code easier to follow. Most importantly, the global intent of the program can be made more transparent to the reader. The conscious use of good spacing conventions can even affect and improve upon the original code.

Unfortunately, some implementations remove the extra spaces typed by the programmer and thus make prettyprinting impossible. To these we strongly object. If you are faced with this dilemma, at the least you can still use blank remark lines.

The development of good spacing conventions is, in large part, up to the programmer. Only when the knowledge of the program at hand is clear can the choice of spacing conventions be made with precision. However, there are a number of simple conventions that can go a long way toward the writing of clear programs. Table 7.1 lists some prettyprinting conventions that have been followed throughout this text.

A point of caution: do not think that these conventions themselves are enough. Like anything else in this chapter, the implementation of even these simple ideas requires a great deal of thought.

This brings us full circle to our point of origin, and that is there can never be a substitute for thinking.

"In solving any sort of programming problem, Watson," Holmes once remarked, "the grand thing is simple, human reasoning. It is a very useful and easy accomplishment, though people do not practice it much. There are fifty who can reason synthetically for one who can reason analytically. I tell you, Watson, we have not yet grasped the results which human reason alone can attain to."

TABLE 7.1 *Some Prettyprinting Conventions*

General Considerations

1. The text of a remark line is not aligned with the program text. For example, instead of

```
REM  PREPARE FOR HANDLING NEXT TRAIN
     LET S1 = S2
     LET X1 = X2
```

use something like:

```
REM  -- PREPARE FOR HANDLING NEXT TRAIN
     LET S1 = S2
     LET X2 = X2
```

Notice here how the -- helps the visual separation of the text of a remark from the text of a program statement.

2. The symbol REM in any remark line begins one space over from the corresponding line number; executable statements begin two or more spaces over from each REM symbol. For example, instead of

```
0010 REM --  ESTABLISH KNOWN CLUES
0020 LET R$(4) = "ROOM_10"
0030 LET A$(3) = "GOLD_WATCH"
0040 LET A$(2) = "RUBY_RING"
0050 LET R$(2) = "ROOM_12"
0060 REM
0070 LET S = 1
```

use:

```
0010 REM  -- ESTABLISH KNOWN CLUES
0020      LET R$(4) = "ROOM_10"
0030      LET A$(3) = "GOLD_WATCH"
0040      LET A$(2) = "RUBY_RING"
0050      LET R$(2) = "ROOM_12"
0060 REM
0070      LET S = 1
```

This convention promotes alignment of executable statements without clutter from remark lines, and gives the effect that blank remark lines are truly blank. It also tends to diminish the visual effect of line numbers, most of which are inconsequential to the reader.

Table 7.1   *Continued*

3.   Any remark lines annotating the overall purpose of a program or subprogram are followed by at least one blank line.

   For example,

```
REM  -- THIS REMARK ANNOTATES THE PROGRAM, BUT IF
REM  -- YOU NOTICE IT IS A BIT CLUTTERED.
     INPUT A, B, C
```

looks better as:

```
REM  -- LEADING REMARKS CAN BE MADE TO STAND
REM  -- OUT NICELY FROM THE PROGRAM TEXT.
REM
     INPUT A, B, C
```

Blank Spaces

4.   At least one space appears after each comma(,), colon(:), and semi-colon(;). For example, rather than

```
INPUT A,B,C
PRINT "THE RESULT IS ";X
```

try:

```
INPUT A, B, C
PRINT "THE RESULT IS ";  X
```

5.   At least one space appears before and after each = and each logical operator. For example, the lines

```
LET A=A + 1
IF A>10 THEN 0250
```

look better as:

```
LET A = A + 1
IF A > 10 THEN 0250
```

6.   In an unparenthesized expression with several operators, spaces are used to show the precedence of the operators. For example, rather than

Table 7.1 *Continued*

```
A + B * C - D * E
```

a reader will be less confused with:

```
A + B*C - D*E
```

Alignment and Indentation

7.   Each statement within a FOR loop is indented three or more spaces from the FOR and NEXT statements bracketing the loop. For example, instead of

```
FOR S = 1 TO 4
LET H$(S) = "UNKNOWN"
LET A$(S) = "UNKNOWN"
LET R$(S) = "UNKNOWN"
NEXT S
```

use:

```
FOR S - 1 TO 4
   LET H$(S) = "UNKNOWN"
   LET A$(S) = "UNKNOWN"
   LET R$(S) = "UNKNOWN"
NEXT S
```

8.   Each statement within a conditional loop is indented three or more spaces from the controlling IF statement. For example, instead of

```
0010 IF C$ = "LO" THEN 0040
0020 INPUT C$, A1
0030 GOTO 0010
0040 PRINT "CITY IS LONDON"
```

or

```
0010 PRINT "CITIES ARE CODED WITH TWO LETTERS."
0020 PRINT "ENTER CITY CODE AND ARRIVAL TIME:"
0030 INPUT C$, A1
0040 IF C$ <> "LO" THEN 0020
```

use

Table 7.1   *Continued*

```
0010 IF C$ = "LO" THEN 0040
0020    INPUT C$, A1
0030    GOTO 0010
0040 PRINT "CITY IS LONDON"
```

and:

```
0010 PRINT "CITIES ARE CODED WITH TWO LETTERS."
0020    PRINT "ENTER CITY CODE AND ARRIVAL TIME:"
0030    INPUT C$, A1
0040 IF C$ <> "LO" THEN 0020
```

9. The actions in a decision structure are indented three or more spaces
from their leading IF statements. For instance, rather than

```
0010 IF R$(S) <> "ROOM_14" THEN 0030
0020 LET H$(S) = "BLACK"
0030 IF R$(S) <> "ROOM_16" THEN 0050
0040 LET A$(S) = "TATTERED_CUFFS
0050 ...
```

use:

```
0010 IF R$(S) <> "ROOM_14" THEN 0030
0020    LET H$(S) = "BLACK"
0030 IF R$(S) <>  "ROOM_16" THEN 0050
0040    LET A$(S) = "TATTERED_CUFFS"
0050 ...
```

10. In a conditional structure with a compound condition, the leading IF
statements are aligned. For instance,

```
0010 IF C$ <> "DARK" THEN 0050
0020 IF N$ <> "+" THEN 0050
0030 IF P$ <> "YES" THEN 0050
0040    PRINT "CIGAR IS A LATINO"
0050 ...
```

is easier on the eyes as:

```
0010 IF C$ <> "DARK" THEN 0050
0020 IF N$ <> "+"   THEN 0050
0030 IF P$ <> "YES" THEN 0050
0040    PRINT "CIGAR IS A LATINO"
0050 ...
```

Three-pipe Problems

VIII

The Ciphered Message

THE intimate relations that had existed between Sherlock Holmes and myself were, to an extent, modified in those years following my marriage, during which my practice increased steadily. I was occasionally able to follow my old companion's activities in the daily papers, which reported on his service to the Royal Family of Scandinavia and a matter of great importance to the French government, the details of which may never fully reach the public. While these cases brought him fame and princely rewards, they, and the one that I am about to relate, gave him the opportunity of demonstrating a fresh idea in his use of the Analytical Engine.

I called upon him late one winter's evening. As we sat on either side of the fire, Holmes was telling me once again, with great exultation, how he had purchased at a broker's in Tottenham Court Road for only fifty-five shillings a Stradivarius that was valued at over five hundred guineas. He suddenly held up his hand in a gesture of silence.

"We have a visitor," he said softly. "A gentleman of some importance, a government official perhaps."

When Mrs. Hudson showed a fellow dressed more like a gardener than a statesman into his lodgings, I must confess I had a slight feeling of amusement in my heart and hoped that this would be a lesson against the somewhat dogmatic tone he often exhibited.

"Tell me, sir," said Holmes, before any introductions had been exchanged, "do you always tend your flower beds in patent-leather boots, or is this the manner of attire appropriate to Whitehall these days?"

"Mr. Holmes," he replied solemnly, "I come on a matter of the utmost delicacy concerning the security of our nation." As he spoke he handed

Holmes his card, which identified him as an undersecretary in the Home Office.

Holmes rubbed his hands and his eyes glistened. Once our visitor was seated, Holmes leaned forward eagerly in his chair.

"State your case," he said briskly.

Uncomfortable, I rose to excuse myself.

"Please stay, Watson," asked Holmes. Then, turning to our visitor, he said, "this is Dr. Watson. You may say before this gentleman anything which you choose to say to me."

"It is known that you have assisted other heads of state on matters of the utmost confidence," said the man. "I am here, disguised so as not to draw attention to myself, on behalf of the Secretary to ask your help on a delicate matter concerning the transmission of diplomatic messages."

"Surely you are aware," answered Holmes, "that this is the special province of my brother, Mycroft. Though a government accountant, he also serves as an advisor in such matters."

"True, very true indeed, sir. However, as you yourself know very well, work of this nature neither begins nor ends in an armchair. While your brother's services remain indispensable, he lacks a certain energy."

Holmes merely nodded. "Pray continue," he said.

"Diplomatic ciphered messages are being regularly intercepted, deciphered, and acted upon. Acted upon with great damage," the Undersecretary stated in a clear and determined manner. With that, he produced a small packet of papers, unfolded them, and disclosed to us some of their contents. Holmes retrieved a small pince-nez and endeavoured to read them.

"HE ENDEAVOURED TO READ THEM."

"I thought that diplomatic ciphers were extremely difficult to break and that their keys were changed regularly. I understand also that the material they contain is often urgent, so that by the time someone could reasonably be expected to decode it, the information would no longer be important," Holmes said.

"This is true for the most part," replied the Undersecretary. "But some of our clerks are—how shall I say it—incapable of handling a cipher of great complexity or of remembering the scheme required to decipher it, and certainly incapable of relearning a new one as often as necessary. Indeed, the same code, a simple one, is used for months, so that confusion is kept to a minimum."

I am not at liberty to reveal the content of the next hour's discussion. Suffice it to say that the matters discussed were grave indeed.

As our visitor was restoring his papers to an inner pocket, Holmes said, "How may I be of assistance to you, sir?"

"Mr. Holmes, we need a more secure cipher. Will you devise one for us?"

"I shall do my best," said Holmes steadily.

"Very good," replied the Undersecretary, and he then withdrew.

"Well, Watson, what do you make of it?" asked Holmes, once we were again alone.

"A nasty business, I should say, by the sound of things. But I am afraid I cannot help you much, for I am quite unfamiliar with ciphers and codes."

"Perhaps," said Holmes. "But this cipher is one of the simplest imaginable. It is so transparent that even a Scotland Yard official could see through it. The foreign agents who intercepted the messages probably believed the cipher was so elementary that it was a blind for a deeper and more complex cipher, embedded within. Each letter of the alphabet is simply replaced by some other letter. Allow me to show you."

Holmes wrote a sequence of letters on a sheet of paper :

A B C D E F G H I J K L M N O P Q R S T U V W X Y Z

"Assume now that our cipher letters are given in the following sequence :

H I J K L M N O P Q R S T U V W X Y Z A B C D E F G

Now we write the message on top, and below it the ciphered message :

```
TWELVE SHIPS WILL LEAVE ...
ADLSCL ZOPWZ DPSS SLHCL ...
```

Thus we get a letter for each letter of the message; and as long as we have a standard table to use, enciphering the message is an easy task."

"Well, all this seems childishly simple to me," I said.

"Too simple; and therein lies our problem, Watson."

"But surely, Holmes, you must know of some other cipher the Home Office could substitute for this one."

"I am fairly familiar with all forms of secret writings; and am myself the author of a trifling monograph upon the subject, in which I analyze one hundred and sixty separate ciphers. This one, however, as I have already stated, is by far the simplest—and I need not remind you with whom we are dealing."

After a considerable pause he returned to his sample ciphering sequence. "Here again is the sequence I have just written :

H I J K L M N O P Q R S T U V W X Y Z A B C D E F G

We can shift this sequence by one letter and get :

I J K L M N O P Q R S T U V W X Y Z A B C D E F G H

We can do likewise for a shift by two letters or three letters or even twenty-five letters. Each of these permutations is displayed in this table."

Holmes then showed me the table that I have duplicated here as Exhibit 8.1.

"Now for the key, Watson. From time to time passwords, or keywords, if you will, can be provided to the clerks. For demonstration, suppose the keyword is WATSON."

"I am flattered, Holmes," I remarked quite involuntarily.

"Now," Holmes continued, "we write the password over the message, like this :

```
WATSON WATSO NWAT SONWA ...
TWELVE SHIPS WILL LEAVE ...
```

For the first letter (T) of the message, we look at the W row of the cipher table under the column T. We get a W. For the next message letter (W), look at the A row under column W. We get a D. Simply continuing as prescribed, the message is coded as :

```
WDEKQY VOION QLSL KZUYL ...
```

Elementary, is it not?"

"Quite," I replied. "And I suppose that you intend to hand this material over to the Analytical Engine?"

"Precisely. Think of it, Watson, a device made of wood and metal that will actually print the results of its most complicated calculations as soon as they are obtained, without any intervention of human intelligence, or lack of it, as this case would suggest. Our Engine will guarantee the mathematical accuracy of its work, so ciphering the message will be flawless."

MESSAGE LETTER

```
    | A B C D E F G H I J K L M N O P Q R S T U V W X Y Z
  --+--------------------------------------------------------
  A | H I J K L M N O P Q R S T U V W X Y Z A B C D E F G
  B | I J K L M N O P Q R S T U V W X Y Z A B C D E F G H
  C | J K L M N O P Q R S T U V W X Y Z A B C D E F G H I
  D | K L M N O P Q R S T U V W X Y Z A B C D E F G H I J
  E | L M N O P Q R S T U V W X Y Z A B C D E F G H I J K
  F | M N O P Q R S T U V W X Y Z A B C D E F G H I J K L
  G | N O P Q R S T U V W X Y Z A B C D E F G H I J K L M
  H | O P Q R S T U V W X Y Z A B C D E F G H I J K L M N
  I | P Q R S T U V W X Y Z A B C D E F G H I J K L M N O
  J | Q R S T U V W X Y Z A B C D E F G H I J K L M N O P
  K | R S T U V W X Y Z A B C D E F G H I J K L M N O P Q
  L | S T U V W X Y Z A B C D E F G H I J K L M N O P Q R
  M | T U V W X Y Z A B C D E F G H I J K L M N O P Q R S
  N | U V W X Y Z A B C D E F G H I J K L M N O P Q R S T
  O | V W X Y Z A B C D E F G H I J K L M N O P Q R S T U
  P | W X Y Z A B C D E F G H I J K L M N O P Q R S T U V
  Q | X Y Z A B C D E F G H I J K L M N O P Q R S T U V W
  R | Y Z A B C D E F G H I J K L M N O P Q R S T U V W X
  S | Z A B C D E F G H I J K L M N O P Q R S T U V W X Y
  T | A B C D E F G H I J K L M N O P Q R S T U V W X Y Z
  U | B C D E F G H I J K L M N O P Q R S T U V W X Y Z A
  V | C D E F G H I J K L M N O P Q R S T U V W X Y Z A B
  W | D E F G H I J K L M N O P Q R S T U V W X Y Z A B C
  X | E F G H I J K L M N O P Q R S T U V W X Y Z A B C D
  Y | F G H I J K L M N O P Q R S T U V W X Y Z A B C D E
  Z | G H I J K L M N O P Q R S T U V W X Y Z A B C D E F
```

Exhibit 8.1 *Holmes's Cipher Table*
(Keyword letters are given on the left)

One of the most remarkable characteristics of Sherlock Holmes was his ability to put his brain out of action, switching his thoughts to lighter things whenever he had satisfied himself that he could no longer work to advantage. With a casual remark that this was indeed one of the most unimaginative tasks he had been called upon to deliver, he lapsed into our earlier discussion of violins. This led him to Paganini; and before I departed we sat for another hour over a bottle of claret, while he told me anecdote after anecdote of that extraordinary man.

I promised to return the next evening, and did so promptly at eight. Upon entering, I found Holmes peering into the internals of the device on the centre-table, which had been cleared of everything else. From where I stood I could see a very closely packed collection of meshing gears and cams. There appeared to be a cover that was swung upwards, forwards, and out of the way. Holmes studied the box for a moment and then beckoned to me.

"An amazing machine, Watson. The way Babbage uses the gears and cams to store his data is truly ingenious. We are now faced with the problem of how we are to proceed with the enciphering programme. I have been giving the matter some consideration and have written down my thoughts in the order that the machine should perform them to accomplish the task. What do you think, Watson?"

On a piece of paper Holmes had written the following :

Set up the cipher table
Input message character

As long as more characters are left, repeat the following:
    select cipher character using keyword and message letter
    print cipher character
    input next message character

Print "CIPHERING COMPLETED."

"Holmes, although this sketch is simple, it will actually be very cumbersome to implement, will it not?"

"How would you do it, Watson?"

I started to write almost without thinking :

If key letter is A and message letter is A then cipher is H
If key letter is A and message letter is B then cipher is I
. . .   .
If key letter is A and message letter is Z then cipher is G

If key letter is B and message letter is A then cipher is I
If key letter is B and message letter is B then cipher is J

. . .   .

and so on.

"My goodness, Holmes, this would take hundreds, if not thousands, of instructions. I do not see how they could possibly fit into the Engine."

"Six hundred and seventy-six, to be precise, Watson. Your method is indeed cumbersome. Perhaps a table—or as our mathematician friends call it, an *array*—would help to reduce the size of the programme. It would also eliminate the element of redundancy that your scheme requires."

"Exactly what is an array?" I enquired.

"An array is much like a chessboard," explained Holmes. "For our problem the cipher table is a 26-by-26 array, a chessboard is an 8-by-8 array.

"Each position in the cipher table or chessboard can be identified by naming the particular array and the specific element or position with which we are concerned. In the message, the first cipher letter is the letter residing at the crossing of the W row and the T column. Thus the cipher for the letter T can be obtained with the description:

CIPHER_TABLE ('W', 'T')

Equivalently, if ROW is set to 'W' and COLUMN to 'T', we can say:

CIPHER_TABLE (ROW, COLUMN)

Indeed, the description can be assumed to be the same as the actual element.

"It is a powerful concept for describing data, as it compresses the information into a form that is entirely suitable for a machine such as Babbages's, and is much more economical with the amount of space used. It also removes the need for all the words describing the choices to be made in the cipher. Rather, it uses the position in the array to convey all of this. However, I am still faced with the problem of the keyword and cipher table. If they are not made to reside in the Engine, anyone could steal and use them. They will both reside in the programme, so that we shall have no problems with the operator."

Holmes paced anxiously about the room for a moment and then constructed a sort of Eastern divan in one corner. He perched himself upon it, cross-legged, with a quantity of shag tobacco and a box of matches laid out before him. In the dim light of the lamp I watched him sitting there, an old briar pipe between his lips, his eyes fixed vacantly upon the corner of the ceiling, the blue smoke curling up from him, silent, motionless, with the light shining upon his strong-set aquiline features.

I knew that seclusion and solitude were necessary for my friend in those hours of intense mental concentration, and it was nearly noon the next day when I again found myself in his sitting room. My first impression was that a fire had broken out, for the room was so thick with smoke that I could barely see Holmes in his dressing-gown, coiled up in his armchair by the fireplace.

"So you've been up all the night and all the morning poisoning yourself," I said.

"Actually, Watson, I have just returned from the Home Office," he answered.

"You have been there in spirit, perhaps?"

"Exactly. The body of Sherlock Holmes has remained here in this armchair and has, I regret to report, consumed in my absence two large pots of coffee and an incredible amount of tobacco."

"And what have you brought back with you to Baker Street?"

He then unrolled a large document upon his knee. On it were the final algorithm and the final programme, which I have duplicated here as Exhibits 8.2 and 8.3, respectively.

As I examined the material he exclaimed, "Well, Watson, let us escape from this weary workaday world by the side door of music. Carina sings tonight at the Albert Hall, and we still have time to dress, drop these off at Whitehall, dine, and enjoy an evening of supreme inspiration."

Definitions:

KEYWORD   : the keyword used for ciphering messages
ROW, COLUMN   : a letter in one of the 26 rows and
                   columns of the cipher table
MESSAGE_CHAR : a character
CIPHER_CHAR   : a character
CIPHER_TABLE : an array giving the cipher letter for each
                   keyword letter and message letter

Algorithm:

Set up keyword letters
Set up cipher letters for each ROW and COLUMN of CIPHER_TABLE
Print "ENTER THE MESSAGE CHARACTERS:"

Input MESSAGE_CHAR
As long as MESSAGE_CHAR ≠ "/" do the following:
   let ROW = next letter of KEYWORD
   let COLUMN = MESSAGE_CHAR
   let CIPHER_CHAR = CIPHER_TABLE (ROW, COLUMN)
   print CIPHER_CHAR
   input next MESSAGE_CHAR

Print "CIPHERING COMPLETED."

Exhibit 8.2   *Algorithm for Holmes's Enciphering Method*

```
0010 REM  -- THIS PROGRAMME READS IN A MESSAGE AND ENCIPHERS EACH
0020 REM  -- LETTER BASED ON THE LETTER AND THE NEXT LETTER OF A
0030 REM  -- KEYWORD. THE ENCIPHER LETTER IS OBTAINED FROM A TABLE
0040 REM  -- OF LETTER PAIRS.
0050 REM
0060 REM  -- THE PROGRAMME PRINTS THE ENCIPHERED LETTERS.
0070 REM
0080 REM  -- DICTIONARY OF NAMES:
0090 REM
0100 REM  -- R      A ROW NUMBER
0110 REM  -- C      A COLUMN NUMBER
0120 REM  -- I      INDEX OF THE NEXT KEYWORD LETTER
0130 REM  -- K$     THE ARRAY OF KEYWORD LETTERS
0140 REM  -- T$     THE TABLE OF CIPHER LETTER PAIRS
0150 REM  -- C1$    A CHARACTER IN THE INPUT MESSAGE
0160 REM  -- C2$    A CHARACTER IN THE KEYWORD
0170 REM  -- C3$    A CHARACTER IN THE OUTPUT MESSAGE
0180 REM
0190      DIM  K$(6), T$(26, 26)
0200 REM
0210 REM
0220 REM  -- SET UP TABLES
0230      FOR I = 1 TO 6
0240        READ K$(I)
0250      NEXT I
0260      FOR R = 1 TO 26
0270        FOR C = 1 TO 26
0280          READ T$(R, C)
0290        NEXT C
0300      NEXT R
0310 REM
0320 REM  -- ENCIPHER MESSAGE
0330      PRINT "ENTER MESSAGE CHARACTERS:"
0340      LET I = 1
0350      INPUT C1$
0360      IF C1$ = "/" THEN 0510
0370        LET C2$ = K$(I)
0380 REM      -- CONVERT LETTERS TO ROW AND COLUMN NUMBERS
```

Exhibit 8.3 *Holmes's Enciphering Programme*

```
0390            LET R = ASC(C2$) - 64
0400            LET C = ASC(C1$) - 64
0410            LET C3$ = T$(R, C)
0420            PRINT C3$
0430            IF I = 6 THEN 0460
0440                LET I = I + 1
0450                GOTO 0480
0460                LET I = 1
0470                GOTO 0480
0480            INPUT C1$
0490            GOTO 0360
0500 REM
0510        PRINT "CIPHERING COMPLETED."
0520        STOP
0530 REM
0540 REM
0550 REM
0560 DATA  W,A,T,S,O,N
0570 REM
0580 DATA  H,I,J,K,L,M,N,O,P,Q,R,S,T,U,V,W,X,Y,Z,A,B,C,D,E,F,G
0590 DATA  I,J,K,L,M,N,O,P,Q,R,S,T,U,V,W,X,Y,Z,A,B,C,D,E,F,G,H
0600 DATA  J,K,L,M,N,O,P,Q,R,S,T,U,V,W,X,Y,Z,A,B,C,D,E,F,G,H,I
0610 DATA  K,L,M,N,O,P,Q,R,S,T,U,V,W,X,Y,Z,A,B,C,D,E,F,G,H,I,J
0620 DATA  L,M,N,O,P,Q,R,S,T,U,V,W,X,Y,Z,A,B,C,D,E,F,G,H,I,J,K
0630 DATA  M,N,O,P,Q,R,S,T,U,V,W,X,Y,Z,A,B,C,D,E,F,G,H,I,J,K,L
0640 DATA  N,O,P,Q,R,S,T,U,V,W,X,Y,Z,A,B,C,D,E,F,G,H,I,J,K,L,M
0650 DATA  O,P,Q,R,S,T,U,V,W,X,Y,Z,A,B,C,D,E,F,G,H,I,J,K,L,M,N
0660 DATA  P,Q,R,S,T,U,V,W,X,Y,Z,A,B,C,D,E,F,G,H,I,J,K,L,M,N,O
0670 DATA  Q,R,S,T,U,V,W,X,Y,Z,A,B,C,D,E,F,G,H,I,J,K,L,M,N,O,P
0680 DATA  R,S,T,U,V,W,X,Y,Z,A,B,C,D,E,F,G,H,I,J,K,L,M,N,O,P,Q
0690 DATA  S,T,U,V,W,X,Y,Z,A,B,C,D,E,F,G,H,I,J,K,L,M,N,O,P,Q,R
0700 DATA  T,U,V,W,X,Y,Z,A,B,C,D,E,F,G,H,I,J,K,L,M,N,O,P,Q,R,S
0710 DATA  U,V,W,X,Y,Z,A,B,C,D,E,F,G,H,I,J,K,L,M,N,O,P,Q,R,S,T
0720 DATA  V,W,X,Y,Z,A,B,C,D,E,F,G,H,I,J,K,L,M,N,O,P,Q,R,S,T,U
0730 DATA  W,X,Y,Z,A,B,C,D,E,F,G,H,I,J,K,L,M,N,O,P,Q,R,S,T,U,V
0740 DATA  X,Y,Z,A,B,C,D,E,F,G,H,I,J,K,L,M,N,O,P,Q,R,S,T,U,V,W
0750 DATA  Y,Z,A,B,C,D,E,F,G,H,I,J,K,L,M,N,O,P,Q,R,S,T,U,V,W,X
0760 DATA  Z,A,B,C,D,E,F,G,H,I,J,K,L,M,N,O,P,Q,R,S,T,U,V,W,X,Y
0770 DATA  A,B,C,D,E,F,G,H,I,J,K,L,M,N,O,P,Q,R,S,T,U,V,W,X,Y,Z
0780 DATA  B,C,D,E,F,G,H,I,J,K,L,M,N,O,P,Q,R,S,T,U,V,W,X,Y,Z,A
0790 DATA  C,D,E,F,G,H,I,J,K,L,M,N,O,P,Q,R,S,T,U,V,W,X,Y,Z,A,B
0800 DATA  D,E,F,G,H,I,J,K,L,M,N,O,P,Q,R,S,T,U,V,W,X,Y,Z,A,B,C
0810 DATA  E,F,G,H,I,J,K,L,M,N,O,P,Q,R,S,T,U,V,W,X,Y,Z,A,B,C,D
0820 DATA  F,G,H,I,J,K,L,M,N,O,P,Q,R,S,T,U,V,W,X,Y,Z,A,B,C,D,E
0830 DATA  G,H,I,J,K,L,M,N,O,P,Q,R,S,T,U,V,W,X,Y,Z,A,B,C,D,E,F
0840 END
```

Exhibit 8.3   *Continued*

8.1 Arrays

Up until now we have been dealing with items like a room number, a hair color, a type of cigar, and the time of day. All of these items have a common characteristic: they denote a single piece of data in the real world. With the introduction of Holmes's enciphering table, we come to an entirely different kind of entity, that of a composite object. A composite object has components that bear some relation to each other. In Holmes's enciphering program, the cipher table is a composite object consisting of the cipher characters corresponding to each possible pair of letters.

The enciphering table brings up a very general issue. In many instances we have collections of related data. To turn such data into a usable tool, we need some means of organizing the data to reflect the way they are used.

We turn here to one of the most important schemes for organizing data, the *array*. In later chapters we will examine how data may be organized into a file or a record structure. But the various methods for structuring data have the same objective: the ability to describe organized patterns of information.

You can think of an array as an ordinary table of entries. A table expresses a correspondence; that is, for each one of several items, we have a corresponding item.

For example, each of the following correspondences can be expressed in a table:

suspect → corresponding hair color
month → corresponding number of days
coin → corresponding value

In the first case, drawn from the murder at the Metropolitan Club, we have four suspects, each having some corresponding color of hair. In the second case, the correspondence is between the name of a month and the number of days in the month. In the third case, taken from our problem to count change, we have six coins, each with a corresponding value in cents. A simple table describing the correspondence between coins and values is given in Figure 8.1.

An array has two fundamental properties. The first is its set of indices, and the second is the set of components that may be stored within it. For example, the table of coin values may be described in Basic as follows:

```
DIM V(6)
```

This array, named V, contains six values, indexed by the numbers 1 through 6. The components of the array, the coin values, are integers. The

COIN	VALUE
Penny	1
Nickel	5
Dime	10
Quarter	25
Half Dollar	50
Dollar	100

Figure 8.1   *Table of Coin Values*

integers give corresponding values for each of the six coins. Notice that the maximum index, 6, is specified in the array definition.

In Basic, the above statement describing the array T is called a *dimension* statement. A dimension statement must occur before any reference to the given array, preferably at the beginning of a program. The integer given in the dimension statement gives the maximum index; the minimum index is 1, although almost every version of Basic lets you go to 0. We prefer not to use the index 0, as it can easily lead to some tricky programs.

Naturally we want to do something with arrays, and this means we want to refer to their components. Just as we can say

```
LET I = 1
```

to assign a value to a simple variable, we can say

```
LET V(2) = 5
```

to assign a value to an array component. Similarly, just as we can refer to the value of a simple variable in an expression like

```
I + 2
```

we can also refer to the value of an array component in an expression like:

```
V(2) * N
```

The general rule here is that we can treat a reference to an array component just the same as a simple variable. We simply give the name of the array followed by an expression in parentheses. The value of the expression denotes the index of the given component.

In the above examples the indices are integer values; this must be the case in Basic. Things get a bit sticky when the indices do not conceptually correspond to integers. In our coin table, for instance, instead of saying something like

```
LET V("NICKEL") = 5
```

which is a nice way of stating that the value of a nickel is 5 cents, we must instead say:

```
LET V(2) = 5
```

Here we assume that the coins penny, nickel, dime and so on are represented by the integers 1, 2, 3, and so on.

A similar problem arises in Holmes's program. Conceptually, the indices of the cipher table I$ should be the letters "A" through "Z". Somehow we need to convert the letters to the numeric equivalents 1 through 26. In every implementation, the available characters are represented inside the computer by numeric codes. One common set of codes is called ASCII. With this code the letters "A" through "Z" are represented by the numbers 65 through 90.

To get the ASCII code for a character, we can use the predefined function ASC. For instance

```
ASC("A") = 65
ASC("B") = 66
```

and so on. Thus

```
ASC("A") - 64 = 1
ASC("B") - 64 = 2
```

and so on. Finally, the statements

```
LET R = ASC(C1$) - 64
LET C = ASC(C2$) - 64
```

in Holmes's program perform the needed trick to convert arbitrary letters into the corresponding row and column numbers needed for the cipher table. We will have more to say on this topic in the next chapter when we discuss characters and strings in detail.

Many of the above ideas are illustrated in Example 8.1, yet another program for counting change. Here the values of the individual coins are stored in the array named V. The first six LET statements simply set the values of each coin to their respective value in pennies. In the computation of the total change, the value of each individual coin is obtained from the array V. The remainder of the program remains as it was in previous versions.

```
0010 REM   -- THIS PROGRAM INPUTS SIX INTEGER VALUES, RESPECTIVELY
0020 REM   -- REPRESENTING THE NUMBER OF PENNIES, NICKELS, DIMES,
0030 REM   -- QUARTERS, HALF DOLLARS, AND SILVER DOLLARS IN COINAGE.
0040 REM   -- THE PROGRAM OUTPUTS THE TOTAL VALUE OF THE COINS IN
0050 REM   -- DOLLARS AND CENTS.
0060 REM
0070 REM   -- DICTIONARY OF NAMES:
0080 REM
0090 REM   -- N  A NUMBER OF COINS, FOR INSTANCE THE NUMBER OF DIMES
0100 REM   -- T  TOTAL CHANGE
0110 REM   -- D  NUMBER OF DOLLARS
0120 REM   -- C  NUMBER OF CENTS
0130 REM   -- K  LOCAL COUNTER
0140 REM
0150       DIM V(6)
0160 REM
0170       LET V(1) =    1
0180       LET V(2) =    5
0190       LET V(3) =   10
0200       LET V(4) =   25
0210       LET V(5) =   50
0220       LET V(6) =  100
0230 REM
0240       LET T = 0
0250       PRINT "ENTER THE NUMBER OF EACH COIN:"
0260       FOR K = 1 TO 6
0270          INPUT N
0280          LET T = T + V(K)*N
0290       NEXT K
0300 REM
0310       LET D = INT(T/100)
0320       LET C = T - 100*D
0330       PRINT "CHANGE IS "; D; " DOLLARS AND "; C; " CENTS."
0340 END
```

Example 8.1　*Counting Change Using an Array of Coin Values*

8.2   Data Statements

The subject of arrays brings up a handy feature of Basic known as the READ statement. Consider the following six statements:

```
LET V(1) =    1
LET V(2) =    5
LET V(3) =   10
LET V(4) =   25
LET V(5) =   50
LET V(6) = 100
```

These statements set up the values needed for the array of coin values mentioned above.

Next consider the following two statements:

```
READ V(1), V(2), V(3), V(4), V(5), V(6)

DATA 1, 5, 10, 25, 50, 100
```

Here a READ statement is given with six variables, the six components of the array; the following DATA statement gives the values of the components. This pair of statements has exactly the same effect as the above LET statements.

Next, consider:

```
FOR I = 1 TO 6
    READ V(I)
NEXT I

DATA 1, 5, 10, 25, 50, 100
```

Again, the effect is the same.

More generally, a READ statement can be used to establish the values of variables just as with an INPUT statement. However, instead of taking the values from a terminal or some other input device, the values are taken from a DATA statement given in the program itself. READ and DATA statements are especially useful with arrays. Instead of entering each component of the array by means of an INPUT statement, or having a series of LET statements to establish each value, you can list all the values in one or more DATA statements.

A READ statement has a form similar to an INPUT statement, that is:

```
READ list-of-variables
```

Execution causes the variables to be assigned values, in order, from DATA statements.

DATA statements can appear anywhere in a program. Values from the collection of all DATA statements are considered as a single sequence of values. The order in which the values appear textually in the program determines the order in which the values are read. Thus

```
READ A, B, C, D
. . .
DATA 1, 2, 3, 4
```

is the same as

```
READ A, B, C, D
. . .
DATA 1
DATA 2
DATA 3
DATA 4
```

and the same as

```
READ A,B
READ C,D
. . .
DATA 1, 2, 3
DATA 4
```

Returning to Holmes's enciphering program, we see that

```
FOR I = 1 TO 6
   READ K$(I)
NEXT I
```

causes the characters in line 0560 to be established as keyword letters. Similarly

```
FOR R = 1 TO 26
   FOR C = 1 TO 26
      READ T$(R, C)
   NEXT C
NEXT R
```

makes heavy use of DATA statements. Each of the characters in lines 0580 to 0830 are used to establish the cipher table. All of this works just as you might expect.

It is common practice to put DATA statements at the end of a program. We support this practice, as it provides good separation between the part of a program to be executed and its data.

IX

An Advertisement
in the Times

HAD seen little of Sherlock Holmes for many months, my marriage and my return to practice in the Paddington district having caused us to drift apart. One night in early August, as my way led through Baker Street, I was seized by a keen desire to see Holmes and to know to what use he was making of his extraordinary Engine. I found him lounging upon the sofa, a pipe-rack within his reach and a pile of crumpled newspapers, apparently recent, near at hand. A lens and a number of columns that had been neatly cut from the papers were lying upon the sofa beside him, which suggested he had been in the process of examining them when I entered.

"You are engaged, I see," said I. "Perhaps I am interrupting your work."

"On the contrary, you could not have come at a better time, my dear Watson," he said cordially. "You would confer a great favour upon me should you lend me an ear, for nothing clears up a problem so much as stating it to another person. I think that your time will not be misspent," he continued as he reached for a paper. "This case has its points of interest and, especially, of instruction."

I gave the pile more careful scrutiny and realized that it was largely made up of back editions, for they were yellowed, of the *Times*.

"You are searching for something?" I asked.

"Indeed, Watson. I am searching for a series of trifles," he remarked. "You know my method. It is founded upon the premise that it is usually in unimportant matters that there is a field for observation."

He flipped rapidly through the paper, finally thrusting it under his sofa and taking up another.

"As you know, I customarily read nothing but the criminal news and the personal announcements. I have of late included the advertisements, which are proving instructive."

I waited silently, accommodating my companion's flair for the dramatic, to which I was long accustomed. He lit his pipe nonchalantly and continued.

"You may have read yourself, over the past eight months, of the series of daring burglaries that have been taking place throughout London's most fashionable districts. Scotland Yard is absolutely baffled."

"I have seen what the *Daily Telegraph* and the *Chronicle* have had to say, but not the *Times*," I replied.

"It is theorized that there are two persons involved," he continued, "and although two suspects have been under investigation, the authorities have never been able to establish their presence at the scenes of the crimes. There is nothing more stimulating than a case where everything goes against you. This particular matter is further complicated by the fact that neither suspect ever seems to communicate with the other. Now unless Scotland Yard can prove some means of communication, or better still, determine this means, intercept their messages, and catch them in the act, it is feared that these burglars will remain free. It is necessary to prove that they were indeed conspirators before they can be brought before a magistrate."

"I take it, Holmes, you have come across something in the *Times* linking these two with the crimes that the police have failed to note?"

"Yes, Watson, the *Times* is a paper that is seldom found in any hands but those of the highly educated. Crime is common but logic is rare, and I sense an extremely complex mind behind this. Therefore, it is upon the logic rather than upon the crime that one should dwell. Just when I thought that the criminal mind had lost all enterprise and originality, enter these singularly interesting specialists.

"This is one of those cases where the art of the reasoner should be used for the sifting of details rather than for the acquisition of fresh evidence. This is where Scotland Yard has wasted its energy. I, on the other hand, have considered how I might communicate with a silent partner."

Holmes rose from the sofa and walked towards the hearth rug while scanning the paper he had picked up earlier. I took this opportunity to stretch out in the comfortable armchair which I had occupied so many times before. I looked dreamily up to the mantelpiece, recollecting old adventures we had shared. I started from my reverie as Holmes abruptly pounced upon an advertisement.

"HOLMES ABRUPTLY POUNCED UPON AN ADVERTISEMENT."

"Here!" he exclaimed. "The most recent one, and at the correct time. That accounts for all seven robberies, by my calculations."

He then showed me the item which had arrested his interest.

> For Sale: Copies of the *Strand* numbering from 23 to 276 with various duplicates. Also, 3 Twybridge carriage wheels in excellent condition. Please enquire: Box 37 GPO

"I do not recognise the carriage name," I replied, "but some of those issues of the *Strand* have chronicles of your achievements."

"The magazine itself is of little import, Watson, but the numbers of these issues are. The newest volume number minus the oldest volume is a number that fits well into my theory, as is the number of carriage wheels. As for these Twybridge carriage wheels, I can safely attest that there are no such items in existence. I am familiar with forty-two impressions left by carriage wheels, having written a short monograph on the subject.

"I believe the 3 represents three o'clock in the morning, the hour the last burglary took place. Also, is it not curious, Watson, that this carriage, whose name is unfamiliar to us, should have the same name as the street on which the last victim resides?"

Holmes pulled another well-worn newspaper from the stack near him.

"Here is another from last month's paper, offering for sale 209 'Brewster' pigeons; and a robbery did occur on Sunday, July 28th."

I pondered for a moment and asked, "Holmes, I believe you may have something. But about the date, are you sure?"

"Absolutely. If we subtract the lower number from the upper number of the supposed volumes of the *Strand*, we get 253. The 253rd day of the year was September 10th, a Tuesday and the date of the last robbery. July 28th was nearly seven weeks ago. It was the 209th day of the year, a Sunday, and the date of the previous robbery. And, I might add, there are no pigeons of a type called Brewster."

"Amazing, Holmes, but how did you determine the date from just the number?"

"That is the flower that comes from this little seed, Watson. I must take care to explain it to you in detail so that you may appreciate it fully.

"Obviously, Watson, a programme on the Analytical Engine which arrives at the date from the number would be a way to achieve an efficient solution to this problem. The first of January was a Tuesday. If we enter the number

253

the programme will calculate the date

Tuesday, September 10

the date that is the 253rd day of the year. I am sure that these scoundrels just count the days off on the current calendar, but counting is tedious and prone to error. Such a solution lacks elegance and can hardly be considered of broad use."

"There are some other uses you have in mind for this programme?" I asked.

"It is what we learn from the particular construction of this programme that will be of continued use to us, Watson," said Holmes. "We are faced here with finding a means of working on a numerical device with items that have many and varying properties. We are dealing here with a theory of *types*, the representation of things from the real world.

"I have given this notion considerable thought and have taken the trouble of constructing a diagram," he said, handing me a small chart which ran this way :

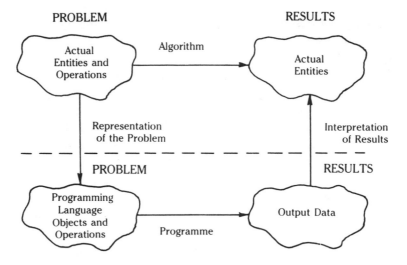

"A type, Watson, characterizes a class of objects and the operations that can be performed upon them.

"The current problem has several classes of objects with differing operations possible for them. Consider the days of the week. There are only seven days of the week—Sunday, Monday, Tuesday, Wednesday, Thursday, Friday, Saturday.

"Some of the common operations that we can perform upon them are:

1. Computing the day after: Given a day of the week, we can determine the following day, for example,

DAY_AFTER(MONDAY) is TUESDAY
DAY_AFTER(FRIDAY) is SATURDAY

2. Comparison of days: In a given week we can determine if any one day precedes another, for example,

MONDAY precedes SATURDAY
MONDAY precedes WEDNESDAY

When we write programmes, we deal with many such types of objects— names, varieties of cigar ash, amounts of money, months, days, and so forth."

Holmes then displayed his algorithm for computing the date from the number of days given in the advertisements. The algorithm is reproduced here as Exhibit 9.1. I had no problem in following his simple logic.

Definitions:

DAY_OF_WEEK   :   one of the days SUNDAY through SATURDAY
MONTH   :   one of the months JANUARY through DECEMBER
DAY_OF_MONTH: a number from 1 to 31

CURRENT_NUM   :   a number from 1 to 365
NUM_OF_DAYS   :   a number from 1 to 365

Algorithm:

Let MONTH = JANUARY
Let DAY_OF_MONTH = 1
Let DAY_OF_WEEK = TUESDAY

Input NUM_OF_DAYS

For CURRENT_NUM set to 2 through NUM_OF_DAYS, do the following:
   Let DAY_OF_WEEK = DAY_AFTER(DAY_OF_WEEK)
   If (MONTH = JANUARY)   and (DAY_OF_MONTH = 31)
   or (MONTH = FEBRUARY)   and (DAY_OF_MONTH = 28)
   or (MONTH = MARCH)   and (DAY_OF_MONTH = 31)
   or (MONTH = APRIL)   and (DAY_OF_MONTH = 30)
   or (MONTH = MAY)   and (DAY_OF_MONTH = 31)
   or (MONTH = JUNE)   and (DAY_OF_MONTH = 30)
   or (MONTH = JULY)   and (DAY_OF_MONTH = 31)
   or (MONTH = AUGUST)   and (DAY_OF_MONTH = 31)
   or (MONTH = SEPTEMBER and (DAY_OF_MONTH = 30)
   or (MONTH = OCTOBER)   and (DAY_OF_MONTH = 31)
   or (MONTH = NOVEMBER) and (DAY_OF_MONTH = 30) then
      let MONTH = MONTH_AFTER(MONTH)
      let DAY_OF_MONTH = 1
   else
      let DAY_OF_MONTH = DAY_OF_MONTH + 1

Print DAY_OF_WEEK, MONTH, DAY_OF_MONTH

Exhibit 9.1   *Holmes's Algorithm to Compute Dates*

"Now for the representation of the problem. When we use the Engine, we have only a small number of commonly used fundamental types at our disposal, for example, integers, characters, and strings. Each of these types has its own special operations defined in the programming language, so we do not have to bother ourselves constantly with defining them. For example, we have :

addition: We can add two numbers and get their sum.

comparison: We can compare two numbers to see which is
              greater.

negation: We can negate an integer or a Boolean truth value.

printing: We can print a number or a string.

"Now, Watson," he continued, "the essence of working with any actual type of data is that the objects, such as amounts of money, days of the week, and months, must be defined in terms of the programming language. We must not only choose a particular representation for an object; we must also make sure that operations upon it, as represented in the language, correctly reflect its actual properties.

"For example, we can perform all numeric operations on numeric data; but when the number represents some real entity, like the year 1889, some operations are meaningless. The difference of two years is a useful operation because it is actually sensible to consider the interval of time between two dates. On the other hand, the square root of a year has no useful meaning associated with it. To multiply two years is likewise senseless.

"Specifically, our calendar problem requires us to write an algorithm which correctly depicts the three data types:

months
days of the week
days of the month

The days of the month running from 1 to 31 can easily be represented in Basic using integers. The 'day after' a day of the month H is :

```
H + 1
```

Of course, when the value of H is the last day of the month, the day after is not

```
H + 1
```

but 1. This shows that although we operate on days of the month as integers, they are not really integers; this must be kept in mind or large problems will certainly result.

"Consider next the days of the week. We could represent them as integers: Sunday with 1, Monday with 2, and so forth. Of course, days of the week are not at all numbers, and the special rule for the last day of the week is needed to correctly represent the real world. In a Basic programme, with a day of the week variable D, we would have something like:

```
0010 REM  -- COMPUTE THE DAY AFTER
0020      IF D <> 7 THEN 0050
0030         LET D = 1
0040         GOTO 0070
0050         LET D = D + 1
0060         GOTO 0070
0070 ...
```

"Quite simple, Holmes," I commented.

"Precisely, Watson," replied Holmes. "But we must never trust to general impressions, rather concentrate upon details. An erroneous conclusion would show us how dangerous it is to reason from insufficient data. In this case, we must consider another operation on the days of the week, that of printing the name of the day. Once we have arrived at our result, Thursday, let us say, we must have it printed in a suitable form. Printing the number 5 is hardly illuminating."

"This certainly makes sense, Holmes," said I. "But what are you proposing?"

"Permit me to demonstrate, Watson," he answered. "Assume that we have determined the numeric value of the day D."

I quickly read his sketch which ran this way :

```
0010 REM  -- PRINT DAY NAME
0020      ON D GOTO  0030, 0050, 0070, 0090, 0110, 0130, 0150
0030         LET D$ = "SUNDAY"
0040         GOTO 0170
0050         LET D$ = "MONDAY"
0060         GOTO 0170
0070         LET D$ = "TUESDAY"
0080         GOTO 0170
0090         LET D$ = "WEDNESDAY"
0100         GOTO 0170
0110         LET D$ = "THURSDAY"
0120         GOTO 0170
0130         LET D$ = "FRIDAY"
```

```
0140              GOTO 0170
0150              LET D$ = "SATURDAY"
0160              GOTO 0170
0170         PRINT D$
0180
```

"Here D$ would take on the proper string value corresponding to the number D," he explained.

As soon as he had finished with this elaborate explanation, Holmes crumpled up his programme, adding it to a pile of newspapers and refuse stored under his sofa.

"I am afraid this is quite unsatisfactory, Watson, as we still have not addressed the problem of representing the months of the year," he remarked. "There are twelve months, not seven, as with the number of days in the week. Again we run into this difficulty.

"Alternatively, Watson, we could represent the days of the week as strings—Monday being "MONDAY", Tuesday being "TUESDAY", and so forth. Then we would have the following structure."

Holmes started sketching the following example :

```
0010 REM   -- COMPUTE THE DAY AFTER
0020       IF D$ <> "SUNDAY" THEN 0050
0030          LET D$ = "MONDAY"
0040          GOTO 0230
0050       IF D$ <> "MONDAY" THEN 0080
0060          LET D$ = "TUESDAY"
0070          GOTO 0230
0080       IF D$ <> "TUESDAY" THEN 0110
0090          LET D$ = "WEDNESDAY"
0100          GOTO 0230
     ...       ...
0230 REM   -- CONTINUATION OF PROGRAM
```

"But Holmes," I interjected, "this second approach is most certainly laborious."

"Correct, Watson," said he. "But you must admit that it does make the operation for printing the name of a day absurdly easy. We simply print the value of D$."

He seemed to fall into depressed spirits once again and this latest programme was added to the pile.

"Ah, Watson," he groaned. "If there is not some compensation in the hereafter, then the world is a cruel jest. This is clearly a three-pipe problem, and I beg that you won't speak to me for the next hour."

I was quite accustomed to his moods and withdrew to the breakfast table, where I attempted to while away the time with one of several scientific journals that lay scattered about. After a while Holmes took up his violin from the corner of the mantelpiece and began to play some low, dreamy air.

I must have been lulled to sleep, for the next thing I was aware of was Holmes shaking my shoulder, eager to show me a long document he held.

"This is ground we've already covered, Watson!" he exclaimed. "The answer has been staring us in the face all along. Using an array, we can represent the correspondence of our seven numbers to their particular names as days of the week, and likewise for our 12 numbers and their corresponding month names. In this way, the days of the week are treated, within our programme, as simple integers and the operation for determining the following day remains an elementary one. If we want to print the name of any given day, we simply obtain it from a table included in our programme.

"You see, Watson, how crucial the proper representation of data is for proper problem solving with the Engine?"

I did not know quite what to say after this great exposition on the theory of types and the days of the week. It was plainly evident that I was both confused and intimidated, for Holmes quickly produced the programme that I have reproduced in Exhibit 9.2. It seemed excessively elaborate to me. After a moment of study, I enquired why he did not say

```
LET D$ = D$ + 1
```

in order to compute the day following a given day.

"It would certainly make sense to us," he replied, "but not to the Engine. A day of the week, Watson, is neither a number nor a character string. Indeed, whichever of these representations we choose to employ has its unpleasant features."

"Well, then," I remarked after a while. 'It all seems clear to me now. You plan to catch them in the act, unless I am not mistaken?"

"Oh, hardly my dear Watson," he replied. "You know that I look upon unnecessary bodily exertion as an extreme waste of energy. This is surely now a matter for the Police. After all, Watson, I am not retained by Scotland Yard to supply their deficiencies."

It was one of the peculiarities of his proud, self-contained nature that was always averse to anything in the shape of public applause, and he bound me in the most stringent terms to say no further word of the calculating engine or of his methods. Nothing amused Holmes more at the end of a successful case than to hand over the actual exposure to some orthodox official.

```
0010 REM  -- JANUARY 1, 1889 WAS A TUESDAY
0020 REM  -- THIS PROGRAMME INPUTS AN INTEGER REPRESENTING
0030 REM  -- THE NUMBER OF DAYS SINCE JANUARY 1.
0040 REM  -- THE PROGRAM PRINTS THE CORRESPONDING DATE.
0050 REM
0060 REM  -- DICTIONARY OF NAMES:
0070 REM
0080 REM  -- D   DAY NUMBER, FROM 1 (MONDAY) TO 7 (SUNDAY)
0090 REM  -- D$  ARRAY OF DAY NAMES
0100 REM  -- M   MONTH NUMBER, FROM 1 (JANUARY) TO 12 (DECEMBER)
0110 REM  -- M$  ARRAY OF MONTH NAMES
0120 REM  -- H   DAY OF THE MONTH, FROM 1 TO 31
0130 REM  -- N   NUMBER OF DAYS SINCE JANUARY 1
0140 REM  -- K   LOCAL COUNTER
0150 REM
0160 REM
0170      DIM D$(7), M$(12)
0180 REM
0190 REM  -- ESTABLISH TABLES
0200      FOR D = 1 TO 7
0210         READ D$(D)
0220      NEXT D
0230      FOR M = 1 TO 12
0240         READ M$(M)
0250      NEXT M
0260 REM
0270 REM  -- ESTABLISH TUESDAY, JANUARY 1
0280      LET D = 3
0290      LET M = 1
0300      LET H = 1
0310 REM
0320      PRINT "ENTER NUMBER OF DAYS:"
0330      INPUT N
0340 REM
```

Exhibit 9.2 *Holmes's Programme to Compute Dates*

```
0350        FOR K = 2 TO N
0360          IF D <> 7 THEN 0390
0370            LET D = 1
0380            GOTO 0430
0390            LET D = D + 1
0400            GOTO 0430
0410 REM    END IF
0420 REM
0430          IF M <> 1    THEN 0460
0440          IF H <> 31   THEN 0800
0450            GOTO 0770
0460          IF M <> 2    THEN 0490
0470          IF H <> 28   THEN 0800
0480            GOTO 0770
0490          IF M <> 3    THEN 0520
0500          IF H <> 31   THEN 0800
0510            GOTO 0770
0520          IF M <> 4    THEN 0550
0530          IF H <> 30   THEN 0800
0540            GOTO 0770
0550          IF M <> 5    THEN 0580
0560          IF H <> 31   THEN 0800
0570            GOTO 0770
0580          IF M <> 6    THEN 0610
0590          IF H <> 30   THEN 0800
0600            GOTO 0770
0610          IF M <> 7    THEN 0640
0620          IF H <> 31   THEN 0800
0630            GOTO 0770
0640          IF M <> 8    THEN 0670
0650          IF H <> 31   THEN 0800
0660            GOTO 0770
0670          IF M <> 9    THEN 0700
0680          IF H <> 30   THEN 0800
0690            GOTO 0770
0700          IF M <> 10   THEN 0730
0710          IF H <> 31   THEN 0800
0720            GOTO 0770
0730          IF M <> 11   THEN 0800
0740          IF H <> 30   THEN 0800
0750            GOTO 0770
0760 REM
```

Exhibit 9.2   *Continued*

```
0770          LET M = M + 1
0780          LET H = 1
0790          GOTO 0820
0800          LET H = H + 1
0810          GOTO 0820
0820      NEXT K
0830 REM
0840          PRINT D$(D); ", "; M$(M); " "; H
0850          STOP
0860 REM
0870 REM
0880 DATA  SUNDAY, MONDAY, TUESDAY, WEDNESDAY, THURSDAY, FRIDAY, SATURDAY
0890 REM
0900 DATA  JANUARY, FEBRUARY, MARCH,     APRIL,   MAY,      JUNE
0910 DATA  JULY,     AUGUST,    SEPTEMBER, OCTOBER, NOVEMBER, DECEMBER
0920 END
```

Exhibit 9.2   *Continued*

I read about the arrests a week later in all the papers. Of course, there was no mention of either Holmes or the Analytical Engine. It was, I surmise, his thought that widespread dissemination in the popular press of this sophisticated coding mechanism would naturally come to the attention of the more undesirable elements of the city. How well I recall him once commenting, "I could not rest, Watson, I could not sit quietly in my chair, if I thought that the Analytical Engine had fallen into the hands of some diabolical mastermind, walking the streets of London unchallenged."

9.1 Representing Data

This latest excursion down Baker Street has introduced the general problem of describing data that are not intrinsically numbers or strings. Problems of this sort, as Watson has learned, require careful thought in program design. They also illustrate two essential programming concerns:

- the need to describe objects and their properties with precision and clarity.

- the need to guarantee that the operations over objects do not violate their intrinsic properties.

This brings us to the concept of *types* of data. To motivate this discussion we first consider describing types of data whose values can be readily enumerated.

We begin with an example from Holmes's program, the days of the week. This is a familiar type of data, with seven possible values:

Sunday, Monday, Tuesday, Wednesday, Thursday, Friday, Saturday

In writing a program dealing with the days of the week, the challenge is representing them in Basic. The answer is not always easy, and depends on what you want to do with them.

In Basic you must ultimately make a choice between numbers and strings. In Holmes's program we see the difficulty with either choice: representing the days of the week with numbers is somewhat cryptic, while using strings is tedious.

To help you decide what to do, a good strategy is to list all of the operations required for using the data in your program. In Holmes's case we have only two basic operations:

Day after : compute the day following a given day.
Print   : print the name of a given day.

Holmes's choice to represent the days of the week with numbers makes it easy to compute the following day. The use of a table to print the name of a day is a compromise to the use of strings.

Problems of this sort are very common. Consider the following:

Types of Data	*Possible Values*
Day name	Sunday, Monday, Tuesday, Wednesday, Thursday, Friday, Saturday
Suspect	Col. Woodley, Mr. Holman, Mr. Pope, Sir Jasper
Cigar texture	Caked, Flaky, Fluffy, Granular, Varied

Coin	Penny, Nickel, Dime, Quarter, Half Dollar, Dollar
Halfday	A.M., P.M.
Army rank	Private, Corporal, Sergeant, Lieutenant, Captain, Major, Colonel, General
Major city	London, Oxford, Bristol, Birmingham, Plymouth, Liverpool, York, Manchester
Shape	Triangle, Quadrangle, Pentagon, Hexagon
Direction	North, East, South, West
Weapon	Gun, Knife, Candlestick, Rope, Wrench
Response	Yes, No, Unknown
Report status	Unwritten, Drafted, Edited, Completed, In press, Missing

Each of the above types of data contain a limited set of possible values; there are, for example, only seven possible answers to the question 'what day of the week is it?'

In most of the programs in this text, we have tried to represent such types of data with strings; normally reading such programs is considerably easier. It is in cases like that of *An Advertisement in The Times*, we may be compelled to use numeric representations.

One particularly good use of string types is for describing states of knowledge. Suppose, for example, we wish to write a program to determine which one of a number of suspects matches a given list of characteristics. In searching the list of suspects, we may wish to keep track of whether or not we have found a match. To do this, we might use a variable M$ to indicate whether a match has been found. Such a variable will take on one of two values:

```
"FOUND"
"NOT_FOUND"
```

At the beginning of our program, since we clearly have not found a match, we can say:

```
LET M$ = "NOT_FOUND"
```

Later in our program we will, of course, change this value to "FOUND" when a matching suspect is found. The status of such a variable may be used in a condition, for example:

```
1000  IF F$ = "FOUND" THEN 1050
1010     PRINT "MESSAGE DESCRIBING WHAT TO DO IF SUSPECT NOT FOUND"
1020     GOTO 1050
1030     PRINT "MESSAGE DESCRIBING WHAT TO DO IF SUSPECT FOUND"
1040     GOTO 1050
1050  ...
```

Each of the above types has only a few values and captures the essence of a fact to be determined. Furthermore, whenever we write a program and wish to keep track of a piece of information that can have only one of these values, we can represent our state of knowledge with a simple string-valued variable.

The issue of representing data is central to programming. To make full use of Basic in representing data, there is a bit more to add. We now turn to some more elaborate features for using strings; these features are common to many, but not all, versions of Basic.

9.2   Characters, Strings, and Substrings

Suppose we wish to read in a list of names and print them in alphabetical order. To do this we would have to compare names to see which one is "greater." You would hope that A is less than B, B is less than C, and so on. That is indeed the case.

To get to the bottom of this matter, we should talk about ASCII (which stands for the American Standard Code for Information Interchange). When a computer stores information, each piece of data is stored with numeric codes. Strings are no exception. Each character in a string has its own code, as illustrated in Table 9.1. These codes, and the characters they represent, make up the ASCII character set.

Notice, for instance, that the numeric code for the uppercase letter "A" is 65, and the code for a lowercase letter "a" is 97. Much as you might dislike it, the code for the character "1" is not 1, but 49. Notice also the appearance of nonprinting characters, such as BEL or CR. These characters have various uses, depending on your terminal and implemention. For instance, the character BEL causes a bell to ring on a terminal (if it has one) and CR causes a carriage return.

Normally you need not be particularly concerned with the details of ASCII, unless you are engaged in doing some fancy programming. For now, you will want to keep in mind that the letters and digits are in their normal order and that you can compare characters just as you would compare numbers. For instance:

TABLE 9.1   *The ASCII Character Set*

Code	Char	Common Use	Code	Char	Common Use	Code	Char	Common Use
0	NUL	Null	41	)	Right paren	85	U	Uppercase U
1	SOH	Start of heading	42	*	Asterisk	86	V	Uppercase V
2	STX	Start of text	43	+	Plus Sign	87	W	Uppercase W
3	ETX	End of text	44	,	Comma	88	X	Uppercase X
4	EOT	End of	45	–	Minus sign	89	Y	Uppercase Y
		transmission	46	.	Period	90	Z	Uppercase Z
5	ENQ	Enquiry	47	/	Slash	91	[	Left bracket
6	ACK	Acknowledge	48	0	Zero	92	\	Reverse slash
7	BEL	Bell	49	1	One	93	]	Right bracket
8	BS	Backspace	50	2	Two	94	^	Circumflex
9	HT	Horizontal tab	51	3	Three	95	_	Underline
10	LF	Line feed	52	4	Four	96	`	Grave accent
11	VT	Vertical tab	53	5	Five	97	a	Lowercase a
12	FF	Form feed	54	6	Six	98	b	Lowercase b
13	CR	Carriage return	55	7	Seven	99	c	Lowercase c
14	SO	Shift out	56	8	Eight	100	d	Lowercase d
		(turn cursor on)	57	9	Nine	101	e	Lowercase e
15	SI	Shift in	58	:	Colon	102	f	Lowercase f
		(turn cursor off)	59	;	Semicolon	103	g	Lowercase g
16	DLE	Data link escape	60	<	Less than	104	h	Lowercase h
17	DC1	Device control 1	61	=	Equals sign	105	i	Lowercase i
18	DC2	Device control 2	62	>	Greater than	106	j	Lowercase j
19	DC3	Device control 3	63	?	Question mark	107	k	Lowercase k
20	DC4	Device control 4	64	@	At sign	108	l	Lowercase l
21	NAK	Neg. acknowledge	65	A	Uppercase A	109	m	Lowercase m
22	SYN	Synchronous idle	66	B	Uppercase B	110	n	Lowercase n
23	ETB	End trans. block	67	C	Uppercase C	111	o	Lowercase o
24	CAN	Cancel	68	D	Uppercase D	112	p	Lowercase p
25	EM	End of medium	69	E	Uppercase E	113	q	Lowercase q
26	SUB	Substitute	70	F	Uppercase F	114	r	Lowercase r
27	ESC	Escape	71	G	Uppercase G	115	s	Lowercase s
28	FS	File separator	72	H	Uppercase H	116	t	Lowercase t
29	GS	Group separator	73	I	Uppercase I	117	u	Lowercase u
30	RS	Record separator	74	J	Uppercase J	118	v	Lowercase v
31	US	Unit separator	75	K	Uppercase K	119	w	Lowercase w
32	SP	Space	76	L	Uppercase L	120	x	Lowercase x
33	!	Exclamation point	77	M	Uppercase M	121	y	Lowercase y
34	"	Quotation mark	78	N	Uppercase N	122	z	Lowercase z
35	#	Number sign	79	O	Uppercase O	123	{	Left brace
36	$	Dollar sign	80	P	Uppercase P	124	|	Vertical line
37	%	Percent sign	81	Q	Uppercase Q	125	}	Right brace
38	&	Ampersand	82	R	Uppercase R	126	~	Tilde
39	'	Apostrophe	83	S	Uppercase S	127	DEL	Delete
40	(	Left paren	84	T	Uppercase T			

```
"C" < "D"
"E" < "Q"
"1" < "5"
```

To alphabetize our names, we have to compare strings of characters. For strings containing only letters, most versions of Basic follow the normal alphabetic ordering found in a dictionary. This means:

```
"CANDLE" < "CANDLESTICK"
"CANDLE" < "CANDY"
"CANDLE" < "ROPE"
```

Notice that CANDLE is less than CANDY even though CANDY is shorter.

For strings that contain characters other than letters, we're back to ASCII. Consider the two strings:

```
"PINCE NEZ"
"PINCE-NEZ"
```

Which comes first? If we look at our table of ASCII codes, we see that the code for a space is 32, and for a hyphen (or minus sign) is 45. The answer? `"PINCE NEZ"`. The general rule here is that for strings with non-alphabetic characters we simply compare their ASCII codes. Thus:

```
"SUSPECT1" < "SUSPECT2"
"1B"       < "1AA"
"$16.20"   < "$450.33"
```

Now suppose we need to examine the parts of a string, or compose new strings from existing ones. Recall Holmes's program of Exhibit 8.3 in the previous chapter. Here the input and output of a message is performed a character at a time. Suppose we wanted instead to process a word or even a line at a time. To do this we need some way of breaking a string into pieces and composing the result.

More generally, consider the following problems:

■   Read in the full name of a person and print the initials.

■   Read in a line of text and print the line with any extra spaces removed.

■   Read in the text of a program and print all lines with an occurrence of the variable A$.

■   Read in the text of a program, renumber the lines in increments of 10, change the corresponding line numbers within each statement, and print the resulting program text.

■   Read in the text of a document and print the document
with a given line length and an even right margin.

These problems have a wide range of difficulty, but all have in common the
need to examine and compose strings.

Before moving deeper into this topic, we must point out an annoying
fact—there are numerous differences among versions of Basic when it
comes to the features described below. These differences can make it hard
to read someone else's program, to read a text on Basic, or more
importantly, to use a program written for another computer. In what
follows we have tried to choose the simplest set of features common to most
popular versions of Basic. Nevertheless, be careful; you will have to check
your manual or do some live testing before writing any full programs.
Some of the problems at the end of this chapter may help you if your
version of Basic is different from that presented here.

Table 9.2 lists some common string functions in Basic, two of which
have already been discussed. Given a string argument (normally a single
character), the function ASC returns the ASCII numeric code of the first
character. Thus:

```
ASC("1")   = 49
ASC("+")   = 43
ASC("A")   = 65
ASC("ABC") = 65
```

The reverse function, CHR$, returns the character for a given numeric
code. Thus:

```
CHR$(65) = "A"
CHR$(49) = "1"
CHR$(43) = "+"
```

The function STR$ turns a numeric value into a string representation,
while its mate VAL does the reverse. Thus:

```
STR$(123.4)  = "123.4"
VAL("123.4") = 123.4
```

Of most interest to us here are the functions LEFT$, MID$, RIGHT$,
and LEN. These functions are useful for breaking a string into its parts. For
instance, if we say

```
LET S$ = "THE TROOPS ARE ADVANCING"
```

then we have:

```
LEN(S$)       = 24
LEN("THE")    = 3

LEFT$(S$, 1)   = "T"
LEFT$(S$, 3)   = "THE"

MID$(S$, 1, 3) = "THE"
MID$(S$, 4, 1) = " "
MID$(S$, 5, 6) = "TROOPS"
MID$(S$, 5)    = "TROOPS ARE ADVANCING"

RIGHT$(S$, 1)  = "G"
RIGHT$(S$, 9)  = "ADVANCING"
```

Two small points. First, the length of an empty string (a string with no characters) is zero. Second, the functions LEFT$, MID$, and RIGHT$ must be applied to strings of sufficient length to yield the desired substring. If you say

```
LEFT$("THE", 4)
```

or

```
MID$("THE", 2, 3)
```

on most Basics you will get an error. Often, when working with a string variable, you will need to check the length of its value before obtaining a substring.

The above functions are elementary to any problem in which strings must be dissected. To complement these functions, many versions of Basic allow you to compose new strings from individual pieces with the + operator. For instance

```
"SHERLOCK " + "HOLMES"
```

gives:

```
"SHERLOCK HOLMES"
```

This operator is often called the *concatenation* operator.

Let us now revisit Holmes's decoding problem of the previous chapter and a related problem, that of deciphering a line at a time. To do this, we need an operation for obtaining the next character in the input line and an operation for obtaining the remainder of the line. We also need an operation for adding a character to a line. Suppose we obtain a line to be deciphered with the statement:

```
INPUT L1$
```

To obtain the first character of L1$ we need only say

```
LET C1$ = LEFT$(L1$, 1)
```

and to update L$ to the remainder of the line we can say:

```
LET L1$ = RIGHT$(L1$, LEN(L1$) - 1)
```

Finally, if L2$ holds the string value of the deciphered line and C2$ is the next deciphered character then

```
LET L2$ = L2$ + C2$
```

adds the new character to the ciphered line.

TABLE 9.2   *Some Common String Functions in Basic*

ASC(*string*)	Returns the ASCII numeric code of the first character of the string; normally used with one-character strings. For control code characters like BEL or CR, some implementations allow the use of the 2- or 3-letter mnemonics.
CHR$(*code*)	Returns the one-character string designated by the given ASCII code. For control codes, check your local implementation.
LEFT$(*string*, *n*)	Returns the leftmost *n* characters of the given string.
LEN(*string*)	Returns the length of the given string. All characters, including blanks, are counted.
MID$(*string*, *p*, *n*)	Returns *n* characters of the given string starting at position *p*; if *n* is omitted, returns the rightmost characters of the given string starting at position *p*.
RIGHT$(*string*, *n*)	Returns the rightmost *n* characters of the given string.
STR$(*expression*)	Converts the specified numeric expression (for instance, 123.4) to its string representation (for instance, "123.4").
VAL(*string*)	Converts a string representing a number (for instance, "123.4") to its numeric value (for instance 123.4).

Summary

As mentioned by Holmes, an important part of the programmer's task is to represent objects that exist in the real world in terms of the constructs of a programming language. Whether these objects are varieties of cigar ash, people's names, amounts of money, or calendar dates, they all must be represented in some way in your computer program.

Any programming language comes equipped with certain basic types of data that you must use when writing your programs. In Basic, you have two primitive types that are predefined in the language itself. These are numbers and strings. In addition, Basic allows you to define arrays of numbers and arrays of strings.

Now you certainly do have a choice in the matter. For example, you may give each of the days of the week a numeric value, say 1 through 7; or you may represent them with their string names. You may, if you wish, even code each of the days of the week with a different single letter character. Your choice will be guided by the problem at hand.

In Basic, there is no type distinction between two different string variables or two different numeric variables. It's simply up to you to keep track of the values. For example, if D$ is a variable denoting a day of the week and you say

```
LET D$ = "NICKEL"
```

the computer will not complain. Similarly, if K denotes the day of the month and you say

```
LET K = K + 5
```

where the result is greater than 31, your program will be equally happy. In both cases, the presumption here is that an error has been made, and this will probably be the case. But you will be the only one who can find it.

X

A Study in Chemistry

I T was a singular combination of events in the spring of '91 that found Mr. Sherlock Holmes and myself again sharing his quarters at 221B Baker Street. I need not detail the circumstances attendant upon my temporary return; suffice it to say that with the aid of a noted Harley Street specialist, I was able to persuade Holmes not to undertake a single investigation at that time. It was absolutely imperative that the great detective lay aside all his work and surrender himself to complete rest, should he wish to avoid a complete breakdown.

The morning of the present narrative began abruptly. Holmes was at my bedside, shaking me from a deep and peaceful sleep and attempting to drag me from under my sheets.

"Quick, Watson!" he exclaimed. "On your feet, man, and to the window!" His face was tinged with colour and his brows drawn into two hard black lines with the steely glitter of his eyes shining out from under them. Only in times of great crisis have I observed these battle signals flying, and I scarcely needed to rely on my companion's great muscular strength to get me standing.

I immediately became aware of a loathsome, suffocating odour as I staggered with his aid to the windows. A thick, black cloud was filtering in from the sitting room where Holmes had been experimenting with chemicals, apparently throughout the night. He tossed aside the curtains and threw open the lead-paned windows, and in a moment we were leaning out, side by side, conscious only of the glorious sunshine and the fresh, early-morning air.

Some while later we sat near my bedside wiping our clammy foreheads and surveying each other with some apprehension. "I take it there is some justifiable reason for all of this?" I queried, letting the tone of my voice carry the full weight of my irritation.

"I have, with some success," replied Holmes, his eyes twinkling, "duplicated the poisonous gas employed in the Hyde Park case."

"Indeed you have, and nearly done away with us in the bargain!"

"Well, yes, I suppose I do owe you a word of apology, as I have almost added another chapter to what the papers are calling the Hyde Park Horrors. It was, I admit, an unjustifiable experiment to carry out on oneself and doubly so considering the presence of an unsuspecting friend."

It was difficult to remain angered at Sherlock Holmes for any great length of time. His apology had been put forth with such sincerity that I was considerably touched. My anger at a rude awakening no longer seemed worth pursuing.

"The vapours have diffused by now," he said presently. "It should be safe to return."

"I am greatly disappointed with you, Holmes. You promised to engage your energies in more scholarly pursuits. The first sensational headline to come along and you've broken your word. There you are, off like a racing engine, ready to tear yourself to pieces, with a hospital bed your destination for certain!" I cried.

"On the contrary, my dear Watson," he retorted. "It was just those scholarly pursuits that have led me here, and once you have performed your morning ablutions and breakfasted I shall be pleased to elaborate on how the Analytical Engine may be most helpful in my chemical dabblings. With the Engine at my disposal our predawn discomforts could have been totally avoided. I suggest for now, however, that we take our rashers and eggs at one of London's finer eating establishments, as arsenic vapours are not pleasing to the discriminating palate."

After a pleasing breakfast in Mrs. Woolwich's Tea Rooms, we returned to Baker Street. Holmes continued his discourse at a small card table on which he had set up a makeshift laboratory.

"Do you recollect anything of my friend Dmitri Ivanovich Mendeleeff?" he asked. "A man ahead of his time in many ways."

"A chemist, as I recall."

"Quite so," he replied. "A scientific mind of the first order. Mendeleeff was the first to bring both system and structure to the family of elements: gold, most highly praised of metals, which never tarnishes or rusts; base lead, common and despised; quicksilver, a metal in liquid form; sulphur and carbon, usually powders, sometimes crystals—why, a diamond is merely carbon! Or consider the very air, a mixture of many gases. And these elements combine chemically with one another to produce the amazing variety of materials that sustain us—or that can destroy us, as was nearly the case this morning.

"A CHEMIST, AS I RECALL."

"It has been Mendeleeff's great insight to categorize the various elements in the form of a table for handy reference. In his table, he arranges the elements, with each assigned a specific atomic weight, vertically in groups. The elements within each group bear chemical properties similar to one another. Dmitri Ivanovich has shown that the properties of elements recur periodically, much as the sounds of musical notes recur throughout the octaves—an idea much scorned by the Royal Society when the unfortunate Newlands first suggested it some years ago."

Holmes then produced a chart from the great bundle of papers that littered his desk. It showed the elements arranged vertically in groups. Naturally I had come across this table, which I have reproduced as Exhibit 10.1, during my medical studies at the University of London.

"This is all very interesting," I said, after looking over the chart. "But of what use is it to you? Surely it is of no importance to a criminal investigator?"

"Ah, but the value of the table to me is practical. Since it lists the atomic weights of the elements, I can use the information to calculate the weight of any compound I choose. Consider, for example, the poisonous arsenic vapors

$$As_4O_6$$

Series	Group I	Group II	Group III	Group IV	Group V	Group VI	Group VII	Group VIII
1	H=1							
2	Li=7	Be=9.4	B=11	C=12	N=14	O=16	F=19	
3	Na=23	Mg=24	Al=27.3	Si=28	P=31	S=32	Cl=35.5	Fe=56, Co=59, Ni=59
4	K=39	Ca=40	—=44	Ti=48	V=51	Cr=52	Mn=55	
5	Cu=63	Zn=65	—=68	—=72	As=75	Se=78	Br=80	
6	Rb=85	Sr=87	?Yt=88	Zr=90	Nb=94	Mo=96	—=100	Ru=104,Rh=104, Pd=106
7	Ag=108	Cd=112	In=113	Sn=118	Sb=122	Te=125	I=127	
8	Cs=133	Ba=137	?Di=138	?Ce=140	—	—	—	
9	—	—	—	—	—	—	—	
10	—	—	?Er=178	?La=180	Ta=182	W=184	—	Os=195, Ir=197, Pt=198
11	Au=199	Hg=200	Tl=204	Pb=207	Bi=208	—	—	
12	—	—	—	Th=231	—	U=240	—	

Exhibit 10.1 *Mendeleeff's Periodic Table of the Chemical Elements*

that I produced this morning. According to Mendeleeff's table, arsenic weighs 75 units and oxygen weighs 16 units. The weight of a molecule of the gas is then:

$$(75 * 4) + (16 * 6) = 396$$

"As you can see, Watson, the calculation is trivial. But there are many elements, all of differing weights. Obtaining correct results can be tedious and subject to error when there are many such calculations to make. I would like to develop a tool for use on the Analytical Engine to assist me in calculating molecular weights. Thus I wish to enter formulae of this sort and receive as output the molecular weight."

"Yes, Holmes," I remarked. "But the problem is not so simple as you make it appear. You must instruct the Engine to make sense of the formulae, and you must store Mendeleeff's table in the Engine's memory."

"Excellent, Watson! Compound of the Busy Bee and Excelsior!" cried Holmes. "That is precisely what must be done. You see, storing Mendeleeff's table in the Engine is of great value, and having the Engine recognise the atomic abbreviations will save my brain for more important matters. This is exactly where the method of instructing the Engine is of particular interest."

In an instant Holmes was at the Engine, continuing with his lecture.

"Now, Watson, pay close attention. Here is a general algorithm that will allow the Engine to solve the problem of molecular weights."

He showed me the following :

```
Set up atomic weight tables
Let WEIGHT = 0.0
Get next ELEMENT

As long as there are more elements, repeat the following:
    Let WEIGHT = WEIGHT + (NUM_ATOMS * ATOMIC_WEIGHT)
    Get next ELEMENT

Print WEIGHT
```

"As you remarked earlier, there are two interesting lines. The first is :

```
Set up atomic weight tables
```

This requires the Engine to fill a table with Mendeleeff's atomic weights and another with the names of the element abbreviations. The second is:

Get next ELEMENT

This requires that the programme ask what the next element is—for example H means hydrogen and AS means arsenic—and how many atoms there are of that element.

"The point is, Watson, that by expressing the algorithm in this way, we have reduced the larger problem to two smaller subproblems, each of which is easier and simpler to develop than the original problem.

"We can now face the two subproblems precisely. Just as for any problem, there are the

input — the "givens"
output — the "finds"

For the first subproblem, there is no input; and the output is to be the completed table of atomic weights. For the second subproblem the input is the molecular formula; the output is the next element and the number of times it occurs in the molecular formula."

Holmes then produced the sketch that I have duplicated as Exhibit 10.2. His illustration shows the main algorithm, giving first the definitions of the variables used and then the algorithm itself. The main algorithm refers to the two subproblems. These are called algorithms SET_UP_TABLES and GET_ELEMENT.

Holmes noted the ease with which I understood the algorithm, and then produced a second sketch that I have reproduced as Exhibit 10.3. This contained the solutions to the two subproblems.

"Notice Watson," he continued, "that the algorithm for each subproblem is separate and self-contained.

"Every problem becomes elementary when once it is explained to you," said Holmes. "You see, Watson, a man possessing special knowledge and powers such as my own is encouraged often to seek a simpler approach to a seemingly complex problem. Notice how childishly simple this all is when you divide the problem into smaller components? One might say, divide and conquer."

"Or divide and calculate!" I rejoined.

"You are developing a certain vein of pawky humour, Watson, against which I must learn to guard myself."

"So now we turn to the programme itself, I presume."

"Yes, Watson, we may nicely express this fundamental concept directly in Basic with a 'sub-programme' or 'subroutine.' Like a programme, a subroutine has inputs and outputs. The algorithm, however, is given separately."

Definitions:

NUM_ATOMS   :   an integer number
ATOMIC_WEIGHT: the atomic weight of an element
WEIGHT   :   the atomic weight of a molecule

ATOMIC_WEIGHT_TABLE: table of atomic weights
ABBREVIATION_TABLE :   table of abbreviations

Algorithm:

Perform algorithm SET_UP_TABLES giving ATOMIC_WEIGHT_TABLE
                                                    and ABBREVIATION_TABLE
Let WEIGHT = 0.0
Perform algorithm GET_ELEMENT giving ATOMIC_WEIGHT
                                          and NUM_ATOMS

As long as there are more elements, repeat the following:
    let WEIGHT = WEIGHT + (NUM_ATOMS * ATOMIC_WEIGHT)
    perform algorithm GET_ELEMENT giving ATOMIC_WEIGHT
                                              and NUM_ATOMS

Print WEIGHT

Exhibit 10.2   *Holmes's Algorithm to Determine Molecular Weights*

Algorithm SET_UP_TABLES—giving ATOMIC_WEIGHT_TABLE
                                            and ABBREVIATION_TABLE

For each element of Mendeleff's table, do the following:
    read abbreviation of element into ABBREVIATION_TABLE
    read atomic weight of element into ATOMIC_WEIGHT_TABLE

Note: Data for the tables is stored within the program, for example:
    Abbreviation of Hydrogen is H;   Atomic_Weight of Hydrogen is 1
    Abbreviation of Lithium is LI;   Atomic_Weight of Lithium is 7

Algorithm GET_ELEMENT—giving ATOMIC_WEIGHT and NUM_ATOMS

Repeat the following:
    obtain next element
    compute ATOMIC_WEIGHT
    obtain NUM_ATOMS
until legal element is entered or last element is given

Exhibit 10.3   *Algorithms for the Two Subproblems*

It sounded simple, but I was still a bit puzzled. I did not quite understand how the so-called "subroutines" would be used.

"To invoke a subroutine in a programme," Holmes continued, "we give the keyword GOSUB followed by the line number where the subroutine is written, as in:

```
GOSUB 1000
```

This is called a *subroutine call*, and means, quite simply, 'do it.' That is, the Engine is commanded to perform the algorithm as spelled out in the subroutine. When the subroutine is completed, the atomic weight and number of atoms of the next element will have been established. The essential idea is that the effect of solving the subproblem is summarized by these calculated values."

To appreciate this sudden bounty of instruction I found it necessary to see the actual programme. It is here duplicated as Exhibit 10.4 and on some reflection it was apparent that the wisest approach was breaking such complex programmes into smaller, more manageable parts.

Holmes forged on. "Notice, incidentally, that in the subroutine GET_ ELEMENT, an improperly written abbreviation will be detected. In these cases, the programme simply allows the user to enter a new abbreviation for the element."

"Enough, Holmes!" I moaned. "I can absorb no more. Are you absolutely certain that all of these complexities involve less work than simply calculating the molecular weights yourself?"

Sherlock Holmes merely smiled.

```
0010 REM  -- THIS PROGRAMME INPUTS THE COMPONENTS OF A CHEMICAL
0020 REM  -- FORMULA, FOR INSTANCE H2 O or AS4 O6. THE ABBREVIATION
0030 REM  -- AND QUANTITY OF EACH ELEMENT OF THE FORMULA ARE
0040 REM  -- REQUESTED BY THE PROGRAMME.
0050 REM  -- THE PROGRAMME PRINTS THE MOLECULAR WEIGHT OF THE
0060 REM  -- FORMULA ACCORDING TO MENDELEEFF'S TABLE.
0070 REM
0080 REM  -- DICTIONARY OF NAMES:
0090 REM
0100 REM  -- T1$  ABBREVIATION TABLE
0110 REM  -- T2   ATOMIC WEIGHTS TABLE
0120 REM  -- E$   AN ELEMENT OR THE WORD "DONE"
0130 REM  -- N    THE NUMBER OF ATOMS
0140 REM  -- A    THE ATOMIC WEIGHT OF AN ELEMENT
0150 REM  -- W    THE WEIGHT OF A MOLECULE
0160 REM  -- K    LOCAL COUNTER
0170 REM  -- F$   LEGAL ELEMENT FLAG, "FOUND" OR "NOT_FOUND"
0180 REM
0190      DIM T1$(63), T2(63)
0200 REM
0210 REM
0220 REM  -- SET_UP_TABLES
0230      GOSUB 1000
0240 REM
0250      LET W = 0.0
0260      PRINT "ENTER EACH ELEMENT; WHEN DONE, ENTER THE WORD DONE."
0270 REM  -- GET_ELEMENT
0280      GOSUB 2000
0290 REM
0300      IF E$ = "DONE" THEN 0360
0310          LET W = W + N*A
0320 REM      -- GET_ELEMENT
0330          GOSUB 2000
0340          GOTO 0300
0350 REM
0360      PRINT "THE MOLECULAR WEIGHT IS "; W
0370      STOP
```

Exhibit 10.4   *Holmes's Molecular Weight Programme*

```
1000 REM  -- SET_UP_TABLES
1010 REM
1020 REM  -- THIS SUBROUTINE ESTABLISHES THE TABLE OF ABBREVIATIONS
1030 REM  -- AND THE TABLE OF ATOMIC WEIGHTS.
1040 REM
1050 REM
1060      FOR K = 1 TO 63
1070          READ T1$(K), T2(K)
1080      NEXT K
1090 REM
1100 REM
1110 REM
1120 DATA  H,1,      LI,7,      BE,9.4,     B,11,      C,12,      N,14
1130 DATA  O,16,     F,19,      NA,23,      MG,24,     AL,27.3,   SI,28
1140 DATA  P,31,     S,32,      CL,35.5,    K,39,      CA,40,     TI,48
1150 DATA  V,51,     CR,52,     MN,55,      FE,56,     CO,59,     NI,59
1160 DATA  CU,63,    ZN,65,     AS,75,      SE,78,     BR,80,     RB,85
1170 DATA  SR,87,    YT,88,     ZR,90,      NB,94,     MO,96,     RU,104
1180 DATA  RH,104,   PD,106,    AG,108,     CD,112,    IN,113,    SN,118
1190 DATA  SB,122,   TE,125,    I,127,      CA,133,    BA,137,    DI,138
1200 DATA  CE,140,   ER,178,    LA,180,     TA,182,    W,184,     OS,195
1210 DATA  IR,197,   PT,198,    AU,199,     HG,200,    TL,204,    PB,207
1220 DATA  BI,208,   TH,231,    U,240
1230 REM
1240      RETURN
```

Exhibit 10.4 *Continued*

```
2000 REM  -- GET_ELEMENT
2010 REM
2020 REM  -- THIS SUBROUTINE PROMPTS THE USER FOR AN ELEMENT
2030 REM  -- OF A CHEMICAL FORMULA.
2040 REM
2050 REM
2060     LET F$ = "NOT_FOUND"
2070         PRINT "ENTER ELEMENT ABBREVIATION:"
2080         INPUT E$
2090         FOR K = 1 TO 63
2100            IF T1$(K) <> E$ THEN 2150
2110               LET F$ = "FOUND"
2120               LET A  = T2(K)
2130               PRINT "ENTER QUANTITY OF ELEMENT:"
2140               INPUT N
2150         NEXT K
2160         IF E$ = "DONE"  THEN 2200
2170         IF F$ = "FOUND" THEN 2200
2180            PRINT "ELEMENT NOT RECOGNISED."
2190            GOTO 2070
2200     RETURN
2210 END
```

Exhibit 10.4 *Continued*

10.1 Packaging and Subroutines

With Holmes's program for calculating molecular weights we encounter the idea of breaking a problem into parts and packaging each part as a subroutine. In its essence, a subroutine is a language unit that embodies the solution to a subproblem. As we attempt to scale up our programming skills to solve larger and more complex problems, the use of subroutines becomes almost indispensable.

All subroutines have two general characteristics:

■ *Inputs and outputs*, which summarize the effect of the subroutine to the rest of the program. These are its givens and finds.

■ *A body*, which specifies the method by which the subroutine is solved. It includes the statements for carrying out the algorithm needed to solve the subproblem.

We now turn to the particulars for writing subroutines in Basic.

Λ *subroutine* is a section of program that causes some desired effect. Consider, for instance, the simple subroutine of Example 10.1. When executed, the three lines of text

```
          THE LOST BASIC PROGRAMMES
                    OF
              SHERLOCK HOLMES
```

are printed, centered within each line. This is the so-called effect of the subroutine.

```
1000 REM  -- PRINT_TITLE
1010 REM
1020 REM  -- THIS SUBROUTINE PRINTS THREE HEADER LINES.
1030 REM
1040 REM
1050      FOR K = 1 TO 23
1060          PRINT " ";
1070      NEXT K
1080      PRINT "THE LOST BASIC PROGRAMMES"
1090 REM
1100      FOR K = 1 TO 35
1110          PRINT " ";
1120      NEXT K
1130      PRINT "OF"
1140 REM
1150      FOR K = 1 TO 29
1160          PRINT " ";
1170      NEXT K
1180      PRINT "SHERLOCK HOLMES"
1190 REM
1200      RETURN
```

Example 10.1 *A Simple Subroutine*

A subroutine is considered a "subprogram," because, as you'll note, it has a form as well as an effect similar to that of a program. In addition, a subroutine can have both remark lines and executable statements. Following Holmes's lead, we shall refer to such subroutines by a name. The name, in this case PRINT_TITLE, will be given in the first line as a remark.

In order to cause the actions of a subroutine to be carried out, we use a GOSUB statement. For example, the subroutine of Example 10.1 can be invoked with the call:

```
GOSUB 1000
```

When this statement is executed, the algorithm specified by the subroutine will be carried out. Execution of the subroutine continues until a RETURN statement is encountered, at which point execution returns to the caller.

Consider the sequence:

```
0010 PRINT "START"
0020 GOSUB 1000
0030 PRINT "FINISH"
```

When this sequence is executed, the following actions take place.

1. The word "START" is printed.

2. The subroutine is executed, causing the three lines of text to be printed, after which control returns to the caller and execution continues at line 0030.

3. The word "FINISH" is printed.

This demonstrates for us two precepts, elementary yet hard-and-fast to the fundamentals of sound problem solving:

■   The solution to a subproblem may be written as a subroutine.

■   The actions specified by the subroutine are carried out when the subroutine is invoked by means of a GOSUB statement.

The use of several subroutines in one program is commonplace as you start to solve larger and more intricate problems. Furthermore, doing this in Basic is quite easy. You simply write the subroutines one after another.

For example, consider the general structure of Holmes's program for calculating molecular weights:

```
0010 REM  -- THIS PROGRAMME INPUTS THE COMPONENTS OF A CHEMICAL
 . . .        . . .
 . . .        Main routine
 . . .        . . .
0370          STOP

1000 REM  -- SET_UP_TABLES
 . . .        . . .
 . . .        subroutine
 . . .        . . . .
1240          RETURN
```

```
2000 REM  -- GET_ELEMENT
...       ...
...       subroutine
...       ....
2200      RETURN

2210 END
```

This program uses the two subroutines SET_UP_TABLES and GET_ELEMENT. The program terminates execution when the STOP statement is executed in the main program; the subroutines, which appear later, are invoked by the main program and so return to the main program. The entire sequence ends with an END statement. This gives rise to the following rule in Basic:

> ■ A program consists of a main routine, a sequence of subroutines, and an END statement.

The main routine must appear first. Otherwise, the order of subroutines is immaterial. Notice that one subroutine can invoke another. This causes no problem, for execution always returns to the calling subroutine.

10.2 Using Subroutines

Consider the following simple subroutine:

```
2000 REM  -- SKIP_SPACES
2010 REM
2020      FOR K = 1 TO N
2030         PRINT " ";
2040      NEXT K
2050      RETURN
```

When this subroutine is executed, it prints the number of spaces given by N.

Now consider a revised version of the subroutine PRINT_TITLE given earlier in Example 10.1:

```
1000 REM  -- PRINT_TITLE
1010 REM
1020 REM  -- THE SUBROUTINE PRINTS THREE HEADER LINES.
1030 REM
1040 REM
```

```
1050      LET N = 23
1060      GOSUB 2000
1070      PRINT "THE LOST BASIC PROGRAMMES OF"
1080 REM
1090      LET N = 35
1100      GOSUB 2000
1110      PRINT "OF"
1120 REM
1130      LET N = 29
1140      GOSUB 2000
1150      PRINT "SHERLOCK HOLMES"
1160 REM
1170      RETURN
```

While this subroutine has the same effect as Example 10.1, the subroutine PRINT_TITLE explicitly invokes another subroutine, SKIP_SPACES, as defined above.

The use of the subroutine SKIP_SPACES within PRINT_TITLE demonstrates an essential point—a subroutine may refer to the variables also used outside the subroutine, in the main program or a calling subroutine. Here, for instance, the variable N is established by the caller PRINT_TITLE and used within the called subroutine SKIP_SPACES. This variable is said to be *global* to the subroutine. It is through such global variables that the subroutine has its effect.

You may have noticed that a subroutine call like

```
GOSUB 2000
```

hardly leaves any clue to the meaning of the called routine. Basic requires that you refer to a subroutine by its starting line number. To get around this annoyance, we will adopt Holmes's convention of not only naming each subroutine in an initial remark line, but of prefixing each *call* with a remark that supplies the name of the subroutine. Thus we will have calls like:

```
REM  -- SKIP_SPACES
     GOSUB 2000
```

From here on, we will use this convention throughout.

10.3   Functions

Consider Example 10.2a. Here we see a simple subroutine named GET_AREA, which, when given a value for a radius, computes the area of a circle having this radius. If, say, the value of R is 3.0, the procedure call

```
GOSUB 1000
```

results in assigning to A the area of a circle of radius 3.0, or 28.2743.

Next consider the *function* of Example 10.2b. This example defines a function named FNA which has a single argument, a real value. It computes the area of a circle having this argument as a radius. The function is defined in line 0040:

```
DEF FNA(R) = 3.14159 * (R*R)
```

Like the predefined functions in Basic, this function can be called within an expression. Again, if the value of R is 3.0, and an evaluation of the expression

```
FNA(R)
```

yields the area of the circle.

A *function* specifies a formula for computing a value. Generally speaking, functions are used in place of *expressions* to return *values*, whereas subroutines are used in place of *statements* to perform *assignments* to variables. Thus the ability to define functions in Basic is a counterpart to the ability to define subroutines.

Conceptually a function behaves just like a function in ordinary arithmetic. That is, given one or more values, we can compute some result. For example, consider the following informally described functions:

■   Given a Fahrenheit temperature, the result is its value in Celsius degrees.

■   Given the circumference of a circle, the result is the area of a circle.

■   Given the initial velocity of a projectile, its angle, and a duration of time, the result is the distance traveled.

■   Given a string, the result is the same string with the first character removed.

In each of these cases we have one or more givens and a single result.

The rules for declaring functions in Basic are quite simple. In particular, a function specification has the form

```
DEF FNx(parameters) = expression
```

where *x* is a letter or, for string-valued functions, a letter followed by a $. Here we see that a function may have parameters and that the expression defines the value of the result.

a. *A Simple Subroutine*

```
0010 REM  -- THIS PROGRAM COMPUTES THE AREA OF A CIRCLE
0020 REM  -- WITH RADIUS R.
0030 REM
0040 REM
0050      INPUT R
0060 REM  -- GET_AREA
0070      GOSUB 0120
0080      PRINT "THE AREA IS "; A
0090      STOP
0100 REM
0110 REM
0120 REM  -- GET_AREA
0130 REM
0140      LET A = 3.14159 * (R*R)
0150      RETURN
0160 END
```

b. *A Simple Function*

```
0010 REM  -- THIS PROGRAM COMPUTES THE AREA OF A CIRCLE
0020 REM  -- WITH RADIUS R.
0030 REM
0040      DEF FNA(R) = 3.14159 * (R*R)
0050 REM
0060 REM
0070      INPUT R
0080      LET A = FNA(R)
0090      PRINT "THE AREA IS "; A
0100      STOP
0110 END
```

Example 10.2 *Functions versus Subroutines*

Each of the functions above may be defined in Basic as follows:

```
REM  -- DICTIONARY OF NAMES:
REM
REM  -- F    FAHRENHEIT TEMPERATURE
REM  -- C    A CIRCUMFERENCE
REM  -- V    VELOCITY
REM  -- A    ANGLE
REM  -- T    TIME
REM  -- S$   A STRING
```

```
REM
DEF   FNC(F) = (5/9)*(F - 32)
DEF   FNA(L) = (L*L) / (4 * 3.14159)
DEF   FND(V, A, T) = V*SIN(A)*T
DEF   FNL$(S$) = RIGHT$(S$, LEN(S$) - 1)
```

Such functions can be used in statements like:

```
INPUT T
PRINT FNC(T)
LET D  = FND(10.1, 0.7, 10.0) + 1.0
LET M$ = FNL$("$12.95")
```

The facility for defining functions in standard Basic is extremely limited since the definition of the function must fit on a single line. (Some versions of Basic allow multi-line functions; a few allow functions with richer facilities.) Otherwise, things work pretty much as you expect. For instance, you may have parameters that denote arrays, strings, or numbers. Furthermore, the expressions describing the result returned by the function may be as complex as you like, and, of course, even contain calls to other functions.

XI

The Coroner's Report

HE murder of the Honourable Colin Wiggs, with its curious, if not to say extraordinary circumstances, had long ceased to be a subject of interest in Fleet Street, where for months the front pages of London's many daily papers had trumpeted the disturbing details as they unfolded. Thus I was surprised to find that, more than a year after this tragedy was laid to rest, it had again become a subject of interest in Baker Street. Early one October evening I called upon my friend Sherlock Holmes, who had had a considerable share in clearing up the Wiggs case. I found him deeply engrossed in reviewing the details attendant upon the matter.

I was apprehensive of what Holmes's humour might be that evening, for his eccentricities became more pronounced when he was engaged on a case and at times his curious habit and mood, which some would call reticent, succeeded in alarming even such an old companion as myself.

To my surprise and pleasure, however, Holmes ushered me into his quarters with an exuberant gesture of welcome and propelled me into the only chair that was not cluttered with books, papers, and scientific specimens.

"You will remember, Watson," he said, "how the dreadful business in which Colin Wiggs was engaged ultimately led to his tragic end, and how the matter was first brought to my notice by a small scar on his left shoulder. A trifling point at first overlooked by the coroner."

"Indeed," said I, "and I well recall your indignation at Scotland Yard's handling of that affair. The case might have dragged on indefinitely had you not chosen to inspect the body yourself."

"Exactly, Watson, why I have now undertaken to reconstruct the material circumstances of that case. I wish to design a systematic, yet simple, means of organizing notes, documented observations, and other data that are used in compiling special presentations, such as a coroner's report."

I listened intently to this explanation, which Holmes delivered between puffs on his cigar. It was evident by a pile of manuscripts within my sight that he had contrived just such a plan for use by the Analytical Engine.

"You have devised some new programme, I take it," I ventured, "though I fear it may lie beyond my comprehension."

"I assure you, my dear Watson, that the algorithm is elementary. If you have understood our other exercises with the Engine, I believe you will find little difficulty with this one."

Holmes thereupon removed a few slips of paper from one of several notebooks that lay open nearby.

"Observe, if you will, the total disarray of these papers, which contain crucial information pertaining to the Wiggs autopsy," he said, handing them to me. "Would it not be more practical to store these data in the Engine's memory, where they would be infinitely more secure and from which a concise report could be called upon whenever necessary?"

"OBSERVE THE TOTAL DISARRAY OF THESE PAPERS."

Holmes then displayed a summary of the data usually given in a medical examiner's report, as follows :

General Information: 1. Coroner's name, 2. Subject's name, 3. Subject's stated age.

Data and Test Results: 4. Subject's height in inches, 5. Subject's hair colour, 6. Subject's eye colour, 7. Subject's sex, 8. Results of alcohol test, 9. Test for salicylates, 10. Bile morphine indication, 11. Gastric content, 12. Presence of bruises, 13. Presence of lacerations, 14. Presence of lesions, 15. Detected haemorrhages, 16. Fractures.

Remarks: 17. Coroner's observations.

"Now, Watson, in designing a programme to store and recall this information, I dealt with several important points. In the first place, you will observe that the data in each section of the report are of variable length and appearance. Thus when we enter the data into the machine, we do not wish to be confined to a predetermined scheme of punctuation, letters, and numbers. Rather, we wish to use a so-called *quoted string* format, which will allow us to include blanks and commas in the data items. The end of the data will be marked with a slash.

"Notice also that it is always a good idea to prepare a sample of the input before coding the programme, as I have also done here. This helps clarify the task at hand. Do you follow me this far, Watson?"

Holmes's sample data are summarized in the chart that I have duplicated as follows :

General Information: 1. Dr. Harrison, 2. Colin Wiggs, 3. 42.

Data and Test Results: 4. 68, 5. Black, 6. Grey, 7. Male, 8. Negative, 9. Negative, 10. +, 11. Negative for organic bases, 12. Face, neck, 13. None, 14. Neck, 15. None, 16. Upper windpipe.

Remarks: 17. Subject was apparently struck on the left side of the neck. Double fracture of the upper windpipe, just below the larynx, suggesting strangulation. A small scar was detected on the left shoulder.

I nodded that his explanation was extremely clear to me and begged him to continue.

"Very good," said Holmes, resuming his manner of a patient lecturer. "Now, so far as the output is concerned, our main objective is to provide a report that is at once complete, orderly, and readily intelligible to the clerks and investigators who are likely to use it. This principle is what I call the *consideration of human factors.* One must remember at all times that one is devising a programme for the benefit of other persons, not only for the Engine—though I cannot refrain from observing that our artificial brain has more aptitude for deduction than many of the natural ones employed by Scotland Yard."

Holmes paused a moment to take another cigar and then continued, as I sat attentively beside him.

"There are two simple concepts involved in the creation of output," he said as he blew a thin stream of smoke into the room.

"First, note that each item of data is viewed as a string of characters. Upon output, each is printed in a specific place.

"Second, the data are grouped into lines, and there must be some predetermined design for the appearance of the report. Thus, when the programme has printed the desired item, advancement to a new line may be called for."

"Really Holmes," I interrupted. "I fear this is all a bit much for my mind to digest at one time."

"No, no, Watson, there are unexplored possibilities about you to which you have given small attention amid your exaggerated estimates of my own performances. If you will bear with me for another moment, I am sure this will all become quite clear to you."

As he spoke he tore two more sheets from his notebook which I have reproduced as Exhibits 11.1 and 11.2.

"Here are my specimens," he remarked as I examined them, "which should shed some light on these concepts. Tell me, Watson, if they are sufficiently clear, as I intend to offer them to Scotland Yard for their own instruction."

Accordingly, I studied Holmes's diagrams, paying special attention to the appearance of his sample output. The specimens looked perfectly clear and readable, and once again I was astonished at the practical use that resulted from a few simple principles applied by an eminently logical mind.

"Why, Holmes," I said, "if the Engine can be programmed to fulfill a wide variety of similar purposes, the entire profession of clerking may well be undermined within a few years!"

"Nonsense, Watson!" snapped Holmes. "The Engine will surely never replace the need for human intelligence. Rather, it will free mankind from mundane tasks, those that shackle the mind and keep it from more challenging and rewarding exercises.

"Moreover," he continued, "once the Engine has been programmed correctly, it will always perform correctly, or at least with negligible chance of a random error. Time invested in programmes is cumulative, always adding to the precision of the process."

I have included Holmes's entire programme, Exhibit 11.3, so that the diligent reader can follow the exact steps taken by Holmes to accomplish the task described herein.

"You see, Watson," Holmes remarked, "the programme is a simple collection of procedures that extract each stored piece of information that

```
                    CORONER'S REPORT
                    --------- ------


CORONER:  ...                    SUBJECT'S NAME:  ...
                                 STATED AGE    :  ...



BASIC DATA
----- ----

        HEIGHT IN INCHES:  ...
        HAIR COLOUR    :   ...
        EYE COLOUR     :   ...
        SEX            :   ...



TOXICOLOGY DATA
---------- ----

        ALCOHOL TEST    :  ...
        SALICYLATES     :  ...
        BILE MORPHINE   :  ...
        GASTRIC CONTENT :  ...



ANATOMIC DATA
-------- ----

        BRUISES       :   ...
        LACERATIONS   :   ...
        LESIONS       :   ...
        HAEMORRHAGES  :   ...
        FRACTURES     :   ...



GENERAL REMARKS
------- -------

        ...
```

Exhibit 11.1   *Output Layout of the Coroner's Report*

```
                        CORONER'S REPORT
                        --------- ------


CORONER: Dr. Harrison          SUBJECT'S NAME: Colin Wiggs
                               STATED AGE   : 42


BASIC DATA
----- ----


     HEIGHT IN INCHES: 68
     HAIR COLOUR    : Black
     EYE COLOUR     : Grey
     SEX            : Male


TOXICOLOGY DATA
---------- ----


     ALCOHOL TEST    : Negative
     SALICYLATES     : Negative
     BILE MORPHINE   : +
     GASTRIC CONTENT : Negative for organic bases


ANATOMIC DATA
-------- ----


     BRUISES       : Face, neck
     LACERATIONS   : None
     LESIONS       : Neck
     HAEMORRHAGES  : None
     FRACTURES     : Upper windpipe


GENERAL REMARKS
------- -------


     Subject was apparently struck on the left side of the neck.
     Double fracture of the upper windpipe, just below the larynx,
     suggesting strangulation. A small scar was detected on the left
     shoulder.
```

Exhibit 11.2 *Sample Output from the Coroner's Report Programme*

is given to it. The important point is that the programme makes the information pleasing for the enquirer to read. If it were printed in a haphazard fashion, the Engine would not be used to its full potential to assist a human undertaking."

"A truly useful concept, Holmes, with great possibilities, assuming the Engine always works without mechanical error!"

To this he made no reply, but it was plainly evident that he was pondering the shortcomings of the Engine. Like all great artists, he was easily impressed by his surroundings; and I fear my comment had thrown him into the blackest depression. How I had learned, long ago, to dread periods of inaction for Holmes. His gaze was now fixed on the mantelpiece, where lay scattered a collection of syringes and bottles; and I knew that the sleeping friend was very near waking in times of such idleness.

```
0010 REM  -- THIS PROGRAMME READS IN DATA CORRESPONDING TO THE
0020 REM  -- ITEMS IN A CORONER'S REPORT.
0030 REM  -- IT PRINTS A SUMMARY REPORT OF THE DATA.
0040 REM
0050 REM  -- DICTIONARY OF NAMES:
0060 REM
0070 REM  -- I$   DATA ITEM
0080 REM  -- K    LOCAL COUNTER
0090 REM  -- T    TAB INDENT FOR TEST DATA (6)
0100 REM
0110 REM
0120      LET T = 6
0130 REM  -- PRINT_TITLE_DATA
0140      GOSUB 1000
0150 REM
0160 REM  -- PRINT_BASIC_DATA
0170      GOSUB 2000
0180 REM
0190 REM  -- PRINT_TOXICOLOGY_DATA
0200      GOSUB 3000
0210 REM
0220 REM  -- PRINT_ANATOMIC_DATA
0230      GOSUB 4000
0240 REM
0250 REM  -- PRINT_REMARKS
0260      GOSUB 5000
0270 REM
0280      STOP
```

Exhibit 11.3   *Holmes's Programme for the Coroner's Report*

```
1000 REM  -- PRINT_TITLE_DATA
1010 REM
1020 REM  -- THIS SUBROUTINE PRINTS THE TITLE LINES, THE CORONER'S
1030 REM  -- NAME, SUBJECT'S NAME, AND AGE.
1040 REM
1050 REM
1060      FOR K = 1 TO 7
1070         PRINT
1080      NEXT K
1090      PRINT TAB(26); "CORONER'S REPORT"
1100      PRINT TAB(26); "--------- ------"
1110 REM
1120      PRINT
1130      PRINT
1140      READ I$
1150      PRINT "CORONER: "; I$;
1160      READ I$
1170      PRINT TAB(36); "SUBJECT'S NAME: "; I$
1180      READ I$
1190      PRINT TAB(36); "STATED AGE    : "; I$
1200 REM
1210      RETURN
```

Exhibit 11.3   *Continued*

```
2000 REM  -- PRINT_BASIC_DATA
2010 REM
2020 REM  -- THIS SUBROUTINE PRINTS THE GENERAL CHARACTERISTICS
2030 REM  -- PERTAINING TO THE SUBJECT.
2040 REM
2050 REM
2060      PRINT
2070      PRINT
2080      PRINT "BASIC DATA"
2090      PRINT "----- ----"
2100      PRINT
2110 REM
2120      READ I$
2130      PRINT TAB(T); "HEIGHT IN INCHES: "; I$
2140      READ I$
2150      PRINT TAB(T); "HAIR COLOUR     : "; I$
2160      READ I$
2170      PRINT TAB(T); "EYE COLOUR      : "; I$
2180      READ I$
2190      PRINT TAB(T); "SEX             : "; I$
2200 REM
2210      RETURN
```

Exhibit 11.3   *Continued*

```
3000 REM  -- PRINT_TOXICOLOGY_DATA
3010 REM
3020 REM  -- THIS SUBROUTINE PRINTS THE TOXICOLOGY TEST RESULTS.
3030 REM
3040 REM
3050      PRINT
3060      PRINT
3070      PRINT "TOXICOLOGY DATA"
3080      PRINT "---------- ----"
3090      PRINT
3100 REM
3110      READ I$
3120      PRINT TAB(T); "ALCOHOL TEST    : "; I$
3130      READ I$
3140      PRINT TAB(T); "SALICYLATES     : "; I$
3150      READ I$
3160      PRINT TAB(T); "BILE MORPHINE   : "; I$
3170      READ I$
3180      PRINT TAB(T); "GASTRIC CONTENT : "; I$
3190 REM
3200      RETURN
```

Exhibit 11.3   *Continued*

```
4000 REM  -- PRINT_ANATOMIC_DATA
4010 REM
4020 REM  -- THIS SUBROUTINE PRINTS THE ANATOMIC TEST RESULTS.
4030 REM
4040 REM
4050      PRINT
4060      PRINT
4070      PRINT "ANATOMIC DATA"
4080      PRINT "-------- ----"
4090      PRINT
4100 REM
4110      READ I$
4120      PRINT TAB(T); "BRUISES        : "; I$
4130      READ I$
4140      PRINT TAB(T); "LACERATIONS    : "; I$
4150      READ I$
4160      PRINT TAB(T); "LESIONS        : "; I$
4170      READ I$
4180      PRINT TAB(T); "HAEMORRHAGES   : "; I$
4190      READ I$
4200      PRINT TAB(T); "FRACTURES      : "; I$
4210 REM
4220      RETURN
```

Exhibit 11.3 *Continued*

```
5000 REM  -- PRINT_REMARKS
5010 REM
5020 REM  -- THIS SUBROUTINE PRINTS THE CORONER'S OBSERVATIONS.
5030 REM
5040 REM
5050      PRINT
5060      PRINT
5070      PRINT "GENERAL REMARKS"
5080      PRINT "------- -------"
5090      PRINT
5100 REM
5110      READ I$
5120      IF I$ = "/" THEN 5170
5130         PRINT TAB(T); I$
5140         READ I$
5150         GOTO 5120
5160 REM
5170      RETURN
```

Exhibit 11.3   *Continued*

```
6000 REM  -- DATA FOR REPORT
6010 REM
6020 DATA    "Dr. Harrison", "Colin Wiggs", "42"
6030 DATA    "68", "Black", "Grey", "Male"
6040 DATA    "Negative", "Negative", "+", "Negative for organic bases"
6050 DATA    "Face, neck", "None", "Neck", "None", "Upper windpipe"
6055 REM
6060 DATA    "Subject was apparently struck on the left side of the neck."
6070 DATA    "Double fracture of the upper windpipe, just below the larynx,"
6080 DATA  "suggesting strangulation. A small scar was detected on the left"
6090 DATA    "shoulder."
6100 DATA    "/"
6110 REM
6120 END
```

Exhibit 11.3   *Continued*

11.1   Input

We have been treating the reading of data and printing of results quite casually up to this point, but, as we are well aware, these matters are essential components of any computer program. Holmes's treatment of the coroner's report brings into focus some of the required fine tuning. The basic how-to's of carrying this out are actually quite simple, though they require some careful attention.

Recall from previous chapters that there are two statements in Basic for reading data—the first, INPUT, obtains data from your terminal; the second, READ, obtains data from DATA statements resident in your program. The form for both statements is similar,

```
INPUT  v₁, v₂, ... , vₙ
READ   v₁, v₂, ... , vₙ
```

where v_1 through v_n are variables that will hold the data.

Your initial concern in entering data should be that the data are there and in the correct form; otherwise your program may stop and the computer may issue some strange sort of cease-and-desist order. Many versions of Basic may be more considerate and ask you to enter the data again.

Watch out though, for the following point. If you are supposed to enter a numeric item, the computer will be perfectly happy to accept any number, even if the given number makes no sense at all. The same problem can equally well arise when you enter string data. The general rule here is that the type of data, numeric or string, must match the type of the variable.

What you should do when actually using the computer is second guess it and check for possible errors in input. For simplicity's sake, we've been lax on this point in the text, but in programs you'll be using routinely you should be very careful to check for input mistakes.

For example, suppose you are reading some value into a numeric variable N representing a number of weapons. If you enter

```
6
```

the value 6 will be assigned to N. On the other hand, if you input the real value

```
3.14159
```

the computer will accept it at face value. You will get no indication of a problem until your program finds trouble elsewhere or prints the wrong result. Notice that if you enter the value

-6

the computer will not complain either, even though from a conceptual viewpoint 6 weapons just doesn't make any sense as well. But if you enter a string, such as

    Q1A%

then the computer will surely complain, since it must be given a valid numeric value.

Something you need to understand here is that when reading numeric data, leading and trailing blanks and line boundaries are ignored. Thus, if you are reading the values of two integer variables, say N and M, then you may input the data as

    6, 8

or

    6,   8

As far as the computer is concerned, these cases are the same and they're handled in the same manner.

Now, suppose you are working with string data where an item itself contains blanks, commas, or other special characters. In these cases you can enter the string data as quoted strings. Consider the statement

    INPUT N$, A$

or

    READ N$, A$

to obtain the name and address of someone. If you enter

    HOLMES, LONDON

all is well, but not so with

    SHERLOCK HOLMES,   221B BAKER STREET, LONDON

Here the computer will think you gave it three, not two data items. With quoted strings as data we would instead write

    "SHERLOCK HOLMES", "221B BAKER STREET, LONDON"

giving the desired effect.

Finally, consider the sequence:

```
PRINT "ENTER FIRST NAME:"
INPUT F$
PRINT "ENTER LAST NAME:"
INPUT L$
```

When these statements are executed, the dialogue will look something like

```
ENTER FIRST NAME:
? SHERLOCK
ENTER LAST NAME:
? HOLMES
```

where the strings given after the question mark are entered by the user.

If you wish, most versions of Basic will allow you to override the question mark and provide your own prefix for input. For instance if you say

```
INPUT "ENTER FIRST NAME:", F$
INPUT "ENTER LAST  NAME:", L$
```

the dialogue will look like:

```
ENTER FIRST NAME: SHERLOCK
ENTER LAST  NAME: HOLMES
```

Here the string given after INPUT is used for the prompt. This handy feature can help you improve dialogues with the user.

Another common variant in most Basics allows you to read the entire line typed by the user, including spaces, quotation marks, and commas. If you say, for instance

```
LINE INPUT L$
```

and the user enters

```
221B BAKER STREET, LONDON
```

the value of L$ will be precisely:

```
221B BAKER STREET, LONDON
```

This feature is especially useful when you need to watch carefully what the user types or when the user is entering normal prose.

11.2 Output

For output, your major concern should be its presentation. You and others using your program should be able to understand the results easily. Granted, producing high-quality output can be a tedious task, but your efforts will be well spent even if you are the only person who will use the program. Keep in mind the great detective's comment in "The Adventure of the Veiled Lodger" that "the example of patient suffering is in itself the most precious of all lessons to an impatient world." If you take the occasion to suffer a little now, you will be amply rewarded later.

The printing of data is just like the reading of data, with one important exception: you get to tell the computer how to display the data. If you don't tell it how to display the data, the computer has its own idea about how the data should appear and that may not be what you had in mind. The Basic conventions for displaying data are quite simple, although sometimes inconvenient.

Let's start with a few examples. Recall our program for counting change, given in previous chapters. Suppose this program contained the statement:

```
PRINT "CHANGE IS ", D, "DOLLARS AND ", C, "CENTS."
```

Assume the number of dollars D is 3 and the number of cents C is 41. Depending on your implementation, this statement may print something like

```
CHANGE IS    3           DOLLARS AND  41          CENTS.
```

The output doesn't look quite right since the length of each of the five output fields is fixed by the computer. In particular, a field width of 12 columns is assumed.

If we want to improve the situation, we can change the PRINT statement to the following, that given in the program to count change:

```
PRINT "CHANGE IS "; D; " DOLLARS AND "; C; " CENTS."
```

Notice here that a semicolon (not a comma) separates each pair of items. This will result in printing the following:

```
CHANGE IS  3 DOLLARS AND  41 CENTS.
```

In both cases above, the PRINT statement causes an advance to the next line before printing any more data. If needed, this can be prevented by putting a comma or semicolon after the last item in a PRINT statement. Thus

```
PRINT "CHANGE IS ";
PRINT D; " DOLLARS AND ";
PRINT C: " CENTS."
```

is the same as

```
PRINT "CHANGE IS "; D; " DOLLARS AND "; C; " CENTS."
```

When handling output then, keep in mind these general observations:

■   The items in a print statement are printed in sequence.

■   If an item is followed by a comma, subsequent printing continues in the next print zone.

■   If an item is followed by a semicolon, subsequent printing continues immediately after the item.

■   If an item is the last item and is not followed by a comma or semicolon, subsequent printing continues on the next line.

Normally, the items given in a PRINT statement will fit on one line. It may happen, however, that they won't, for instance if you are printing some long strings or a large number of items. In these cases, an item that will not fit on the line is printed on the subsequent line.

If you want more precise control over the position of items, as is the case in Holmes's program, you can use the tab feature of Basic. Consider:

```
PRINT TAB(10); A; TAB(20); B; TAB(30); C
```

This will print values for A, B, and C beginning in columns 10, 20, and 30 respectively. What if, say, the value for A occupies more than 10 column positions so that the value of B cannot be started in position 20? Printing will continue on the next line, in column 20.

You can write PRINT statements with no items. Here the computer will simply advance to a new line. Thus

```
FOR K = 1 TO 5
   PRINT
NEXT K
```

will print 5 blank lines for you. You can even have empty items in a PRINT statement, such as

```
PRINT A, B, C
PRINT , , D
```

in which case the value of D will be printed beneath the value of C. Normally, you should avoid these empty items, which look a bit odd, and opt for using tabs instead.

Now for the fine print. When your version of Basic prints an item, it obeys a number of rules in deciding exactly what to print. For strings, it is easy; it prints the string. If the string has length zero and thus has no characters, it prints an empty string.

For numbers, the rules are much more complicated, but to make your output really pleasing to read you have to be aware of them. The first is that each number is preceded and followed by a blank space; if the number is negative, it is preceded by a minus sign instead of a space. So if you say

```
LET X = 1
PRINT "X IS"; X
LET X = -1
PRINT "X IS"; X
LET X = +1
PRINT "X IS"; X
```

your output will be:

```
X IS 1
X IS-1
X IS 1
```

Frankly, the extra spaces can be annoying in getting your output to line up. For instance if you say

```
PRINT "X", "Y"
FOR K = 1 TO 3
    LET X = K
    LET Y = K
    PRINT X, Y
NEXT K
```

your output may look like:

```
X           Y
 1           1
 2           2
 3           3
```

Not every version of Basic puts in these extra spaces. If it doesn't, be careful not to write something like

```
LET X = 1
LET Y = 2
PRINT "X IS"; X; "Y IS"; Y
```

which will print

```
X IS 1Y IS 2
```

or even

```
X IS1Y IS2
```

all of which means you can't really win.

The next issue is how Basic actually prints a number. One of the pleasant aspects of Basic is that it is very clever in keeping track of numeric values. For instance, 3, 3.0, and 0.3E+1 are all taken as the same value, and you may freely mix integers, numbers with a decimal point, and numbers in E notation. To know which notation is used for printing depends on a number of factors and varies from computer to computer.

To start with, your computer can only hold integers up to some predetermined maximum value, for arguments sake let's say up to six digits. If the value is a whole number that can be exactly represented with 6 or fewer digits, then that is what you get. This means that

```
LET A = 3
LET B = 3.0
LET C = 0.3E+1
LET D = 2.1 + 0.9
LET E = 9/3
PRINT "THE ANSWERS ARE:"; A; B; C; D; E
```

will print:

```
THE ANSWERS ARE: 3  3  3  3  3
```

For numbers requiring a decimal point a similar convention holds. That is, if the number can be represented with 6 or fewer digits in decimal point form, decimal point notation is used. This means that

```
LET A = 3.3
LET B = 3.300
LET C = 0.33E+1
LET D = 2.4 + 0.9
LET E = 9.9/3
PRINT "THE ANSWERS ARE:"; A; B; C; D; E
```

will print, yes:

```
THE ANSWERS ARE: 3.3  3.3  3.3  3.3  3.3
```

For very large (or very small) numbers that would require more digits, the result will appear in E notation. Thus

```
LET A = 3000000000
LET B = 3.0 * 1000 * 1000 * 1000
LET C = 3000E+6
LET D = 3E-9
LET E = 3.0 / 1000 / 1000 / 1000
PRINT "THE ANSWERS ARE:"; A; B; C; D; E
```

will print:

```
THE ANSWERS ARE: 3.0E+9  3.0E+9  3.0E+9  3.0E-9  3.0E-9
```

We close with a small example. In our program to count change we have the PRINT statement

```
PRINT "CHANGE IS "; D; " DOLLARS AND "; C; " CENTS."
```

which will print something like:

```
CHANGES IS  3 DOLLARS AND  41 CENTS.
```

Suppose we wish to get a bit snazzy and print something like:

```
CHANGE IS $3.41
```

You might try:

```
PRINT "CHANGE IS $"; D; "."; C
```

This will give you

```
CHANGE IS $ 3 . 41
```

which is not bad, but not right. If your version of Basic does not print spaces around numbers, you would get:

```
CHANGE IS $3.41
```

Now for the snag. Suppose the number of dollars D is 3, but the number of cents C is 8. Now you will get either

```
CHANGE IS $ 3 . 8
```

or

```
CHANGE IS $3.8
```

both of which are not at all what you want.

What do you do? There is really only one good alternative — using the predefined function STR$. Consider the following:

```
0010 IF C > 9 THEN 0040
0020    PRINT "CHANGE IS $"; STR$(D); ".0"; STR$(C)
0030    GOTO 0060
0040    PRINT "CHANGE IS $"; STR$(D); ".";  STR$(C)
0050    GOTO 0060
0060 ...
```

Here the function STR$ converts each value to its string representation (without spaces); no matter which position your version takes on printing numbers, this excerpt will print exactly what you want.

Granted, all of this can be quite annoying, but all languages have their little idiosyncrasies; some are just easier to live with than others.

XII

The Adventure
of the Gold Chip

T is really very good of you to come along, Watson," said
Sherlock Holmes, as he rummaged through a litter of
newspapers. We had the carriage to ourselves and were
sitting in the two corner seats opposite each other as our
train moved rapidly along to Reading. We were responding
to a summons from Lestrade which arrived as we were breakfasting.

"It does make a considerable difference, having someone with me on
whom I can thoroughly rely. I am sure the aid we will find in Reading will
be so terribly biased as to render it worthless. You are familiar with the
particulars of this ghastly murder?"

"Not at all," I replied. "My practice has kept me quite busy and I have
not seen a newspaper in days."

"The press have not had very full accounts," he replied. "But it has
been reported that our unfortunate victim was something of a recluse and a
miser, with over three thousand pounds to his name at the time of his
death. It was also widely known that he had numerous acquaintances in
the London blackmail industry, hence the interest of Scotland Yard in the
affair. He was last seen walking away from the village of Eyford late
yesterday morning with a man who witnesses say had a bald patch
crowning his matted hair. While there is no strong evidence that this
stranger was the murderer, the police are left with no other suspects."

It was fairly late in the afternoon when we arrived to find Inspector
Lestrade of Scotland Yard waiting for us upon the platform.

"I have ordered a carriage," said Lestrade, as we disembarked. "I know your energetic nature and that you would not be happy until you had been on the scene of the crime.

"We certainly appreciate your help, Mr. Holmes," added the Inspector. "But let me forewarn you that I myself and my best men could find no clue out here. As you will soon see, there is nothing but a jumble of footprints where the final confrontation apparently took place."

"Judge not too hastily, Lestrade," Holmes replied nonchalantly. "If I had a shilling for every clue your best men have overlooked in the last ten years, I would retire at once to the country and never want for the rest of my days. Surely you know, Lestrade, that there is no branch of detective science so important and so much neglected as the art of tracing footsteps."

A short while later we arrived at the scene. Holmes sprang down from our carriage, his face flushed and dark; once on a hot scent like this, he was transformed.

Like a foxhound, with gleaming eyes and straining muscles, Holmes was down on his knees, and at one point lay flat on the ground. For a long time he remained there, carefully surveying the earth with his pocket lens. Eventually, he scooped something up into a small envelope, which he returned to his pocket.

"Are there any points to which you would draw my attention?" asked Lestrade, as Holmes returned to us.

"Beyond the obvious facts that there were three men present here at the time of the incident, that the man who led our victim down this path

"FOR A LONG TIME HE REMAINED THERE."

wears a size-nine boot and is in good standing with the London financial community, and that the killer himself is a highly underpaid labourer and former officer in the Royal Marine Light Infantry, I can deduce nothing else. After all, Lestrade, one cannot make bricks without clay."

The Inspector opened his mouth to speak, but Holmes quickly added, "And do take the trouble of extinguishing your pipe before examining evidence. That left foot of yours with its inward twist and the ash from your Arcadia mixture are all over the place. A mole could trace your movements. Oh, how much simpler it would be if I could only get a look at things before you and your men come in here like a herd of buffalos, trampling over everything!"

Convinced that there was no further need for his services, Holmes called for the carriage, and we were soon heading for Baker Street again. In the privacy of our carriage he shed some light on our abrupt departure.

"As a rule, when I have observed some slight indication of the course of events, I am able to guide myself by the thousands of other similar cases which occur to my memory," he began. "As you are aware, over the course of my career I have amassed data on well over a thousand criminals. In recent years I have stored these data in files suitable for the memory of the Analytical Engine. Furthermore, I have designed a programme that will read the description of each criminal and then print out the names of all those fitting a given description."

I have reproduced here a small section of my companion's curious assortment of criminal data, which he showed me upon our return to Baker Street.

Name	:	The name of a person
Height	:	Height in inches, ranging from 48 to 84
Hair colour	:	One of the colours brown, black, red, or grey
Eye colour	:	One of the colours brown, blue, or hazel
Hat size	:	A number from 4 to 10
Shoe size	:	A number from 5 to 15
Teeth marks	:	One of the characteristics normal, crooked, gold-filled, partially missing, or (totally) missing
Cigar type	:	One of the cigar types Lunkah, Trichinopoly, Espanada, Heritage, Londoner, MacDuffy, Top Hat, or West Country
Facial scar	:	Yes or no
Hand scar	:	Yes or no
Eye patch	:	Yes or no
Bald patch	:	Yes or no
Leg limp	:	Yes or no
Tattoo	:	Yes or no

"I must confess Watson, as I look over these possibilities, that this case does have its points of interest. We know that the suspect has a slight bald patch and wears a size-nine boot. The most singular clue in this mystery, however, is this gold chip I found in amongst the gravel." He showed me the object. "It is a gold dental filling and surely narrows down our list of candidates. Just as you can tell an old master by the sweep of his brush, I can tell a Moriarty when I see one."

"A Moriarty?" I queried.

"The power behind half that is evil and nearly all that is undetected in this great city, Watson. I have been at great pains to work out all my programmes for the Analytical Engine before he becomes aware of its utility, for Moriarty is a mathematical mind of the highest order; and I shudder to think what he could carry out with the Engine at his command."

"What are the ingredients of this particular programme?" I asked, after a considerable pause.

"The most important feature of this programme is, aptly enough, called a *file*," replied Holmes. "As you might presume, a file is a collection of data on some item of interest. In this instance, of course, the file is a collection of facts about known criminals. It is organized into records, each containing data on a given criminal.

"For simplicity, the data such as colour values and shoe sizes are entered as strings," said Holmes, jotting illustrations of his ideas on a scrap of paper, as follows :—

Hair Colour: UNKNOWN   BROWN   BLACK   RED   GREY

"Here is a sample of my record structures," he continued, handing me a sheet from his portfolio.

What he showed me is duplicated here :—

Name   :   COLONEL SEBASTIAN MORAN
Height   :   66
Hair colour   :   BLACK
Eye colour   :   BLUE
Hat size   :   8
Shoe size   :   10
Teeth marks   :   NORMAL
Cigar type   :   UNKNOWN
Facial scar   :   NO
Hand scar   :   YES
Eye patch   :   NO
Bald patch   :   YES

Leg limp   :   NO
Moustache   :   YES

"In all cases, if a value is unknown, its place is held by the string UNKNOWN."

"How can you possibly use these data to find the name of a suspect?" I asked, for I still had no idea how he could use such data advantageously.

"Easily," remarked Holmes. "The data on each criminal are resident in a file that I have created. These data can, of course, be called into the prgramme when needed.

"What our programme will do, Watson, is read in the characteristics of a suspect, such as a bald patch or a size-nine boot, and then print out the names of all those criminals in its files that fit the description. Let's give it a try, shall we? I can tell you well in advance, however, whose signature we shall find on this latest criminal masterpiece."

Holmes then carefully entered the data according to the programme which I have duplicated here as Exhibit 12.1. He was careful to enter all suspect values as UNKNOWN except for shoe size (9), teeth marks (GOLD_FILLED), and bald patch (YES). We watched for several minutes before the names of three criminals within the file had been printed.

"Moriarty," Holmes whispered. "These other two, Watson, are certainly capable of carrying out such a crime. However, I happen to know one of them is in Newgate; and if I am not mistaken, this other is awaiting trial here in London."

"Surely you haven't enough evidence to convict Moriarty," I protested.

"Oh, hardly, Watson," replied Holmes. "But count on it, this crime fits into something much larger which we fail to see presently, for there are certain subtleties that even our Engine cannot detect. True, it has removed much of the painstaking drudgery from our work; but it is up to us to find where and how this piece fits into the larger scheme of things.

"For now, Watson, there is a cold partridge on the sideboard and a bottle of Montrachet here. Let us renew our energies before we make fresh calls upon them."

```
0010 REM  -- THIS PROGRAMME INPUTS VALUES CORRESPONDING TO
0020 REM  -- DATA KEPT ON KNOWN CRIMINALS. FOR EACH DATA
0030 REM  -- ITEM, A PROMPT IS GIVEN.
0040 REM  -- THE PROGRAMME OUTPUTS THE NAME OF EACH CRIMINAL FOR WHICH
0050 REM  -- THE INPUT VALUES MATCH THOSE ON THE CRIMINAL'S RECORD.
0060 REM
0070 REM  -- DICTIONARY OF NAMES:
0080 REM
0090 REM  -- S$  ARRAY OF SUSPECT DATA ENTERED FOR THE SUSPECT
0100 REM  -- C$  ARRAY OF CRIMINAL DATA FOR A GIVEN CRIMINAL
0110 REM  -- E$  END OF FILE FLAG, "MORE_DATA" OR "NO_MORE_DATA"
0120 REM  -- N$  NAME OF A CRIMINAL
0130 REM  -- K   LOCAL COUNTER
0140 REM
0150 REM
0160      DIM S$(13), C$(14)
0170 REM
0180      LET E$ = "MORE_DATA"
0190      OPEN #1: NAME "CRIMINAL_FILE", ACCESS INPUT
0200 REM
0210 REM  -- GET_SUSPECT_DATA
0220      GOSUB 1000
0230 REM
0240      IF E$ = "NO_MORE_DATA" THEN 0310
0250 REM     -- GET_CRIMINAL_RECORD
0260         GOSUB 2000
0270 REM     -- TEST_FOR_MATCH
0280         GOSUB 3000
0290         GOTO 0240
0300 REM
0310      PRINT "ALL ENTRIES HAVE BEEN CHECKED."
0320      CLOSE #1
0330      STOP
```

Exhibit 12.1   *Holmes's Programme for the Criminal Search*

```
1000 REM  -- GET_SUSPECT_DATA
1010 REM
1020 REM  -- THIS SUBROUTINE OBTAINS THE DATA KNOWN ABOUT A SUSPECT.
1030 REM
1040 REM
1050      PRINT "ENTER SUSPECT DATA REQUESTED."
1060      PRINT "IF ANY ITEM IS UNKNOWN, ENTER THE WORD UNKNOWN"
1070 REM
1080      PRINT "ENTER HEIGHT IN INCHES:"
1090      INPUT S$(1)
1100 REM
1110      PRINT "ENTER HAIR COLOUR - BROWN, BLACK, RED, OR GREY:"
1120      INPUT S$(2)
1130 REM
1140      PRINT "ENTER EYE COLOUR - BROWN, BLUE, GREEN, OR HAZEL:"
1150      INPUT S$(3)
1160 REM
1170      PRINT "ENTER HAT SIZE:"
1180      INPUT S$(4)
1190 REM
1200      PRINT "ENTER SHOE SIZE:"
1210      INPUT S$(5)
1220 REM
1230      PRINT "ENTER TEETH DESCRIPTION - NORMAL, CROOKED"
1240      PRINT "GOLD_FILLED, PARTIAL, OR MISSING:"
1250      INPUT S$(6)
1260 REM
1270      PRINT "ENTER CIGAR TYPE - LUNKAH, TRICHONOPOLY, ESPANADA,"
1280      PRINT "HERITAGE, LONDONER, MACDUFFY, TOP_HAT, OR WEST_COUNTRY:"
1290      INPUT S$(7)
1300 REM
1310      PRINT "FOR EACH OF THE FOLLOWING, ENTER YES OR NO:"
1320      PRINT "FACIAL SCAR? HAND SCAR? EYE PATCH? BALD PATCH? ";
1330      PRINT "LEG LIMP? MOUSTACHE?"
1340      INPUT S$(8), S$(9), S$(10), S$(11), S$(12), S$(13)
1350 REM
1360      RETURN
```

Exhibit 12.1   *Continued*

```
2000 REM  -- GET_CRIMINAL_RECORD
2010 REM
2020 REM  -- THIS SUBROUTINE READS IN THE NEXT RECORD IN THE
2030 REM  -- MASTER CRIMINAL FILE.
2040 REM  -- IF THE END OF FILE IS REACHED, A FLAG IS SET.
2050 REM
2060 REM
2070      INPUT #1 AT EOF 2130: N$
2080      FOR K = 1 TO 13
2090         INPUT #1: C$(K)
2100      NEXT K
2110      RETURN
2120 REM
2130      LET E$ = "NO_MORE_DATA"
2140      RETURN
```

Exhibit 12.1   *Continued*

```
3000 REM  -- TEST_FOR_MATCH
3010 REM
3020 REM     THIS SUBROUTINE TESTS IF THE SUSPECT DATA MATCH
3030 REM  -- THOSE FOR A GIVEN CRIMINAL.
3040 REM  -- IF ANY DATA ITEM FOR THE SUSPECT OR CRIMINAL IS UNKNOWN,
3050 REM  -- IT IS TAKEN AS A MATCH.
3060 REM
3070 REM
3080      IF E$ = "MORE_DATA" THEN 3110
3090         RETURN
3100 REM
3110      LET M$ = "MATCH"
3120      FOR K = 1 TO 13
3130         IF C$(K) = S$(K)       THEN 3170
3140         IF C$(K) = "UNKNOWN" THEN 3170
3150         IF S$(K) = "UNKNOWN" THEN 3170
3160            LET M$ = "NO_MATCH"
3170      NEXT K
3180 REM
3190      IF M$ <> "MATCH" THEN 3220
3200         PRINT "POSSIBLE SUSPECT: "; N$
3210 REM
3220      RETURN
```

Exhibit 12.1   *Continued*

12.1 Files

Certainly one of the most useful features of a computer is its ability to store large amounts of data. The use of files to store data is common to many implementations of Basic. Typically, whenever we have a large collection of information, it is stored in a file external to the program. The file may reside on a tape cassette or a magnetic disk (often on a "floppy" disk). Usually the information is collected into records, and the purpose of the program is to analyze the information in some way.

Now this would suggest that there are, in essence, two kinds of data. On one hand there are data that are designed for human consumption, such as when we read and write numbers and character strings during input and output. On the other hand, there are data such as files that are designed entirely for use by machine. The computer's ability to maintain huge amounts of data can only be accomplished with external files.

All files have certain properties. For one, a file may have an arbitrary number of items. In Holmes's case, the file of criminal records may contain data on 10, 50, or even 500 criminals. Second, the last item in the file is always followed by a special marker called an "end-of-file." This marker is put there so you can know when you have read all of the data.

The actual facilities for handling files in Basic can vary greatly from version to version, but the underlying ideas are similar. Here especially we assume some particular conventions, and you will have to check your local dialect for its own variation. In what follows we describe only *serial* (or *sequential*) files, those in which the data are accessed in the sequence in which they are stored.

The basic operations on a file are simple:

1.   *Opening a file:* To work with a file of data, you have to create it or use an existing one.

2.   *Writing data:* If data are generated, you will want to put the data onto a file for later use.

3.   *Reading data:* Once a file is established, you will want to read the data into your program for processing.

4.   *Closing a file:* Once you are finished with the file, you often need to tell the computer you are done with it.

The methods for performing these operations in Basic are also simple.

To open a file you need to give its external name and identify whether the file is to be used for reading or writing data. Normally you cannot read and write a file at the same time. In addition, you must establish a number for the file; this number must be used when you refer to the file elsewhere in your program.

For instance, if you are going to read the contents of a file, you might say:

```
OPEN #1: NAME "CRIMINAL_FILE", ACCESS INPUT
```

If you want to create a file, you might say:

```
OPEN #2: NAME "NEW_DATA", ACCESS OUTPUT
```

Normally your system will have its own requirements for using such files. For instance, it may require information about its size and location on storage, or may require that file names have at most six characters.

Once you have opened a file, reading or writing data can be accomplished similar to that for reading or writing on a terminal. For instance

```
INPUT #1: X, Y, Z
```

reads in the next three values in file 1 and assigns the values to X, Y, and Z. Similarly

```
PRINT #2: A, B, C
```

will add the values of A, B, and C to file 2. Just as for reading and writing data on a terminal, both string and numeric variables can be used in an INPUT statement, and string and numeric expressions can be used in a PRINT statement.

If you are working with files of text, you will probably need to read the text line by line. This is easy, and can be handled with a LINE INPUT statement. For instance

```
LINE INPUT #1: L$
```

will read the next full line of text in file 1 and assign the text to the string variable L$.

When reading data on file, you need some way of knowing when the end of file is reached. In Basic this is usually handled with an EOF clause, as in:

```
INPUT #1 AT EOF 0500: X
```

Here the clause

```
AT EOF 0500
```

will cause a transfer of control to line 0500 when no value remains for X.

When you have finished reading or writing data, you can tell the system to close each file with a CLOSE statement, such as:

```
CLOSE #1
```

This may not be necessary on your particular version of Basic.

That's really all we have to say about files in Basic, though here especially, your own version of Basic may provide much more elaborate features. But remember, as the great detective remarked in "The Adventure of the Dancing Men," involving a complex code, "Every problem becomes very childish when once it is explained to you."

The Last Bow

XIII

Holmes Delivers
A Lecture

NO record of the doings of Mr. Sherlock Holmes and his contributions to the development and understanding of the Analytical Engine would be complete without a report on his brilliant address to the Royal Society in the late autumn of 1895. Shortly after the conclusion of the case involving Arthur H. Staunton, the rising young forger, came the publication of the great detective's much celebrated monograph, "Upon the Use of the Analytical Engine in the Work of the Criminal Investigator," which earned him an invitation to speak before the annual meeting of the Royal Society.

It may be remembered that I had sold my Kensington practice a year earlier and that I was again sharing lodgings with my old companion at 221B Baker Street. He insisted that I accompany him to the assembly, and it was my great privilege to do so. I offer here an account of his address, which I have reconstructed from my notes.

A special carriage was sent for us bearing two emissaries of the Royal Society. These gentlemen escorted us to a stately house situated off Pall Mall, to the rooms that were home to the learned group, where a reception was already in progress. Here Holmes and I had the opportunity to mingle with some of Britain's most renowned scientific figures.

At a certain point, Holmes was escorted to a podium and, following a brief introduction, commenced his lecture.

"Gentlemen and fellow scientific investigators," Holmes began. "It is without doubt an honour to appear before this assembly tonight in order to share a few of my ideas on the use of the Analytical Engine.

"A SPECIAL CARRIAGE WAS SENT FOR US."

"Though all of you are doubtless already aware of the advantages that the Engine promises to bestow upon science, and although many of you may be considering applying this new device to your own areas of investigation, it is likely that you have as yet had little experience in designing programmes for the Engine. It is my hope that my lecture will furnish you with a general, logical method for organizing programming tasks and attacking scientific problems with the Analytical Engine. This method I have called "programming from the top-down," although elementary in its fundamental concepts, it is invaluable as a technique for constructing all types of programmes, including the most complex ones you are likely to encounter.

"In my engagements as a criminal investigator I have always been careful to arrange all clues systematically and devise a complete hypothetical approach to a case before taking a single step out of my rooms in pursuit of a solution. This principle applies equally well to the use of the Analytical Engine. No matter how simple the task, it is necessary at the outset to formulate a *clear* and *complete* statement of the problem at hand, as well as a basic plan for solving it. The programmer should prepare sample input and output formats and design a general algorithm before writing any programme. This precaution ensures that a minimal amount of confusion and lost time will result during interactions with the Engine.

"Let me now enumerate the characteristics of the top-down approach.

"The first concept essential for a grasp of programming top-down is the idea of *design in levels*. The programmer should construct his programme according to a conceptual hierarchy. The upper levels of his hierarchy should indicate the more general features of the problem, with details and elaborations introduced at the lower levels.

"The highest level is thus the initial conception of the solution. The individual paths from each level represent the possible solutions at each conceptual stage. Each lower level thus elaborates the preceding level. Here is a chart," said Holmes, "that illustrates this idea."

I have reproduced this graphic representation as Exhibit 13.1.

"Secondly, the language used to formulate this preliminary model need not be the special language of the Engine, and for this reason the top-down method is described as being *language independent*. At this early stage of programming, ordinary English will generally be sufficient. Later, of course, it should be possible to encode the programme in a form intelligible to the Engine.

"Thirdly, as in all forms of scientific reasoning, it is advisable to attain a firm grasp of the broad aspects of a problem before proceeding to the minute details of analysis. Accordingly, in the top-down approach, *details should be deferred* to lower levels. Typical of such detail is the internal representation of data.

"Fourthly, before advancing to a lower level, the programmer must ascertain that the solution is stated in *precise* terms. By this I mean that instead of using a very vague statement that has no immediate consequences, the programmer should seek a more meaningful statement that entails one or more submodules.

"Fifthly, as a new level unfolds in the programme's development, the programmer must take pains to *verify the solution*. You will conserve appreciable amounts of time and energy by detecting errors in style or content as early as possible, rather than after numerous subprogrammes have already been generated and the errors must be traced to their sources further up in the hierarchy.

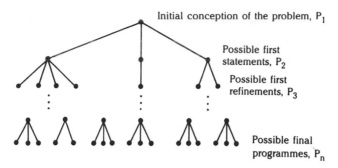

Exhibit 13.1   *The Top-Down Approach*

"And finally, each step of the programme must be elaborated, improved, and meticulously examined until it is ready to be transformed into the Engine's special language.

"Although this lengthy process of refinement may seem tedious to the lofty theorists among you, I assure you that there is no other way to use the computing machine efficaciously. In fact, as you become more adept at designing programmes, this stage of the task will become less and less burdensome; and you may well discover that you enjoy the intellectual exercise it affords.

"I myself found no difficulty in adapting to the requirements of programme design, for my career as a detective has sharpened my faculties to such a degree that I routinely dissect cumbersome problems into manageable components with little effort.

"Now, gentlemen, if my explication is entirely clear to you thus far, I should like to offer some further observations concerning the art, or science, as you would perhaps prefer to designate it, of programming from the top-down. I cannot emphasize too strongly that you must thoroughly understand the given task and its solution before attempting to write a programme.

"Therefore, you should initially be far less concerned with your notation—for example, ordinary English would suffice—than with your overall comprehension of the problem. This is especially important at the top levels of the hierarchy. Eventually, of course, sub-programmes must be explicitly stated; and in particular all input and output arguments must be described.

"Again, allow me to emphasise the importance of scrupulous examination and refinement of each stage of a top-down model. One should always look for possible errors and provide against them.

"Here is an example at an intermediate level of refinement," continued Holmes, gesturing towards another illustration that I have duplicated as follows :

```
depending on the DAY_OF_THE_WEEK, do one of the following:
    MONDAY:          -- generate last weeks criminal summary
    TUESDAY:         -- do nothing
    WEDNESDAY:       -- update criminal records
    THURSDAY:        -- process new reports
    FRIDAY:          -- generate lab item reports
    SATURDAY:        -- generate weekly statistics
    SUNDAY:          -- do nothing
end
```

"The language in this illustration is obviously informal, yet each statement can be transformed into instructions as required for the Engine. Of course, the programme must ultimately provide explicit instructions for performing each operation, such as the updating of criminal records, but this occurs at a later stage of the refinement process.

"Once again, gentlemen, may I direct your attention to our first illustration (Exhibit 13.1). As I remarked previously, this is a graphic representation of the top-down concept. The highest level, P_1, constitutes the most general description of the problem; and the downward branchings represent the alternative methods of programme design available to the programmer at each step. As the programmer reaches each successive level, he must choose the branches that best fit the stated purposes. If all the branches at a certain level seem unsuitable, it may be necessary to return upward in the tree and select a different solution at a higher level. In advancing from P_1 to the bottom of the tree, the programmer thus moves from a general statement of the problem, through a series of decisions about the design, and finally to a working programme.

"Let us turn our attention to this illustration of the top-down structure of a particular programme containing five levels."

Holmes directed their attention to the chart I have included here as Exhibit 13.2.

"Observe how individual paths from P_1, as they were designated in our first illustration (Exhibit 13.1), are elaborated to produce the individual parts charted in this illustration (Exhibit 13.2).

"I imagine that by this time my learned listeners have conceived some applications of the top-down method to their own investigations in various scientific disciplines. As a man acquainted with several branches of natural

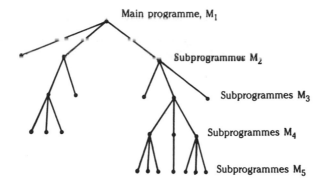

Exhibit 13.2 *Top-Down Structure of a Programme*

science, and especially chemistry, I am confident that the principles outlined in this lecture can be of service to investigators in all fields, mundane as well as academic."

As could only be expected, the members of the Royal Society greeted Holmes's lecture with considerable applause and afterwards detained him for nearly an hour with their questions concerning the details of the top-down method. Many of them were delighted to meet the famous detective, whose adventures they confessed to having followed in my modest chronicles; and they pressed Holmes to discuss his latest endeavours in criminal investigation.

Once we were back at our comfortable lodgings in Baker Street, sitting on either side of the fire, Holmes, who was always amenable to flattery, allowed his more sombre and cynical spirit to comment on the evening's course of events.

"Do you realize, Watson, that none of our distinguished company this evening enquired as to my plans for applying the Analytical Engine in my future criminal investigatoins? If these are the greatest minds our generation can offer, I fear that the world may not yet be ready or deserving of this magnificent Engine. It was indeed a disappointment, for I would surely like to contemplate tomorrow's challenges as well as yesterday's laurels."

"I fear, Holmes, that I am entirely to blame for this," I remarked. "My highly exaggerated accounts of your doings, as you yourself have called them, have given the public a distorted view of the seriousness with which you go about your business."

"On the contrary, Watson. You have given prominence not so much to the many sensational causes in our cases together, but rather to those seemingly trivial incidents that have given room for those faculties of deduction that I have made my special province. For this, I am eternally grateful. As for the Analytical Engine, I offer my work to the next generation of scientific investigators—to those young boys still in boarding school, capsules they are, hundreds of bright little seeds from which will doubtless spring a wiser, and indeed better, England."

13.1   Revisiting the Top-Down Approach

There are many different approaches to a programming problem. Holmes's use of the top-down approach is in marked contrast to other methods. Consider the following list:

1.   Linear approach
2.   Bottom-up approach
3.   Inside-out or forest approach
4.   Imitation approach

The first method is the "linear" approach. Here you immediately start writing code as it will appear when executed, first line first, second line second, and so forth. The drawback with this approach is the need to make specific, detailed decisions with very little assurance that they will be appropriate to the problem at hand.

It is a capital mistake to theorize before one has data, as Holmes has remarked on a number of occasions, because one begins to twist facts to suit theories, instead of theories to suit facts. It is just so with programming; if one begins to construct a program without sufficient data one must be prepared to accept the consequences. The linear technique may seem obviously poor, but the temptation to use it can be very strong, especially on those problems that appear "easy." But beware of this temptation—the little, easy problems have a way of ending up much more complicated than they first appear.

In the "bottom-up" approach, the programmer designs and writes the lower components first, and the upper levels later. The bottom-up approach is in a sense the inversion of the top-down approach. It suffers severely by requiring the programmer to make specific decisions about the program before the overall problem and algorithm are understood.

In between the top-down and bottom-up approaches, we have the "inside-out" or "forest" approach, which consists of starting in the middle of the program and working down and up at the same time. Roughly speaking, it goes as follows:

1. *General idea*. First we decide upon the general idea for programming the problem.

2. *A rough sketch of the program*. Next we write any "important" sections of the program, assuming initialization in some form. In some sections we write portions of the actual program. In doing this, we hope that the actual intent of each piece of program will not change several times, necessitating rewriting parts of our sketch.

3. *Programming the first version*. After Step 2, we write the entire program. We start with the lowest level module. After an individual component has been programmed, we debug it and immediately prepare a description of what it does.

4. *Rethinking and revising*. As a result of Step 3, we should be close to a working program, but it may be possible to improve on it. So we continue by making improvements until we obtain a complete working program.

It is probably fair to say that many programmers, even experienced ones, often work inside out, starting neither very close to the top or to the bottom level. Instead they start in the middle and work outward until a program finally appears on the horizon. The approach is a poor one, for the program may undergo many changes and patches and thus seldom achieves a clear logical structure.

As another method, consider the "imitation" approach, a method superficially resembling the top-down approach. This approach is discussed in detail because many programmers *think* that the top-down approach is really the way they have always programmed. There are, however, subtle but important differences. The imitation approach is described as follows:

1. *Thinking about the program*. Having been given a programming task, take the time to examine the problem thoroughly before starting to program. Think about the details of the program for a while, and then decide on a general approach.

2.   *Deciding on subprograms.* After having thought about the problem in detail, decide on what sections will be sufficiently important to merit being made into subprograms.

3.   *Writing of subprograms.* At this point write each subprograms. After each is completed, write down what it expects as input, what it returns as output, and what it does. The subprograms should be written in a hierarchical manner: the most primitive first, calling routines second, and so forth. Doing this will ensure that the subprograms are fully written before the upper-level program structures are finalized.

4.   *Writing the main program.* After all subprograms have been written, write the main program. The purpose of the main program is to sequence and interface the subprograms.

The imitation approach has some important similarities to the top-down approach:

■   The problem must be understood thoroughly before writing the program.

■   The actual writing of the program is postponed until after certain decisions have been made.

■   The problem is broken up into clear, logical units.

However, there are important differences between the two approaches:

■   In the top-down approach, a *specific* plan of attack is developed in stages. Only the issues relevant to a given level are considered, and these issues are formalized completely.

■   Furthermore, whenever the programmer decides to use a subprogram, the interfaces (arguments, returned values, and effects) are decided *first*. The inputs and outputs are formalized before developing the subprograms; that is, the subprograms are made to fit the calling routine instead of the other way around.

■   Most important, at *every step* in the top-down approach, the programmer must have a complete, correct "program."

The disadvantages of the imitation approach are that it is more likely to produce errors, to require extensive program modifications, or to result in a somewhat ill-conceived program. Choosing a partially specified attack may require serious changes to the program. Writing subprograms first may result in confusing program logic if the subprograms do not integrate easily into the upper-level code designed later.

In summary, think carefully about programming technique. The top-down approach, as described by Holmes, may provide the best alternative.

XIV

The Final Programme

ITH Mr. Sherlock Holmes at Baker Street, one's morning paper presented infinite possibilities. The air of London remains all the sweeter for his absence but the days of the great cases are past following his retirement to the Sussex Downs.

During this period of my life, Holmes passed almost entirely beyond my ken, save for an occasional weekend pilgrimage I might make to his little villa at Fulworth. I was surprised and delighted, therefore, when one morning in June the maid brought in a small package and a note from my old companion. Removing the wrappings I found a slim volume entitled, *Practical Handbook of Bee Culture, with Some Observations upon the Segregation of the Queen.* The accompanying note read :

> *Watson,*
>
> *As you can see, I have been considering some of the problems furnished by Nature, rather than those of a more superficial character for which our artificial state of society is wholly responsible. Of late, however, I have been tempted to direct my thoughts towards the Analytical Engine. Can you spare me a few days? Air and scenery are perfect.*
>
> *Holmes*

Owing to my experience in the rough-and-tumble camps of Afghanistan, I was quite a ready traveller. My bag was packed and I was rattling out of Victoria station within the hour.

Mrs. Hudson, his old housekeeper, showed me into Holmes's sitting room where I found him engaged in conversation with a distinguished gentleman, vaguely familiar to me.

"Surely you remember Major General Henry Prevost Babbage?" said Holmes

"Of course," I replied. "We met at the annual meeting of the Royal Society. I am delighted to meet you again, sir."

"The pleasure is mine, Dr. Watson," he answered, extending his hand. We sat for a while and, naturally enough, the conversation turned to the Analytical Engine.

"NATURALLY THE CONVERSATION TURNED TO THE ANALYTICAL ENGINE."

"As you know, Watson, I am now preparing the *magnum opus* of my career, a comprehensive treatise of my methods entitled *The Whole Art of Detection*, with illustrations from my most noteworthy cases. As you may imagine, this is the longest and most difficult work I have ever attempted, over five hundred pages in its entirety. I have spent countless hours and many sleepless nights verifying minute points and making hundreds of emendations.

"The content and style of this manuscript have so engrossed my attention that I simply have no patience left for the more mundane aspects of its creation, such as typing and proofreading. Yet I dare not entrust the copying and editing of such an important work to just anyone. Do you understand, Watson?"

"Yes, quite, Holmes," I replied, with some apprehension lest he ask me to serve as his scribe. A sudden thought came to me. "Perhaps the Engine can be put to good use here?"

"Precisely what I had in mind, Watson. Now, you may well wonder how the Engine is equipped to serve in this capacity. Imagine, if you will that I have scribbled out a paragraph of my manuscript without observing the conventions of margins, indentation, *et cetera*, as in this fragment.

He placed before Babbage and me a card with the following inscription :

Although the   criminal investigator
typically does
not consider himself a   disciple
of empirical science,
his work, like   the chemist's,
consists in a logical and systematic
quest   for Truth.

"Obviously I could not submit a collection of such fragments to a publisher. I am trying to design a programme that will, among other things, arrange such fragments of text correctly, as follows."

He thereupon handed us another card on which was written an emendation of the first :

Although the criminal investigator typically does
not consider himself a disciple of empirical science,
his work, like the chemist's, consists in a logical
and systematic quest for Truth.

"Notice here that the words are arranged to fill the line properly," Holmes continued. "You see, the typing and editing process can be made considerably simpler. I can enter the text at leisure; and if a mistake is encountered or a change is deemed necessary, I can simply correct the original version. The Engine can then be commanded to print a perfect, corrected copy. Here I have made an outline of the desired format for my entire manuscript."

I inspected the proffered conventions, which are reproduced here :

1. Page Size (standard 8 1/2-by-11 page)
    85 characters per line
    66 lines per page

2. Margins
    Left: 15 characters in from left edge of page
    Right: 10 characters in from right edge of page

Top: 6 lines down from top of page
Bottom: 6 lines up from bottom of page

3. Printing Area (standard 10 point spacing)
    60 characters per line
    54 lines per page

4. Page Numbers
    3 lines down from bottom margin, centered between the left and
    right margin, and enclosed by hyphens, for example:

                              -14-

I immediately thought of my own writings and the great amount of time
that could be saved with the implementation of such a scheme. It would
sometimes take up to a year for my manuscripts to be edited by my literary
agent, Dr. Arthur Conan Doyle, again by *his* editors, and finally appear in
their printed form. I noted that in addition to spacing each line of text
properly, the Engine would ensure that the margins were observed and that
page numbers were correctly incremented.

"Well, Holmes," I said after a time, "this idea of yours will undoubtedly
spare you much of the tedium authors ordinarily suffer."

"True, Watson," he replied, "but this is only the beginning of my work.
Remember that before approaching the Engine it is imperative to define
the problem completely and exactly, using the top-down approach. In
particular, one must enumerate every possible detail of the input and
output. On these pages I have described the commands for formatting text
and worked out a hypothetical input with its corresponding output."

Holmes then showed us the commands as well as samples of the input
and output to his programme. I have replicated them here as Exhibits 14.1
and 14.2, respectively.

"The Engine would also be employed to control the general scheme of
the printed page, that is to say, it would handle the paragraphing and
indentation patterns. Thus a command such as

```
:INDENT 10
```

would cause following lines of text to be indented ten spaces. Then if one
wished to return to the left margin, the command

```
:INDENT 0
```

would suffice."

Commands	Meaning
:PARAGRAPH	Marks the beginning of a paragraph. All following lines of text up to the next command line are treated as a sequence of words without line boundaries. The words are printed with end-of-line markers inserted so that each line (except the last) will be filled with one space between each pair of words. The first line of each paragraph is indented 5 spaces. The right margin is ragged.
	If the paragraph is followed by a blank line or one or more commands (excluding the **VERBATIM** command), then the next line of text will be considered the beginning of a new paragraph.
:VERBATIM	Marks the beginning of a series of lines that are to be output exactly as given, except for possible indentation. All lines (excluding command lines) between the **VERBATIM** command line and the next **PARA-GRAPH** command line (or the end of the input) are to be printed verbatim.
:INDENT n	Causes all following lines of text to be indented n spaces from the left margin (n from 0 through 60).
:CENTER n	Causes the following n lines of text ($n > 0$) to be centered between the left and right margins. If n is omitted, then only the next line will be centered.
:SPACE n	Causes n blank lines ($n > 0$) to be printed. If n is omitted, then one blank line is printed. Note that a blank line of text in the input is treated exactly as a ":SPACE 1" command line.
:PAGE	Causes the next line to be printed at the top of a new page. This is also done automatically whenever a page is filled.

Exhibit 14.1   *Text Formatting Commands*

Sample Input

```
:CENTER 2
THIS IS A TITLE
---- -- - -----

:PARAGRAPH
The text of a paragraph is adjusted
on a line to fit on
a line with at most 60 characters.

:INDENT 10
One or more lines can be indented from the left margin
with an INDENT command.

:INDENT 0
One can also specify that lines are to be printed
verbatim, as in the following short table:

:VERBATIM
     ITEM          AMOUNT
       1             18
       2              6
       3             11
```

Corresponding Output

```
                    THIS IS A TITLE
                    ---- -- - -----


        The text of a paragraph is adjusted on a line to fit on
a line with at most 60 characters.

                  One or more lines can be indented from the
            left margin with an INDENT command.

        One can also specify that lines are to be printed
verbatim, as in the following short table:

     ITEM          AMOUNT
       1             18
       2              6
       3             11
```

Exhibit 14.2   *Sample Input and Output*

"I beg your pardon, Mr. Holmes," Babbage interjected at this point. "But what exactly do you have in mind when you speak of enumerating every possible detail of the input and output?"

"I am delighted that you asked, Mr. Babbage," said Holmes, "for that is the most difficult aspect of this programme's design. When creating a programme intended for intimate use by a person such as this, we must always ask ourselves such questions as: What sorts of command are useful? What precisely are the actions these perform? What sorts of error might one make while using the programme? What would happen if one incorrectly entered some input to the Engine? And what are all the possible ways of entering input incorrectly?"

"But Mr. Holmes," interrupted Babbage. "With all due respect, my first impression is that all this detail and fussing only complicates the problem before one even begins to solve it. My research has trained me to find the shortest possible route to a problem's solution and then take that route without a glance at the more convoluted byways. Does this top-down approach not result in considerable wasted time?"

"On the contrary, my dear Babbage," Holmes replied, as he reclined in his sofa and reached for a cigarette case on a table near at hand. He lit one end of a cigarette and blew a thin cloud of smoke into the room before he continued. "You must know the value of taking pains in any scientific endeavour. It has long been an axiom of mine that the little things are infinitely the most important, and that one must realize the need for analyzing a situation thoroughly before making a single attempt to call upon the Engine.

"You will recall my address to the Royal Society, when we had occasion to meet for the first time, and your own brilliant paper in the Proceedings of the British Association. Keep in mind that we are not merely seeking a single answer to a perfectly defined problem, as an engineer does many times in his daily work. Rather, we must instruct the Engine to deal with an entire host of problems. Our first and foremost task is to define these problems, as it remains impossible to solve them without first grasping an understanding of the general situation and all its ramifications. This procedure may appear very time-consuming at the outset. However, it usually results in an accurate programme requiring few emendations; thus our method will actually save us time."

Holmes then produced yet another chart, given here as Exhibit 14.3. I now began to see that his problem was not a simple one at all. The Engine would have to keep track of many details and even be tolerant to the errors

1. An input line beginning with a colon is not followed by a legitimate command.

   Response. The line is output verbatim with five asterisks in the left margin to call attention to the problem.

2. The argument given for an INDENT command is not numeric or too large (> 60); the argument given for a CENTER or SPACE command is not numeric or too large (> 99).

   Response: As above.

3. One of the lines to be centered with a CENTER command is a command line.

   Response: The line is output centered with five asterisks in the left margin to call attention to the problem.

4. A line to be output extends beyond the right margin. This can be a verbatim line that is too long or a word in a paragraph line that is too long (for example, if the indent happens to be 50 characters and a word will not fit in the remaining ten spaces).

   Response: Allow the line to be output up to, but not beyond, the edge of the page. Place five asterisks in the left margin to call attention to the problem.

5. A text line is seen before either a PARAGRAPH or VERBATIM command is seen.

   Response: Assume that a PARAGRAPH command has been seen at the very beginning.

Exhibit 14.3 *Holmes's List of Exceptional Conditions*

of its employer. He had obviously spent a considerable amount of time thinking about the design of the programme.

"I have asked you out for the weekend, Watson," said Holmes, turning his attention to me, "to call upon your remarkable powers of stimulating genius, which I have, of late, found in short supply. I have been lost without my Boswell. I would appreciate your company also, Mr. Babbage; and, at any rate, there is no return train to London tonight and I have unwittingly condemned you to the horrors of my hospitalities. I have oysters and a brace of grouse, with something a little choice in red wines."

We enjoyed a pleasant meal together and continued our discussion of the Analytical Engine well into the evening, with a bottle of claret among us. When the conversation again turned to the design of a top-down outline of a programme for formatting Holmes's manuscripts, Babbage tried his hand at sketching a preliminary design.

"I am not wholly certain how far to delve into your list of exceptions and details, or where to draw the line," said Babbage. "Perhaps something like this would suffice." He then scribbled on a sheet of paper and handed it to Holmes. It read :

Initialize programme variables

As long as INPUT_FILE is not empty, do the following:
    read NEXT_CHARACTER
    process NEXT_CHARACTER

Print last PAGE_NUM

"Very good," said Holmes. "But there remain some points in need of clarification. In the first place, what programme variables are to be initialized? And the specification for reading characters is not explicit enough. The characters, you see, may be either part of the text or part of a command; and these two categories must of course be treated differently.

"A line of input falls into the command category if it begins with a colon. Otherwise, it is a line of text. Notice that in practice, lines will tend to occur in groups belonging to one category or the other. Thus we may view the input as groups of one or more lines of a given category.

"Notice also that command lines are treated uniformly, regardless of their context, whereas this is not true of text lines. The treatment of a text line depends upon whether the line is part of a paragraph or is to be printed verbatim. Moreover, this distinction depends on the context. When a PARAGRAPH or VERBATIM command is entered, the Engine must 'remember' the command so that all following text lines can be treated accordingly. The programme is initially assumed to be in paragraph mode in order to accept input text directly, and the mode is altered when a VERBATIM command is entered."

We then waited in silence while Holmes's mind worked uninterrupted. Finally he continued,

"I'm glad you wrote this out, Mr. Babbage, as it has forced me to consider several alternatives. I would now formulate my approach to this problem as follows."

Holmes began to outline a format programme and wrote the following sketch :

```
Assume TEXT_MODE is paragraph mode

Assume INDENTATION is zero

Assume line number is one

Assume page number is one

As long as INPUT_FILE is not empty, do the following:
    if next line is a command then
        process command line
    else -- next line is a text line
        if TEXT_MODE is paragraph mode then
            process paragraph line
        else
            process verbatim line

Print last page number
```

"Yes, now I see," said Babbage. "Your method is becoming clearer and clearer to me. In the first draft of a top-down analysis you want to be very general, yet also account for all the various possibilities as they might logically arise."

"Quite so," replied Holmes. "But I should like to make this analysis even more precise, for no surprises should arise later as a result of initial misjudgment. There are some details this first top-down sketch does not include—for example, the line number on the output page, the page number if a page becomes full, or the possibility of an input line resulting in a change to the indentation."

"Well, Mr. Holmes," said Babbage after some length, "I fear that Dr. Watson and I have been of very little help to you this evening. Perhaps tomorrow will bring more profitable results."

"Nonsense," snapped Holmes. "I cannot agree with those who rank modesty among the virtues. To a logician all things should be seen exactly as they are, and to underestimate oneself is as much a departure from truth as to exaggerate one's own powers. You have both paid me a great service this evening and I am most appreciative."

Here was a different Holmes at work, for historically it had been one of the peculiarities of his proud, self-contained nature that, though he docketed any fresh information very quickly and accurately in his brain, he seldom made any acknowledgment to the provider.

I rose the next morning earlier than usual to find Sherlock Holmes pacing back and forth in his sitting room. He was in excellent spirits. I could see that he had been up the whole night working on his programme and, furthermore, that he had good news to report.

"You have met with success, Holmes," I stated confidently.

"Indeed, Watson, I have," he replied, looking me over curiously. "The top level of the design is completed and sketched in Basic, but the papers are stored away in my desk. How is it that you knew?"

"Obvious, my dear Holmes. What else am I to assume when I see your right cuff so very shiny and spotted with ink for nearly four or five inches, and the left one with the smooth patch at the elbow where it has rested for some length of time upon your desk?"

"I must say, my dear Watson, the faculty of deduction is certainly contagious."

And so I conclude this account of Mr. Sherlock Holmes and his major contributions to the development of the Analytical Engine. A detailed sketch of his final top-level design is reproduced here as Exhibit 14.4, and a detailed sketch of the top-level design as written in Basic is shown as Exhibit 14.5.

I have also included, under the heading of Exhibit 14.6, the complete programme that Holmes worked out a few weeks later. It was my first experience with a programme of this scale, and Holmes's meticulous initial design proved highly useful throughout the project.

His decision to test out the programme on a complete chapter from his forthcoming work, *The Whole Art of Detection*, brought to mind my first encounter with Sherlock Holmes in January of 1881. A chance reunion with young Stamford, a dresser at St. Bartholomew's, brought Holmes and me together. How well I recall Stamford, standing there at the Criterion Bar, saying of Holmes, "I could imagine his giving a friend a little pinch of the latest vegetable alkaloid, not out of malevolence, you understand, but simply out of a spirit of inquiry in order to have an accurate idea of the effects. To do him justice, I think that he would take it himself with the same readiness."

Definitions:

> TEXT_MODE   : paragraph or verbatim
> INDENTATION : the current indentation
> LINE_NUM   : the current line for output
> PAGE_NUM   : the current page being printed

Algorithm:

> Initialize program constants and files
>
> Let **TEXT_MODE** = **PARAGRAPH_MODE**
> Let **INDENTATION** = 0
> Let **LINE_NUM** = 1
> Let **PAGE_NUM** = 1
>
> Get next line
> As long as **INPUT_FILE** is not empty, do the following:
>   If next line is a command then
>   do command line possibly updating **TEXT_MODE, INDENTATION,**
>   **LINE_NUM, PAGE_NUM**
>   else
>   if **TEXT_MODE** = **PARAGRAPH_MODE** then
>   do paragraph line, using **INDENTATION,**
>   possibly updating **LINE_NUM, PAGE_NUM**
>   else
>   do verbatim line, using **INDENTATION,**
>   possibly updating **LINE_NUM, PAGE_NUM**
>   Get next line
>
> Print last **PAGE_NUM**

Exhibit 14.4   *Final Version of Holmes's Top-level Design*

```
0500 REM  -- ** DICTIONARY OF VARIABLES:
0501 REM  --
0503 REM  -- I   CURRENT INDENTATION.
0505 REM  -- L   CURRENT LINE NUMBER.
0506 REM  -- P   CURRENT PAGE NUMBER.
0512 REM  -- E$  END OF FILE INDICATOR: "MORE_DATA" OR "NO_MORE_DATA".
0516 REM  -- S$  STATUS OF INPUT LINE: "COMMAND_LINE" OR "TEXT_LINE".
0517 REM  -- T$  TEXT_MODE: "PARAGRAPH" OR "VERBATIM".
...  ...
0600 REM  -- MAIN PROGRAMME
0602 REM
0603 REM  -- INITIALIZE
0604      GOSUB 1600
0605 REM
0606      LET E$ = "MORE_DATA"
0607      LET T$ = "PARAGRAPH"
0608      LET I  = 0
0609      LET L  = 1
0610      LET P  = 1
0611 REM
0612 REM  -- GET_LINE
0613      GOSUB 1400
0614 REM
0615      IF E$ = "NO_MORE_DATA" THEN 0634
0616         IF S$ = "TEXT_LINE" THEN 0620
0617 REM        -- DO_COMMAND_LINE
0618              GOSUB 0700
0619              GOTO 0630
0620            IF T$ = "PARAGRAPH" THEN 0625
0621 REM          -- DO_VERBATIM_LINE
0622                GOSUB 0900
0623                GOTO 0630
0624 REM          -- DO_PARAGRAPH_LINE
0625                GOSUB 0800
0626                GOTO 0630
0627 REM          END IF
0628 REM        END IF
0629 REM      -- GET_LINE
0630            GOSUB 1400
0631      GOTO 0615
0632 REM
0633 REM  -- FINISH_PAGE
0634      GOSUB 1000
0635 REM
0636      STOP
```

Exhibit 14.5 *Top-level Sketch of Holmes's Formatting Programme*

```
0001 REM  -- ** PROGRAMME TITLE: FORMAT
0002 REM  --
0003 REM  --
0004 REM  -- ** PROGRAMME INTENT:
0005 REM  --    THIS PROGRAMME READS A TEXT FILE AND FORMATS IT ACCORDING
0006 REM  --    TO CONVENTIONS SET BELOW. THE TEXT FILE CONTAINS LINES OF
0007 REM  --    TEXT AND COMMAND LINES. EACH COMMAND LINE BEGINS WITH A
0008 REM  --    COLON, AND MUST BE FOLLOWED BY A LEGAL COMMAND NAME.
0009 REM  --
0010 REM  --
0011 REM  -- ** INPUT AND OUTPUT FILES:
0012 REM  --    OLDTEXT: A FILE CONTAINING TEXT LINES AND COMMAND LINES.
0013 REM  --    NEWTEXT: THE FORMATTED TEXT.
0014 REM  --
0015 REM  --
0016 REM  -- ** GENERAL LAYOUT CONVENTIONS:
0017 REM  --    PAGE SIZE: STANDARD 8 1/2 BY 11 PAGE, 85 CHARACTERS PER
0018 REM  --       LINE, 66 LINES PER PAGE
0019 REM  --
0020 REM  --    MARGINS:
0021 REM  --       LEFT  :  15 CHARACTERS IN FROM LEFT EDGE OF PAGE
0022 REM  --       RIGHT :  10 CHARACTERS IN FROM RIGHT EDGE OF PAGE
0023 REM  --       TOP   :  6 LINES DOWN FROM TOP OF PAGE
0024 REM  --       BOTTOM:  6 LINES UP FROM BOTTOM OF PAGE
0025 REM  --
0026 REM  --    PRINTING AREA: STANDARD 10 PITCH SPACING, 60 CHARACTERS PER
0027 REM  --       LINE, 54 LINES PER PAGE
0028 REM  --
0029 REM  --    PAGE NUMBERS: 3 LINES DOWN FROM BOTTOM MARGIN, CENTERED
0030 REM  --       BETWEEN THE LEFT AND RIGHT MARGIN, AND ENCLOSED BY
0031 REM  --       HYPHENS, FOR EXAMPLE
0032 REM  --
0033 REM  --                         - 14 -
```

Exhibit 14.6   *A Programme to Format Text*

```
0100 REM  -- *'
0101 REM  -- :PARAGRAPH  MARKS THE BEGINNING OF A PARAGRAPH. ALL
0102 REM  --             FOLLOWING LINES OF TEXT UP TO THE NEXT COMMAND LINE
0103 REM  --             ARE TREATED AS A SEQUENCE OF WORDS WITHOUT LINE
0104 REM  --             BOUNDARIES. WORDS ARE PRINTED WITH ENDS-OF-LINES
0105 REM  --             INSERTED SO THAT EACH LINE (EXCEPT THE LAST) WILL
0106 REM  --             BE FILLED, WITH ONE SPACE BETWEEN EACH WORD. THE
0107 REM  --             FIRST LINE OF EACH PARAGRAPH IS INDENTED 5 SPACES.
0108 REM  --             THE RIGHT MARGIN IS RAGGED.
0109 REM  --
0110 REM  --             IF THE PARAGRAPH IS FOLLOWED BY A BLANK LINE OR ONE
0111 REM  --             OR MORE COMMANDS (EXCLUDING THE VERBATIM COMMAND),
0112 REM  --             THEN THE NEXT LINE OF TEXT WILL BE CONSIDERED
0113 REM  --             THE BEGINNING OF A NEW PARAGRAPH.
0114 REM  --
0115 REM  -- :VERBATIM   MARKS THE BEGINNING OF A SERIES OF LINES THAT ARE
0116 REM  --             TO BE OUTPUT EXACTLY AS THEY ARE GIVEN, EXCEPT FOR
0117 REM  --             POSSIBLE INDENTATION. ALL LINES (EXCLUDING COMMAND
0118 REM  --             LINES) BETWEEN A VERBATIM COMMAND LINE AND THE NEXT
0119 REM  --             PARAGRAPH COMMAND LINE (OR THE END OF INPUT) ARE
0120 REM  --             TO BE PRINTED VERBATIM.
0121 REM  --
0122 REM  -- :INDENT N   CAUSES ALL FOLLOWING TEXT LINES TO BE INDENTED N
0123 REM  --             SPACES FROM THE LEFT MARGIN (N FROM 0 THROUGH 60).
0124 REM  --
0125 REM  -- :CENTER N   CAUSES THE FOLLOWING N LINES OF TEXT (N > 0)
0126 REM  --             TO BE CENTERED BETWEEN THE LEFT AND RIGHT MARGINS.
0127 REM  --             IF N IS OMITTED, THEN ONLY THE NEXT LINE
0128 REM  --             WILL BE CENTERED.
0129 REM  --
0130 REM  -- :SPACE N    CAUSES N BLANK LINES (N > 0) TO BE PRINTED. IF N IS
0131 REM  --             OMITTED, THEN ONLY ONE BLANK LINE IS PRINTED. NOTE
0132 REM  --             THAT A BLANK LINE OF TEXT IN THE INPUT IS TREATED
0133 REM  --             EXACTLY AS A ":SPACE 1" COMMAND LINE.
0134 REM  --
0135 REM  -- :PAGE       CAUSES THE NEXT LINE TO BE PRINTED AT THE TOP OF A
0136 REM  --             NEW PAGE. THIS IS ALSO DONE AUTOMATICALLY WHENEVER
0137 REM  --             A PAGE IS FILLED.
```

Exhibit 14.6   *Continued*

```
0200 REM  -- ** SAMPLE INPUT:
0201 REM  --
0202 REM  -- :CENTER 2
0203 REM  -- THIS IS A TITLE
0204 REM  -- ---- -- - -----
0205 REM  --
0206 REM  -- :PARAGRAPH
0207 REM  -- The text of a paragraph is adjusted
0208 REM  -- on a line to fit on
0209 REM  -- a line with at most 60 characters.
0210 REM  --
0211 REM  -- :INDENT 10
0212 REM  -- One or more lines can be indented from the left margin
0213 REM  -- with an indent command.
0214 REM  --
0215 REM  -- :INDENT 0
0216 REM  -- One can also specify that lines are to be printed
0217 REM  -- verbatim, as in the following short table:
0218 REM  --
0219 REM  -- :VERBATIM
0220 REM  --      ITEM        AMOUNT
0221 REM  --        1           18
0222 REM  --        2            6
0223 REM  --        3           11
0224 REM  --
0225 REM  --
0226 REM  --
0227 REM  --
0228 REM  -- ** CORRESPONDING OUTPUT:
0229 REM  --
0230 REM  --                      THIS IS A TITLE
0231 REM  --                      ---- -- - -----
0232 REM  --
0233 REM  --     The text of a paragraph is adjusted on a line to fit on
0234 REM  -- a line with at most 60 characters.
0235 REM  --
0236 REM  --          One or more lines can be indented from the
0237 REM  --          left margin with an indent command.
0238 REM  --
0239 REM  --     One can also specify that lines are to be printed
0240 REM  -- verbatim, as in the following short table:
0241 REM  --
0242 REM  --      ITEM        AMOUNT
0243 REM  --        1           18
0244 REM  --        2            6
0245 REM  --        3           11
```

Exhibit 14.6   *Continued*

```
0300 REM  -- ** ERROR CONDITIONS:
0301 REM  --
0302 REM  --   1. AN INPUT LINE BEGINNING WITH A COLON IS NOT FOLLOWED BY A
0303 REM  --   LEGITIMATE COMMAND.
0304 REM  --
0305 REM  --      RESPONSE:  THE LINE IS OUTPUT VERBATIM WITH FIVE ASTERISKS
0306 REM  --      IN THE LEFT MARGIN TO CALL ATTENTION TO THE PROBLEM.
0307 REM  --
0308 REM  --
0309 REM  --   2. THE ARGUMENT GIVEN FOR AN INDENT COMMAND IS NOT NUMERIC OR
0310 REM  --   TOO LARGE (> 60); THE ARGUMENT GIVEN FOR A CENTER OR SPACE
0311 REM  --   COMMAND IS NOT NUMERIC OR TOO LARGE (> 99).
0312 REM  --
0313 REM  --      RESPONSE:  AS ABOVE.
0314 REM  --
0315 REM  --
0316 REM  --   3. ONE OF THE LINES TO BE CENTERED WITH A CENTER COMMAND IS A
0317 REM  --   COMMAND LINE.
0318 REM  --
0319 REM  --      RESPONSE:  THE LINE IS OUTPUT CENTERED, BUT FIVE ASTERISKS
0320 REM  --      ARE PLACED IN THE LEFT MARGIN TO CALL ATTENTION TO THE
0321 REM  --      PROBLEM.
0322 REM  --
0323 REM  --
0324 REM  --   4. A LINE TO BE OUTPUT EXTENDS BEYOND THE RIGHT MARGIN. THIS
0325 REM  --   CAN BE A VERBATIM LINE THAT IS TOO LONG OR A WORD IN A
0326 REM  --   PARAGRAPH LINE THAT IS TOO LONG (FOR EXAMPLE, IF THE INDENT
0327 REM  --   HAPPENS TO BE 40 CHARACTERS, AND A WORD WILL NOT FIT IN THE
0328 REM  --   REMAINING 20 SPACES).
0329 REM  --
0330 REM  --      RESPONSE:  ALLOW THE LINE TO BE OUTPUT UP TO, BUT NOT
0331 REM  --      BEYOND, THE EDGE OF THE PAGE.  PLACE FIVE ASTERISKS IN THE
0332 REM  --      LEFT MARGIN TO CALL ATTENTION TO THE PROBLEM.
0333 REM  --
0334 REM  --
0335 REM  -- ** NOTE:
0336 REM  --
0337 REM  -- THE SUBROUTINES FOLLOWING THE MAIN PROGRAMME ARE GIVEN IN
0338 REM  -- ALPHABETICAL ORDER BY NAME.
```

Exhibit 14.6   *Continued*

```
0400 REM  -- ** DICTIONARY OF CONSTANTS:
0401 REM  --
0402 REM  -- C1   PAGE SIZE, NUMBER OF LINES FROM TOP EDGE OF PAGE TO
0403 REM  --      BOTTOM EDGE OF PAGE (66).
0404 REM  --
0405 REM  -- C2   TEXT SIZE, NUMBER OF LINES FROM TOP MARGIN TO BOTTOM
0406 REM  --      MARGIN (54).
0407 REM  --
0408 REM  -- C3   LEFT MARGIN, NUMBER OF COLUMNS FROM LEFT EDGE OF
0409 REM  --      PAGE TO LEFT MARGIN (15).
0410 REM  --
0411 REM  -- C4   TEXT WIDTH, NUMBER OF COLUMNS FROM LEFT MARGIN
0412 REM  --      TO RIGHT MARGIN (60).
0413 REM  --
0414 REM  -- C5   MAXIMUM LINE LENGTH, NUMBER OF COLUMNS FROM LEFT
0415 REM  --      MARGIN TO RIGHT EDGE OF PAGE (70).
0416 REM  --
0417 REM  -- C6   TOP MARGIN, NUMBER OF BLANK LINES FROM TOP EDGE OF
0418 REM  --      PAPER TO FIRST LINE OF TEXT (6).
0419 REM  --
0420 REM  -- C7   PAGE NUMBER LINE, THE LINE ON WHICH THE PAGE NUMBER IS
0421 REM  --      PRINTED (57).
0422 REM  --
0423 REM  -- C8   PAGE NUMBER COLUMN, THE FIRST COLUMN USED FOR PRINTING
0424 REM  --      THE PAGE NUMBER (43).
```

Exhibit 14.6 *Continued*

```
0500 REM  -- ** DICTIONARY OF VARIABLES:
0501 REM  --
0502 REM  -- A    ARGUMENT GIVEN WITH A COMMAND.
0503 REM  -- I    CURRENT INDENTATION.
0504 REM  -- J,K  LOCALLY USED INDEX OR COUNTER.
0505 REM  -- L    CURRENT LINE NUMBER.
0506 REM  -- P    CURRENT PAGE NUMBER.
0507 REM  -- P1   CURRENT COLUMN POSITION ON INPUT LINE.
0508 REM  -- P2   CURRENT COLUMN POSITION ON OUTPUT LINE.
0509 REM  --
0510 REM  -- C$   TYPE OF COMMAND LINE: "INDENT", "CENTER", "SPACE", "PAGE",
0511 REM  --      "PARAGRAPH", "VERBATIM", OR "ILLEGAL".
0512 REM  -- E$   END OF FILE INDICATOR: "MORE_DATA" OR  "NO_MORE_DATA".
0513 REM  -- L$   CURRENT INPUT LINE.
0514 REM  -- M$   CURRENT OUTPUT LINE.
0515 REM  -- N$   NEXT CHARACTER ON INPUT LINE
0516 REM  -- S$   STATUS OF INPUT LINE: "COMMAND_LINE" OR "TEXT_LINE".
0517 REM  -- T$   TEXT MODE: "PARAGRAPH" OR "VERBATIM".
0518 REM  -- V$   ARGUMENT STATUS: "VALID_ARGUMENT", "INVALID_ARGUMENT",
0519 REM  --      OR "MISSING_ARGUMENT".
0520 REM  -- W$   THE NEXT WORD ON THE INPUT LINE.
```

Exhibit 14.6   *Continued*

```
0600 REM  -- MAIN PROGRAMME
0601 REM
0602 REM
0603 REM  -- INITIALIZE
0604      GOSUB 1600
0605 REM
0606      LET E$ = "MORE_DATA"
0607      LET T$ = "PARAGRAPH"
0608      LET I  = 0
0609      LET L  = 1
0610      LET P  = 1
0611 REM
0612 REM  -- GET_LINE
0613      GOSUB 1400
0614 REM
0615      IF E$ = "NO_MORE_DATA" THEN 0634
0616          IF S$ = "TEXT_LINE" THEN 0620
0617 REM          -- DO_COMMAND_LINE
0618              GOSUB 0700
0619              GOTO 0630
0620              IF T$ = "PARAGRAPH" THEN 0625
0621 REM              -- DO_VERBATIM_LINE
0622                  GOSUB 0900
0623                  GOTO 0630
0624 REM              -- DO_PARAGRAPH_LINE
0625                  GOSUB 0800
0626                  GOTO 0630
0627 REM          END IF
0628 REM      END IF
0629 REM      -- GET_LINE
0630          GOSUB 1400
0631      GOTO 0615
0632 REM
0633 REM  -- FINISH_PAGE
0634      GOSUB 1000
0635 REM
0636      STOP
```

Exhibit 14.6   *Continued*

```
0700 REM  -- DO_COMMAND_LINE
0701 REM
0702 REM  -- THIS SUBROUTINE PERFORMS THE ACTIONS FOR A COMMAND
0703 REM  -- ILLEGAL COMMANDS ARE TREATED AS VERBATIM TEXT LINES,
0704 REM  -- BUT AN ERROR MARGIN IS PRINTED.
0705 REM
0706 REM
0707 REM  -- FINISH_PARAGRAPH
0708      GOSUB 1100
0709 REM  -- GET_COMMAND
0710      GOSUB 1300
0711 REM
0712      IF C$ = "PARAGRAPH"  THEN 0720
0713      IF C$ = "VERBATIM"   THEN 0723
0714      IF C$ = "INDENT"     THEN 0726
0715      IF C$ = "CENTER"     THEN 0729
0716      IF C$ = "SPACE"      THEN 0735
0717      IF C$ = "PAGE"       THEN 0742
0718      IF C$ = "ILLEGAL"    THEN 0745
0719 REM
0720          LET T$ = "PARAGRAPH"
0721          GOTO 0750
0722 REM
0723          LET T$ = "VERBATIM"
0724          GOTO 0750
0725 REM
0726          LET I = A
0727          GOTO 0750
0728 REM
0729          FOR J = 1 TO A
0730 REM         -- PROCESS_CENTERED_LINE
0731             GOSUB 2000
0732          NEXT J
0733          GOTO 0750
0734 REM
0735          FOR J = 1 TO A
0736 REM         -- START_NEW_LINE
0737             GOSUB 2100
0738          NEXT J
0739          GOTO 0750
0740 REM
```

Exhibit 14.6 *Continued*

```
0741 REM     -- START_NEW_PAGE
0742         GOSUB 2200
0743         GOTO 0750
0744 REM
0745         LET M$ = L$
0746 REM     -- PRINT_ERROR_LINE
0747         GOSUB 1700
0748         GOTO 0750
0749 REM
0750     RETURN
```

Exhibit 14.6   *Continued*

```
0800 REM  -- DO_PARAGRAPH_LINE
0801 REM
0802 REM  -- THIS SUBROUTINE READS THE WORDS ON THE INPUT LINE.
0803 REM  -- EACH WORD IS PRINTED SO AS TO FILL THE OUTPUT LINE AS MUCH AS
0804 REM  -- POSSIBLE. A BLANK LINE MARKS THE BEGINNING OF A NEW PARAGRAPH.
0805 REM
0806 REM
0807      IF LEN(L$) <>  0 THEN 0815
0808 REM     -- FINISH_PARAGRAPH
0809         GOSUB 1100
0810         LET M$ = ""
0811 REM     -- PRINT_NORMAL_LINE
0812         GOSUB 1800
0813         RETURN
0814 REM
0815      LET P1 = 0
0816 REM  -- GET_WORD
0817      GOSUB 1500
0818 REM  -- TEST FOR NEW PARAGRAPH
0819      IF P2 <> 0 THEN 0821
0820         LET W$ = "     " + W$
0821      IF LEN(W$) = 0 THEN 0828
0822 REM     -- PRINT_WORD
0823         GOSUB 1900
0824 REM     -- GET_WORD
0825         GOSUB 1500
0826         GOTO 0821
0827 REM
0828      RETURN
```

Exhibit 14.6   *Continued*

```
0900 REM   -- DO_VERBATIM_LINE
0901 REM
0902 REM   -- THIS SUBPROGRAM PRINTS A VERBATIM LINE, INDENTED WITH THE
0903 REM   -- CURRENT INDENTATION. IF THE LINE IS TOO LONG, AN ERROR
0904 REM   -- MARGIN IS PRINTED.
0905 REM
0906 REM
0907       LET M$ = L$
0908       LET K  = LEN(M$) + I
0909       IF K > C5 THEN 0914
0910       IF K > C4 THEN 0919
0911 REM      -- PRINT_NORMAL_LINE
0912          GOSUB 1800
0913          GOTO 0922
0914          LET M$ = LEFT$(M$, C5 - I)
0915 REM      -- PRINT_ERROR_LINE
0916          GOSUB 1700
0917          GOTO 0922
0918 REM      -- PRINT_ERROR_LINE
0919          GOSUB 1700
0920          GOTO 0922
0921 REM
0922       RETURN
```

Exhibit 14.6   *Continued*

```
1000 REM  -- FINISH_PAGE
1001 REM
1002 REM  -- THIS SUBROUTINE COMPLETES THE CURRENT PAGE AND PRINTS
1003 REM  -- THE PAGE NUMBER AT THE BOTTOM
1004 REM
1005 REM
1006      FOR K = L + 1 TO C7
1007         PRINT
1008      NEXT K
1009 REM
1010      PRINT TAB(C8); "-"; P; "-"
1011 REM
1012      FOR K = C7 + 1 TO C1
1013         PRINT
1014      NEXT K
1015 REM
1016      RETURN
```

Exhibit 14.6   *Continued*

```
1100 REM  -- FINISH_PARAGRAPH
1101 REM
1102 REM  -- THIS SUBPROGRAMME COMPLETES THE PREVIOUS PARAGRAPH IF IT
1103 REM  -- HAS NOT ALREADY BEEN COMPLETED.
1104 REM
1105 REM
1106      IF LEN(M$) = 0 THEN 1109
1107 REM     -- PRINT_NORMAL_LINE
1108         GOSUB 1800
1109      LET P2 = 0
1110      RETURN
```

Exhibit 14.6   *Continued*

```
1200 REM  -- GET_ARGUMENT
1201 REM
1202 REM  -- THIS SUBROUTINE OBTAINS THE ARGUMENT (IF ANY) GIVEN
1203 REM  -- WITH A CENTER, SPACE, OR INDENT COMMAND.
1204 REM
1205 REM
1206 REM  -- SKIP OVER BLANKS
1207      IF P1 = LEN(L$)                 THEN 1212
1208      IF MID$(L$, P1 + 1, 1) <> " " THEN 1212
1209         LET P1 = P1 + 1
1210         GOTO 1207
1211 REM
1212      IF P1 <> LEN(L$) THEN 1216
1213         LET V$ = "MISSING_ARGUMENT"
1214         RETURN
1215 REM
1216      LET P1 = P1 + 1
1217      LET N$ = MID$(L$, P1, 1)
1218      IF ASC(N$) < ASC("0") THEN 1222
1219      IF ASC(N$) > ASC("9") THEN 1222
1220         LET A = VAL(N$)
1221         GOTO 1226
1222         LET V$ = "INVALID_ARGUMENT"
1223         RETURN
1224 REM
1225 REM  -- TEST FOR SECOND DIGIT
1226      IF P1 <> LEN(L$) THEN 1230
1227         LET V$ = "VALID_ARGUMENT"
1228         RETURN
1229 REM
1230      LET P1 = P1 + 1
1231      LET N$ = MID$(L$, P1, 1)
1232      IF ASC(N$) < ASC("0") THEN 1237
1233      IF ASC(N$) > ASC("9") THEN 1237
1234         LET A = A*10 + VAL(N$)
1235         LET V$ = "VALID_ARGUMENT"
1236         RETURN
1237         LET V$ = "INVALID_ARGUMENT"
1238         RETURN
```

Exhibit 14.6   *Continued*

```
1300 REM  -- GET_COMMAND
1301 REM
1302 REM  -- THIS SUBROUTINE DETERMINES THE NAME AND ARGUMENT (IF ANY)
1303 REM  -- OF A COMMAND LINE. ERRONEOUS COMBINATIONS OR LINES WITH
1304 REM  -- EXTRA CHARACTERS ARE REPORTED AS ILLEGAL.
1305 REM
1306 REM
1307      IF LEN(L$) < 10 THEN 1309
1308      IF LEFT$(L$, 10) = ":PARAGRAPH" THEN 1321
1309      IF LEN(L$) < 9 THEN 1311
1310      IF LEFT$(L$, 9) = ":VERBATIM"   THEN 1325
1311      IF LEN(L$) < 7 THEN 1314
1312      IF LEFT$(L$, 7) = ":INDENT"     THEN 1329
1313      IF LEFT$(L$, 7) = ":CENTER"     THEN 1344
1314      IF LEN(L$) < 6 THEN 1316
1315      IF LEFT$(L$, 6) = ":SPACE"      THEN 1356
1316      IF LEN(L$) < 5 THEN 1318
1317      IF LEFT$(L$, 5) = ":PAGE"       THEN 1368
1318         LET C$ = "ILLEGAL"
1319         RETURN
1320 REM
1321         LET P1 = 10
1322         LET C$ = "PARAGRAPH"
1323         GOTO 1372
1324 REM
1325         LET P1 = 9
1326         LET C$ = "VERBATIM"
1327         GOTO 1372
1328 REM
1329         LET P1 = 7
1330         LET C$ = "INDENT"
1331 REM     -- GET_ARGUMENT
1332         GOSUB 1200
1333         IF V$ <> "MISSING_ARGUMENT" THEN 1336
1334            LET C$ = "ILLEGAL"
1335            RETURN
1336         IF V$ <> "INVALID_ARGUMENT" THEN 1339
1337            LET C$ = "ILLEGAL"
1338            RETURN
1339         IF A < C4 THEN 1342
1340            LET C$ = "ILLEGAL"
1341            RETURN
1342         GOTO 1372
```

Exhibit 14.6   *Continued*

```
1343 REM
1344          LET P1 = 7
1345          LET C$ = "CENTER"
1346 REM      -- GET_ARGUMENT
1347          GOSUB 1200
1348          IF V$ <> "MISSING_ARGUMENT" THEN 1351
1349            LET A = 1
1350            RETURN
1351          IF V$ <> "INVALID_ARGUMENT" THEN 1354
1352            LET C$ = "ILLEGAL"
1353            RETURN
1354          GOTO 1372
1355 REM
1356          LET P1 = 6
1357          LET C$ = "SPACE"
1358 REM      -- GET_ARGUMENT
1359          GOSUB 1200
1360          IF V$ <> "MISSING_ARGUMENT" THEN 1363
1361            LET A = 1
1362            RETURN
1363          IF V$ <> "INVALID_ARGUMENT" THEN 1366
1364            LET C$ = "ILLEGAL"
1365            RETURN
1366          GOTO 1372
1367 REM
1368          LET P1 = 5
1369          LET C$ = "PAGE"
1370          GOTO 1372
1371 REM
1372       IF LEN(L$) = P1 THEN 1374
1373          LET C$  = "ILLEGAL"
1374       RETURN
```

Exhibit 14.6   *Continued*

```
1400 REM  -- GET_LINE
1401 REM
1402 REM  -- THIS SUBROUTINE OBTAINS THE NEXT LINE FROM THE INPUT
1403 REM  -- FILE. IT DETERMINES IF THE LINE IS A COMMAND OR A TEXT
1404 REM  -- LINE. WHEN THE END OF FILE IS REACHED, A FLAG IS SET.
1405 REM
1406 REM
1407      LINE INPUT #1 AT EOF 1424:  L$
1408 REM
1409      IF LEFT$(L$, 1) = ":" THEN 1412
1410         LET S$ = "TEXT_LINE"
1411         GOTO 1416
1412         LET S$ = "COMMAND_LINE"
1413         GOTO 1416
1414 REM
1415 REM  -- REMOVE TRAILING BLANKS
1416      LET K = LEN(L$)
1417      IF K = 0 THEN 1422
1418      IF RIGHT$(L$, 1) <> " " THEN 1422
1419         LET K  = K - 1
1420         LET L$ = LEFT$(L$, K)
1421         GOTO 1417
1422      RETURN
1423 REM
1424      LET E$ = "NO_MORE_DATA"
1425      RETURN
```

Exhibit 14.6   *Continued*

```
1500 REM  -- GET_WORD
1501 REM
1502 REM  -- THIS SUBROUTINE OBTAINS THE NEXT WORD FROM THE INPUT LINE.
1503 REM
1504 REM
1505 REM  -- SKIP OVER BLANKS
1506      IF P1 = LEN(L$)                THEN 1511
1507      IF MID$(L$, P1 + 1, 1) <> " " THEN 1511
1508        LET P1 = P1 + 1
1509        GOTO 1506
1510 REM
1511      IF P1 <> LEN(L$) THEN 1515
1512        LET W$ = ""
1513        RETURN
1514 REM
1515      LET P1 = P1 + 1
1516      LET W$ = MID$(L$, P1, 1)
1517      IF P1 = LEN(L$)                THEN 1523
1518      IF MID$(L$, P1 + 1, 1) = " "  THEN 1523
1519        LET P1 = P1 + 1
1520        LET W$ = W$ + MID$(L$, P1, 1)
1521        GOTO 1517
1522 REM
1523      RETURN
```

Exhibit 14.6 *Continued*

```
1600 REM  -- INITIALIZE
1601 REM
1602 REM  -- THIS SUBROUTINE SETS UP THE PROGRAMME CONSTANTS
1603 REM  -- AND ESTABLISHES THE INPUT FILES.
1604 REM
1605 REM
1606 REM  -- PAGE SIZE
1607     LET C1 = 66
1608 REM  -- TEXT SIZE
1609     LET C2 = 54
1610 REM  -- LEFT MARGIN
1611     LET C3 = 15
1612 REM  -- TEXT WIDTH
1613     LET C4 = 60
1614 REM  -- MAXIMIMUM LINE LENGTH
1615     LET C5 = 70
1616 REM  -- TOP MARGIN
1617     LET C6 = 6
1618 REM  -- PAGE NUMBER LINE
1619     LET C7 = 57
1620 REM  -- PAGE NUMBER COLUMN
1621     LET C8 = 43
1622 REM
1623 REM
1624 REM  -- ESTABLISH FILES
1625     OPEN #1:  NAME "MANUSCRIPT", ACCESS INPUT
1626     RETURN
```

Exhibit 14.6   *Continued*

```
1700 REM  -- PRINT_ERROR_LINE
1701 REM
1702 REM  -- THIS SUBROUTINE PRINTS AN ERRONEOUS INPUT LINE
1703 REM
1704 REM
1705      PRINT "******"; TAB(C3 + 1); M$;
1706      LET M$ = ""
1707 REM  -- START_NEW_LINE
1708      GOSUB 2100
1709      RETURN
```

Exhibit 14.6 *Continued*

```
1800 REM  -- PRINT_NORMAL_LINE
1801 REM
1802 REM  -- THIS SUBROUTINE PRINTS A LINE OF TEXT.
1803 REM
1804 REM
1805      PRINT TAB(C3 + I + 1); M$;
1806      LET M$ = ""
1807 REM  -- START_NEW_LINE
1808      GOSUB 2100
1809      RETURN
```

Exhibit 14.6   *Continued*

```
1900 REM  -- PRINT_WORD
1901 REM
1902 REM  -- THIS SUBROUTINE ADDS THE NEXT WORD TO THE OUTPUT LINE.
1903 REM  -- IT UPDATES THE COLUMN POSITION FOR THE FOLLOWING WORD.
1904 REM
1905 REM
1906 REM  -- SET P2 TO POSITION OF THE END OF WORD
1907       IF LEN(M$) <> 0 THEN 1910
1908          LET P2 = LEN(W$)
1909          GOTO 1914
1910          LET P2 = LEN(M$) + LEN(W$) + 1
1911          GOTO 1914
1912 REM
1913 REM  -- CHECK NEED FOR NEW LINE
1914       IF LEN(M$) = 0 THEN 1921
1915       IF I + P2 <= C4 THEN 1921
1916 REM     -- PRINT_NORMAL_LINE
1917          GOSUB 1800
1918          LET P2 = LEN(W$)
1919 REM
1920 REM  -- TEST FOR AVAILABLE SPACE ON LINE
1921       IF I + P2 <= C4 THEN 1928
1922          LET M$ = LEFT$(W$, LEN(W$) - (P2 - C5))
1923 REM     -- PRINT_ERROR_LINE
1924          GOSUB 1700
1925          RETURN
1926 REM
1927 REM  -- WORD IS ACCEPTABLE
1928       IF LEN(M$) <> 0 THEN 1931
1929          LET M$ = W$
1930          RETURN
1931          LET M$ = M$ + " " + W$
1932          RETURN
```

Exhibit 14.6   *Continued*

```
2000 REM  -- PROCESS_CENTERED_LINE
2001 REM
2002 REM  -- THIS SUBROUTINE OBTAINS AND PRINTS A LINE TO BE CENTERED.
2003 REM
2004 REM
2005 REM  -- GET_LINE
2006      GOSUB 1400
2007 REM  -- COUNT LEADING BLANKS
2008      LET K = 0
2009      IF LEN(L$) = K              THEN 2014
2010      IF MID$(L$, K + 1, 1) <> " " THEN 2014
2011         LET K = K + 1
2012         GOTO 2009
2013 REM
2014      LET M$ = RIGHT$(L$, LEN(L$) - K)
2015 REM
2016 REM  -- ADD BLANKS FOR CENTERING
2017      FOR K = 1 TO (C4 - LEN(M$)) / 2
2018         LET M$ = " " + M$
2019      NEXT K
2020 REM
2021      IF LEFT$(L$, 1) = ":" THEN 2027
2022      IF LEN(M$)       > C4   THEN 2027
2023 REM     -- PRINT_NORMAL_LINE
2024         GOSUB 1800
2025         GOTO 2030
2026 REM     -- PRINT_ERROR_LINE
2027         GOSUB 1700
2028         GOTO 2030
2029 REM
2030      RETURN
```

Exhibit 14.6   *Continued*

```
2100 REM  -- START_NEW_LINE
2101 REM
2102 REM  -- THIS SUBROUTINE ADVANCES TO THE NEXT LINE ON A PAGE.
2103 REM
2104 REM
2105      PRINT
2106      IF L = C2 THEN 2110
2107          LET L = L + 1
2108          GOTO 2112
2109 REM      -- START_NEW_PAGE
2110          GOSUB 2200
2111          GOTO 2112
2112      RETURN
```

Exhibit 14.6   *Continued*

```
2200 REM  -- START_NEW_PAGE
2201 REM
2202 REM  -- THIS SUBROUTINE PREPARES FOR PRINTING A NEW PAGE.
2203 REM
2204 REM
2205 REM  -- FINISH_PAGE
2206     GOSUB 1000
2207     LET L = 1
2208     LET P = P + 1
2209     RETURN
2210 END
```

Exhibit 14.6   *Continued*

14.1 The Remaining Subroutines

It is with a heavy heart that we sit down to our word processor to write these, the last words in which we record the singular gifts by which Mr. Sherlock Holmes had distinguished himself as a pioneer in the field of computer programming. His "final programme" is a full scale application of computers that we may employ in many circumstances and with a variety of computers.

Let us begin with the structure of the entire program. It has the form of a tree, much like that in Exhibit 13.2 mentioned by Holmes in his lecture on top-down programming. The root node of the tree is the main program. Each successive node of the tree is a subroutine. The branches emanating from a subroutine node are the subroutines that, in turn, are called from the subroutine.

The individual subroutines are quite straightforward, and we will not elaborate on each. We will describe one subroutine to get a feel for the entire program.

As the sample subroutine, let us look at DO_PARAGRAPH_LINE. The subroutine performs the actions required for adding words to a paragraph. The body of the procedure begins with:

```
0807       IF LEN(L$) <> 0 THEN 0815
0808 REM        FINISH_PARAGRAPH
0809           GOSUB 1100
0810           LET M$ = ""
0811 REM       -- PRINT_NORMAL_LINE
0812           GOSUB 1800
0813           RETURN
0814 REM
0815 ...
```

These statements perform the actions required when a blank line is given as input (i.e. LEN(L$) = 0). In particular, the current paragraph is completed and an empty line is printed.

The major work in the subroutine is accomplished next. The line

```
0815       LET P1 = 0
```

sets the position P1 of the next input character to zero. The subroutine call

```
0816       -- GET_WORD
0817       GOSUB 1500
```

obtains the first word of the input line. The lines

```
0819      IF P2 <> 0 THEN 0821
0820          LET W$ = "     " + W$
0821      ...
```

add five spaces to the first word if the word happens to be the first word of a
new paragraph.

The final lines make up a simple loop:

```
0821      IF LEN(W$) = 0 THEN 0828
0822 REM     -- PRINT_WORD
0823          GOSUB 1900
0824 REM     -- GET_WORD
0825          GOSUB 1500
0826          GOTO 0821
0827 REM
0828      RETURN
```

This loop keeps reading and processing words until the end of the line is
reached (i.e. the length of the next word is zero).

Elementary, but keep in mind that when using the top-down approach
the main program should be so carefully defined and mapped out that each
procedure can be written *independently*. Thus any subprograms that are true
to the behavior expected by the main program will suffice.

As always, the complete, final program comprises the main program
and all the subroutines, as shown in Exhibit 14.6. You may wish to read
over the main program and all its subroutines until you are satisfied that
they work correctly. While doing this you may note several ways of
"speeding up" the program. The fact is, we confess, that efficiency was not a
major design criterion during development, though it could have been.

The Real Story

The development of the text formatting program, with a suitable
change of names and places, is, by and large, accurate. We have, in fact,
attempted to adhere to the top-down approach exactly in composing this
program. In fairness to the reader, we would like to summarize what
actually transpired.

First of all, a program similar to this had been written some months
before, which naturally lead to a deeper insight into the problem. Second,
the inputs and outputs underwent minor revisions as a result of writing the
actual program. This, of course, is to be expected. Third, there were a
number of debates over the strategy used to implement the program.
Debate continues, we might add, over the strategy we used.

Finally, there was much discussion over the details of the subroutines,
for instance the actual error-checking mechanism carried out by the

program. This is a sticky area and the structure of Basic had some effect on our final decisions.

In parting, we would like to underline a few points:

- Like Holmes, we strongly advocate the top-down approach.

- Regardless of the approach a programmer settles upon, we cannot over-emphasize the importance of *thinking*. Recall the great detective's thoughts on human reasoning in earlier chapters, especially *before* attempting to write any code.

- Finally, we should not forget that ultimately computer programs are designed to do useful things, for *human* users.

Sadly, our narrative is all but done. "What is the use of having powers, doctor, when one has no field upon which to exert them?" inquired Holmes in *The Sign of Four*. Surely, dear reader, you have some field of your own to address.

Notes on the Programs

The programs presented by Holmes were written with two major objectives: brevity and simplicity. It was more important to us to illustrate the concept being presented than write, for example, an efficient program or one that would respond to erroneous input. Such programs would be longer and more complicated. We comment on these program issues here.

The program of Exhibit 3.1 does not completely reflect the algorithm from which it was drawn, Exhibit 2.1. In the program, the initial value for the suspect is set before the loop, and updated after each iteration. A more faithful rendition of the program, although longer, would test an individual clue against all four suspects.

Holmes's program of Exhibit 4.2 could stand a major improvement. This would allow the user to enter the hour *and* minutes of high tide. Moreover, it would be nicer here to print the output with only one or two digits after the decimal point.

In Holmes's program to classify cigar ash of Exhibit 5.2, there is a small anomaly. Suppose some different, probably less well known, cigar were found whose texture was granular, color was dark gray, and strength was normal. In this case, the cigar characteristics would not be sufficient to identify the cigar uniquely, and Holmes would have to resolve the matter himself.

The ciphered message program, Exhibit 8.3, brings up another issue—whether the cipher table should be resident in the program or defined externally to the program. This issue, we believe, depends on the application.

The program to compute dates of Exhibit 9.2 is quite straightforward, but it can be made to run faster. The problem arises in counting the days by ones. It's faster, for instance, to count a month at a time until the correct month is found, and then count by ones.

The program for "A Study in Chemistry" really brings out the issue of checking the user's input for errors. The program makes a small attempt to do this, but not enough for an actual application. For example, the number of atoms may not be an integer, or extra spaces may be typed by the user. On a separate matter, the program does not handle "radicals." For example, calcium hydroxide, $CA(OH)_2$ must be entered as 1 calcium, 2 oxygens, and 2 hydrogens.

Exhibit 12.1, the program to search files, could be improved in various ways. Certainly the program should be more tolerant of input errors. A particularly sticky problem is checking for compatibility of input values. A suspect of 6 feet in height would hardly wear a size 2 shoe, although the program will certainly accept these values. Such issues take us far beyond our intent.

As for the final program, Exhibit 14.6, we have not too much to add. Any program of this scale is open to debate, and there are numerous ways to extend it.

Appendix
Basic at a Glance

The following table summarizes the rules for writing the Basic programs given in this text. Local versions of Basic may differ from that presented here, notably with features that enhance this definition. In the table describing our version of Basic, the following conventions have been used.

1. Italicized symbols appearing in the left column, for example,

    let-statement

    give the names of constructs in Basic. Uppercase words, like LET and IF, are program symbols.

2. The symbol → separates the name of a construct from the form for writing the construct in Basic. The symbol → may be read "is written as" or "is defined as."

3. If a construct has two or more alternative forms, the symbol |
    is used to separate each alternative. The symbol | may thus be read "or."

4. Braces, for example, the braces in

    { *sign* }

    enclose optional items.

5. An ellipsis symbol (. . .) following a name or an item in braces, for example the ellipses in

    digit . . .
    { *adding-operator term* } . . .

    specifies that the preceding name or item can be repeated one or more times.

Programs

program	→	*line line* . . .
line	→	*line-number statement*
statement	→	*close-statement* │ *data-statement* │ *def-statement*
		│ *dim-statement* │ *end-statement* │ *for-block*
		│ *gosub-statement* │ *goto-statement* │ *if-statement*
		│ *input-statement* │ *let-statement* │ *on-goto-statement*
		│ *open-statement* │ *print-statement* │ *read-statement*
		│ *remark-statement* │ *return-statement* │ *stop-statement*

Statements

close-statement	→	CLOSE *file-number*
data-statement	→	DATA *data-item* {, *data-item*} . . .
def-statement	→	DEF *function-name*(*parameter-list*) = *expression*
parameter-list	→	*identifier* {, *identifier*} . . .
dim-statement	→	DIM *identifier*(*integer*)
	│	DIM *identifier*(*integer*, *integer*)
end-statement	→	END
for-block	→	FOR *identifier* = *expression* TO *expression*
		line . . .
		NEXT *identifier*
gosub-statement	→	GOSUB *line-number*
goto-statement	→	GOTO *line-number*
if-statement	→	IF *condition* THEN *line-number*
input-statement	→	INPUT *variable* {, *variable*} . . .
	│	INPUT *file-number*: *variable* {, *variable*} . . .
let-statement	→	LET *variable* = *expression*
on-goto-statement	→	ON *expression* GOTO *line-number* {, *line-number*} . . .

open-statement	→	OPEN *file-number*: NAME *string*, ACCESS INPUT
	|	OPEN *file-number*: NAME *string*, ACCESS OUTPUT
print-statement	→	PRINT { *print-item separator* } ... { *print-item* }
	|	PRINT *file-number*: {*print-item separator*} ... {*print-item*}
separator	→	, | ;
read-statement	→	READ *variable* { , *variable*} ...
remark-statement	→	REM {*character*...}
return-statement	→	RETURN
stop-statement	→	STOP

Conditions and Expressions

condition	→	*expression relational-operator expression*
expression	→	*numeric-expression*
	|	*string-expression*
numeric-expression	→	{*sign*} *term*
	|	*term* {*adding-operator term*} ...
term	→	*factor* {*multiply-operator factor*} ...
factor	→	*operand* {^ *operand*}
operand	→	*unsigned-number* | *variable* | (*numeric-expression*)
	|	*function-name*(*argument-list*)
string-expression	→	*string-operand* {+ *string-operand*} ...
string-operand	→	*variable* | *string* | (*string-expression*)
	|	*function-name*(*argument-list*)
argument-list	→	*expression* { , *expression*} ...
sign	→	+ | –
adding-operator	→	+ | –
multiply-operator	→	* | /
relational-operator	→	= | <> | < | <= | > | >=

Variables, Numbers, and Other Program Units

variable	→	*identifier*
	│	*identifier* (*subscript-list*)
subscript-list	→	*expression* { , *expression*}
data-item	→	*number* │ *string*
print-item	→	*number* │ *string* │ *variable* │ TAB(*integer*)
line-number	→	*digit digit digit digit*
file-number	→	*integer*
function-name	→	FN*letter* │ FN*letter* $
identifier	→	*letter* │ *letter digit*
	│	*letter* $ │ *letter digit* $
number	→	{*sign*} *unsigned-number*
unsigned-number	→	*integer* │ *real-number*
integer	→	*digit*...
real-number	→	*integer.integer* {*scale-factor*}
	│	*integer* { *.integer*} *scale-factor*
scale-factor	→	E *sign integer*
string	→	" *character*... "
character	→	*letter* │ *digit* │ *special-character*
digit	→	0 │ 1 │ 2 │ 3 │ 4 │ 5 │ 6 │ 7 │ 8 │ 9
letter	→	A │ B │ C │ D │ E │ F │ G │ H │ I │ J
	│	K │ L │ M │ N │ O │ P │ Q │ R │ S │ T
	│	U │ V │ W │ X │ Y │ Z
special-character	→	+ │ – │ * │ / │ = │ < │ > │ [│] │ , │ '
	│	(│) │ . │ : │ ; │ # │ % │ $ │ ! │ ?

Postscript

This book is the outgrowth of an idea proposed by Andrew Singer during a discussion at Versailles, France, in December 1978. Since that time, the project has served as an extension of our general work in human factors and as a focus for several objectives.

First, we believe that it is possible to capture the fundamental ideas of programming in a simple way. We know that programming is difficult for almost everyone, and often very confusing. Yet the motivation for much of the basis of programming stems from a few elementary ideas. The design of the Watson-Holmes dialogue and the technical points raised by the detective are a deliberate attempt to convey these underlying ideas in a way that is at once easy to follow and enjoyable.

Second, we believe that the best method to teach programming is through problems. The traditional approach has been to convey the programming language first and then try to use it to solve problems. We have taken the road less travelled. In each chapter here, the detective solves a problem — a "real" problem and at the same time a problem in program design. Then the language ideas needed to support the solution are presented by the narrator.

In writing this, we asked ourselves whether the world really needed yet another text on programming. If the question were as simple as that, so too would be the answer. We wanted to write a very serious text on programming, covering not all but most of Basic in a complete manner. In limiting ourselves this way, we believe that what we present here leaves no loose ends.

Last and most obvious, we believe that engaging the learner's interest is fundamental to effective teaching. At the root of this approach is our concern for the reader as a human being. This theme is central to the entire text.

This text was designed as a series. Other members of the series are expected to follow. Versions tailored to specific language implementations using particular computers are also planned.

Three previous works had a strong influence on parts of this work. One of the earlier texts on Basic, *Fundamental Programming Concepts* (Harper and Row, New York, 1972) by Jonathan Gross and Walter Brainerd, set a gently spirited tone for presenting programming, along with excellent exercises. A book by William Lewis, *Problem Solving for Programmers* (Hayden Book Company, Rochelle Park, New Jersey, 1980), sharpened our attention to the real problem-solving issues in programming. *The Fortran Coloring Book* by Roger Kaufman (MIT Press, Cambridge, Massachusetts, 1978), set an example for a radically different style of presentation.

This text was under development for approximately three years; and during this time, many persons contributed their work and wisdom. A special bow goes to E. Patrick McQuaid, who possesses extraordinary knowledge of Sherlock Holmes, and who rewrote and edited this text from top to bottom. Much of its creativity is due to him.

Jon Hueras contributed to the technical content of the book, including a working draft of the "Final Programme," and the idea for the Ciphered Message example.

Karen Herman provided excellent drafts of many of the Holmes stories, integrating the technical content in an easily readable way. John Whiteside was the man behind the scenes for "The Adventure of the Bathing Machine" and "A Study in Chemistry." Ed Judge was the source of the text for "The Ciphered Message" and "The Advertisement in The Times." He also kindly provided on-the-spot ideas at various times.

We are grateful to Michael Marcotty and to Edwin Carter for providing their knowledge of England and many particulars of Victorian language. Edwin Carter also provided the pen of Sherlock Holmes. His daughter, Edwina Carter, kept a vigilant eye on each of the Holmes stories, editing them with a flair for proper British terminology. She has supported the entire effort in many ways since its inception.

Dede Ely-Singer contributed to many of the ideas in this book and was a collaborator in the design of the typography. Ron Lewton, Michael Samuels, Erik Sandberg Diment, and Lillian Singer all contributed in various ways to the development of the project.

Special thanks go to Murray Gallant and E & L Instruments, Inc. for permitting one of the authors (Singer) to take vacation time at the oddest moments.

Stephen Chernicoff provided a superlative review of the entire manuscript; his suggestions on grammar, style, programming, and Sherlock Holmes were used throughout.

We are grateful to Louis Chmura for his thoughtful questions on the matter of teaching programming. To Robbie Moll we owe the idea of having a 20th-century narrator follow each of Dr. Watson's accounts. Many other people, including Cookie Daniels, Rich Scire, and Richard Tenney, offered their assistance. To each we are grateful.

Permission for the photographs of the Analytical Engine, Charles Babbage, and Ada Lovelace was obtained from the British Science Museum, London. Portions of this text contain excerpts from *Basic With Style,* by Paul Nagin and Henry Ledgard, copyright 1978, reprinted with permission of Hayden Book Company.

Holly Whiteside drew the picture of the bathing machine. Gordon Daniels took the photographs of the original Sidney Paget pictures. Jack Tracey, author of *The Encyclopedia Sherlockiana* (Avon Books, New York, 1979), kindly provided key information at various times. Peggy Farrell provided excellent assistance on delicate matters of state.

A very special word of thanks to Linda Strzegowski, a person with many talents. Besides humoring us at critical times, she creatively managed the entry, composition, and production of this text from its first day to its last.

Finally, we are grateful to Sir Arthur Conan Doyle, creator of the true Sherlock Holmes.

HENRY LEDGARD
Number Six Road
Leverett, MA 01054

ANDREW SINGER
P.O. Box 734
Woodbury, CT 06798

Index

About the Authors

Henry Ledgard received his B.A. from Tufts University and his Ph.D from the Massachusetts Institute of Technology in 1969. After a year teaching and doing research at the University of Oxford, he joined the faculty of Johns Hopkins University and later the faculty of the University of Massachusetts. In 1977 he joined the Honeywell design team on the Department of Defense program to develop a new computer language (Ada). In 1979 he started his own consulting and writing practice, Human Factors Limited. He is the author of a series of friendly books on programming style, known as *The Programming Proverbs*. One of these, *Pascal with Style* has had its effect on this work. He is also the author of *Ada: An Introduction* and co-author of a textbook, *A Programming Language Landscape*. His view on his primary research area, making computers more fit for human users, are expressed in a monograph with the stuffy title, *Directions on Human Factors for Interactive Systems*. He lives in Leverett, Massachusets.

As a computer scientist, Andrew Singer has long been fascinated by the problems people have with computers. He is the co-author of a recent research monograph in this area, and his lighter comments on the subject have appeared in the personal computing magazine, *ROM*, for which he was a contributing editor. Mr. Singer is a well-known seminar leader and consultant and has been a member of the research staffs at New York University Medical Center, Haskins Laboratories, and the Department of Social Psychology at Harvard. Since 1979 he has been Vice President for Research and Engineering at E&L Instruments, a manufacturer of products for education in electronics and computing. Mr. Singer holds a Ph.D. and M.S. degrees in Computer Science from the University of Massachusetts. He lives in Woodbury, Connecticut.